MORE MYERS

AN IRISHMAN'S DIARY

1997-2006

KEVIN MYERS

THE LILLIPUT PRESS
DUBLIN

First published 2007 by
THE LILLIPUT PRESS
62–63 Sitric Road, Arbour Hill
Dublin 7, Ireland
www.lilliputpress.ie

ISBN 978 1 84351 130 4

10 9 8 7 6 5 4 3 2 1

A CIP record for this title is available
from The British Library.

Set in 10.5 pt on 13.5 pt Bembo
Printed in England by Athenaeum Press Ltd, Tyne and Wear

MORE MYERS

AN IRISHMAN'S DIARY 1997-2006

Fir
tic
ar
in
b

c3.

Kevin Myers, writer, broadcaster and novelist, was with *The Irish Times* for twenty-five years. An earlier selection of his celebrated 'An Irishman's Diary', *Kevin Myers*, has long been out of print. This gathering, *More Myers*, covers his last years with the paper. He is now a columnist with the *Irish Independent*.

Banks of Green Willow, his novel, appeared in 2001. His best-selling *Watching the Door, A Memoir 1971–1978* was published in 2006 and will be paperbacked in 2008.

Contents

III. IRELAND

IV. THE NORTH

V. WHEELS

VI. DESTINATION IRELAND

VII. THE ARTS AND SO ON

VIII. PEOPLE

The Dead

The Undead

IX. MISCELLANEOUS AND OTHER

Preface and Acknowledgments

The Lilliput Press had obtained permission from *The Irish Times* to publish a selection of my columns long before I left that newspaper in the spring of 2006. However, the publication of my Belfast memoirs, subsequent to that permission, delayed the appearance of this volume. There is, therefore, nothing more to it than this: the following selection of my 'Irishman's Diary' has absolutely no tendentious motive. It certainly is not thumbing a nose at an institution with which I spent over a quarter of a century, and at whose lathe I spent many happy hours, though I think either party would agree that 'toiling' is hardly an apt description for how I earned my crust.

What follows is exemplary evidence of what I produced in return for that crust, and it covers some – though not all – of the areas that were, and remain, of interest to me. Where readers are kind, or foolish enough, to be enticed by what they find within, they will – I hope – now discover further examples of in the pages of the *Irish Independent*.

I retain fond memories of my years in *The Irish Times*, and of the many splendid people I met there. I would like to think this small compendium shall serve as a testament to those happy days.

My gratitude for the preparation of this book must go to Antony Farrell, my publisher, Karen Bolger, his indefatigable assistant who prospected for re-usable ore in the vein of old material, and Djinn von Noorden, his editor, who through the summer grimly wielded a similar hand-axe in the dark and largely unrewarding coal mines of recent columnar history. My thanks to them all, but most of all, and as ever, they go to my wife Rachel.

MORE MYERS

AN IRISHMAN'S DIARY 1997-2006

I. War in the Twentieth Century

I.1. A Most Peculiar Neutrality

This being the week that it is, it's hard now to recall how controversial the issue of remembrance of the Irish dead of two world wars once was. In the 1980s, during the baleful and diseased suzerainty of Charles Haughey, the army was actually prevented from honouring the Irish fallen of two world wars, though he ordered it to attend the annual service at Glencree to commemorate Nazi war-dead. This, surely, was a moral nadir, one which finally matched the dismal abyss achieved by Eamon de Valera in proffering his personal sympathies to Legate Hempel on the Fuherer's tragic death.

– Such a loss, Herr Hempel: so much to give: and relatively so young!

– Mr de Valera, there is more. Heidi, she is dead also.

–What? His dog too? Enough already.

The very first British serviceman to die in the war was probably Pilot Officer William Joseph Murphy, the 23-year-old son of William and Katherine Murphy of Mitchelstown. He and the rest of his colleagues of 107 Squadron of the RAF were slaughtered as they attempted the first daylight raid of the war on German warships, at dawn on Monday 4th September 1939.

As Oliver Murphy's research for Belvedere College suggests, and the war memorial at St Canice's Church of Ireland Cathedral in Kilkenny tends to confirm, Irish involvement in the RAF in the Second World War was far higher than has hitherto been suspected. A trawl through the Commonwealth War Graves

Commission archives gives us a glimpse of these forgotten Irishmen, such as Flight Sergeant Andrew Murphy of Clifden, Kilkenny, who was shot down and killed during the Arnhem operation in 1944. Flying Officer Desmond O'Sullivan of Camolin, County Wexford, had been shot down over Denmark a couple of weeks earlier.

Did Sergeant Michael O'Sullivan, RAF flight engineer, who died on January 15, 1945 and is buried in Castlemahon graveyard, County Limerick, succumb at home to wounds received in action? Did aircraftman 2nd Class Timothy O'Sullivan, aged 20, who died in September 1945, and who is buried at Kilfinane, County Limerick, meet a similar end? And what of aircraftman Patrick Jerry O'Rourke, aged 30, who died in November 1945 and is buried in Bray. Did he too finally perish of injuries so soon after victory was won?

Leading aircraftman Patrick Behan most probably did. He was 21 when he died in December 1945 in 64th Military Hospital in Germany, and he is buried in Celle War Cemetary, Niedersachsen. He left behind a widow, Mary Carmel, in Crumlin in Dublin. What became of her and her young life? Corporal John Patrick O'Neill, from Tullow, County Carlow, Royal Air Force Volunteer Reserve, went to his grave in the Pas de Calais earlier that year, aged 32.

Many more Irishmen than has perhaps been recognised served in the Royal Navy. At least five of them were killed in the opening days of the war when the aircraft carrier HMS *Courageous* was torpedoed. Stoker Joseph Patrick Brunt from Waterford was 22 when he died. Able Seaman Henry McCauley was 39. His body was washed ashore, and it is buried near his home in Ballydare, County Antrim – some consolation for his parents, for the body of his brother Robert, who was killed in the First World War, was never found. No such token consolation for Elizabeth Millar, of Belfast, whose husband Samuel went down on the *Courageous*.

Two of the dead of the *Courageous* came from Cork. One was Commissioned Boatswain Patrick Joseph O'Brien of Leap, and the other was Air Mechanic Michael Anthony McCarthy of Rosscarbery. Also from Cork was Leading Stoker Patrick Joseph Murphy of HMS *Valiant*, son of Denis and Margaret Murphy, of Skibbereen, and who died at the end of the war. These men remind us of the sea going traditions of our maritime communities: hence Ordinary Seaman Patrick Murphy, HMS *Charybdis*, from Westport, County Mayo, killed in action October 1943, or Cornelius Murphy, HMS *Hurworth*, from Lismore, County Waterford, killed in action the same day, and Able Seaman John Murphy, from Fethard, killed on HMS *Matabele* in January 1942.

Finally, we now know about Irish casualties in the British army, 1939–45. Definitive research on the subject by the historian Yvonne McEwen shows that 4543 Irishmen died while serving in the army – 2241 men from the north, 2302 from Éire, as the state was then called. Of those deaths, 1358 occurred in Irish regiments.

She believes about 100,000 Irishmen served in the army alone, a slight majority from the South. The north-south disparity for women was greater: 41 women from the south – nurses and ATS – died in the war, and 11 from the North.

There are no figures (yet) for the RN or the RAF – nor indeed for Irish casualties in the commonwealth and Indian armies, nor the five US services: the USAAF, the USN, the Marine Corps, the army and the Coast Guard. All in all, the Irish involvement in the Second World War was very substantial. Ours, truly, was a most peculiar neutrality.

Irishmen and women served a foreign flag during the last world war for complex reasons – economic need, family tradition, loyalty to the crown, and because they felt that Hitler had to be opposed by force of arms. Most Irish people today are generous enough in their judgment, in their sense of identity, and in their grasp of history to accept that there is reason for pride in what these men and women did; for the cause they served was just, and in the end, victorious. On Sunday, some of us will remember them.

[12 November 2004]

I.2. Israel and the Media

Possibly, you missed the news that Mahmoud Abbas, the President of the Palestinian Authority, last weekend authorised the execution of four men in Gaza – three by hanging, the fourth by firing squad. Indeed, this newspaper was virtually alone in reporting it.

But imagine the publicity such judicial murder would have garnered had the executioners been Jewish and the legal authority responsible for them the state of Israel. Of course, this is hypothesis: the only man lawfully executed in Israel was Adolf Eichmann: otherwise the state of Israel does not indulge in judicial executions. But if it did, and in a single morning sent three men to the gallows and the fourth to the firing squad, would the killings have gone largely without notice around the world?

Now the issue here is not the rights and the wrongs of capital punishment. Virtually without exception, we all approve of capital punishment: who would argue today that Himmler, the architect of the death camps, should have been allowed to end his days in stately old age in a prison cell? If you accept that he should have been hanged – as he would have been if he hadn't managed to poison himself – then you agree in principle with capital punishment: the rest is quibbles.

Nor is the issue the conduct of Israel's deeds in the West Bank, Gaza or anywhere else for that matter, many of which have been reprehensible. Few of us can look with equanimity at what are called 'targeted killings', which could also go by the terms 'assassination' or even 'murder'. But before we get too precious about Israel, let us remember a few details of our own counter-insurgency operations. Let us recall the 77 men summarily murdered by the Free State, or the way de Valera's government used the Emergency Powers Act to change the rules of evidence so as to ensure a conviction and execution of the IRA man George Plant. In more recent times, the Rangers were deployed with orders to kill the kidnappers of Don Tidy, if at all possible, and when the security forces of this Republic, ambushed the INLA leader Dessie O'Hare, their apparent intention was, understandably, to kill him.

No, the real issue here is how our media view the Middle Eastern conflict: is a sub-conscious, pan-European anti-Semitism now at work, when this newspaper was almost alone in reporting last Sunday's executions? Yet we know that if performed by the other side in the conflict, these killings would probably have caused an international outcry. And is this the reason why almost every visual representation of the conflict nowadays consists of Palestinian victims, or palpable signs of Israeli 'aggression', such as the wall along the West Bank? We are all familiar with pictures of dead Palestinians, killed by the Israelis. But how many pictures of any of the hundreds of dead Jews, children or otherwise, who have been killed by Palestinian suicide bombers, have you ever seen?

An anti-Israeli bias has now become a norm in Western European culture at even the most simple level. The reason that Israel still stands a chance of qualifying for the World Cup is because of the performances of its Arab players, yet this uncomfortable truth is explained away with a few embarrassed coughs. That Israeli society generally strives to be fair and just, in almost impossible circumstances, is seldom applauded: instead, there is the usual diet of supercilious sneers and disdain at its failures, as if Israel could be just like Denmark, if only it tried a little harder.

The *Wall Street Journal* recently reviewed European coverage of the Middle East crisis. It reported that in Spain, for example, on 4 June 2001 (three days after a Palestinian suicide bomber killed 21 young Israelis at a disco), *Cambio 16* published a cartoon of the Israeli Prime Minister Ariel Sharon, with a big hook nose, wearing a skull cap and sporting a swastika inside a star of David on his chest, proclaiming: 'At least Hitler taught me how to invade a country and destroy every living insect.'

The week before, *El Pais* – roughly the Spanish equivalent of this newspaper – published a cartoon of a figure carrying a small rectangular-shaped black moustache, flying toward Sharon's upper lip. The caption read: 'Clio, the muse of history, puts Hitler's moustache on Ariel Sharon.' A cartoon in the Catalan daily *La Vanguardia* showed an imposing building bearing the sign 'Museum of the Jewish

Holocaust' and beside it, another building under construction, with a large sign, 'Future Museum of the Palestinian Holocaust'.

A cartoon in Greece's largest newspaper, the daily *Eleftherotypia*, under the title 'Holocaust II', showed an Israeli soldier as a Nazi officer and a Palestinian civilian as a Jewish death camp inmate. In Italy, *La Stampa* ran a cartoon showing an Israeli tank pointing a large gun at the infant Jesus in the manger, while the baby pleads, 'Surely they don't want to kill me again, do they?' A *Corriere Della Sera* cartoon showed Jesus trapped in his tomb, unable to rise, because Ariel Sharon, rifle in hand, was sitting on the sepulchre.

These sacrilegious falsehoods – just a sample of many across a continent which was the home of the Final Solution – are so grotesque as to constitute anti-Semitism, pure and simple; but what makes them most insidious of all is the fact that their perpetrators are – apparently – quite unaware of this. Worst of all, such foul libels conceal the real truth that the only people who desire another holocaust in the Middle East are Israel's fundamentalist enemies.

[15 June 2005]

I.3. The World at War ... and Jane Fonda

'Extremist Muslims' belief that their way is right and everyone else is wrong and is immoral is the same as that of the twisted Christian fundamentalists who have bombed gay venues in Atlanta and London, who seek to ban gay parades in Belfast ...' So wrote Morgan Carpenter to this newspaper the other day.

I'm not sure whether Morgan is a man or a woman, and it matters only in the pronoun that s/he uses. But is s/he serious? Does s/he really believe that an attempt to ban a gay parade in Belfast is the same as murdering 50 people in London, 200 in Madrid and 3000 in New York? Because – speaking for myself, that is: Morgan might have different opinions on this – I think I'd rather be simply banned from walking down a street on a particular day than be blown to pieces all over it at any time.

Moreover, one cannot reasonably compare one isolated bombing at a gay bar in Atlanta in 1997 by a lunatic (who also bombed an abortion clinic in Alabama) or the isolated bombing of another gay bar in London in 1999, two dead, by another lunatic, with the worldwide explosion of genocidal hate in recent years. Or can s/he? It's hard to say. Given the culture of moral equivalence that has swept through our *bien-pensant* classes, in which a perceived insult to one's sexuality registers pretty much the same on the offensiveness-scale as a railway carriage full of dead bodies, who knows?

Nobody represents the showbiz side of moral equivalence more than Jane Fonda. What is perhaps most unnerving about her is the way she can talk of herself, often in the third person, with such voluble and fascinated indefatigability. She clearly believes that she's as interesting as China and as wise as Socrates. Close, actually: in fact, as interesting as a china plate (but cracked) and as wise as a sock.

I know, I know, one shouldn't really be personal about a woman's appearance, but since she has traded on it all her life, in her case she's fair game. So with all those plastic surgeons industriously slicing, sewing and tucking their way across her features, her face now resembles a macaque's bottom.

The macaque's bottom announced the other day that she is going to tour the US calling for an end to American military presence in Iraq. Apparently determined to show us that not merely has she the face of a macaque, but the mind of one also, she proudly boasts she's going to travel in a bus that runs on vegetable oil. That'll go down well in Iraq. Not merely will she be demanding the withdrawal of the only force that is stopping the country from slipping into a catastrophic civil war, she's not even going to use any of Iraq's oil in the process.

However, this is not necessarily all bad news. The discovery that they have Jane Fonda on their side should thin the ranks of the anti-war crowd considerably. Certainly, if I was in the last lifeboat from the *Titanic* and I found old macaque-bottom leering at me from the stern with her little bottle of vegetable oil, I think I'd take my chances in the water.

She – like many others, especially in this country – has not grasped a central feature of the war in Iraq. The US-led coalition is only present in that country by the invitation and legal authorisation of the democratically elected government there. Moreover, what we see happening in that country is truly Manichean, which is what macaque-bottom probably thinks is something that happens to your nails when you go to your beautician: no Janey, in this case, it is a struggle of the forces of good, of law and of popular will against the greatest evil the world has seen since the Fall of Berlin.

Five years ago, such evil was not merely unpredicted but entirely unpredictable. No one in the world would have foreseen the day that hundreds of suicide bombers would be eagerly lining up to kill their fellow Muslims, which is what we now see in Iraq. Not even the most pessimistic prophet could have imagined that a suicide bomber would blow 30 Arab children to pieces because they were queuing up to get sweets from US soldiers. Nor would anyone have believed that images of conscious people being slowly beheaded, from the neck to the spine, would be fed around the world on the internet, to audiences eager to do the same.

In the past five years we have passed more thresholds in our understanding of the nature of human depravity than we had in the previous 50; and believe me, Morgan, not being able to march in gay-pride parades in Belfast wasn't one of them. For the US and its allies to do a Spanish runner and get out of Iraq now because of a terrorist campaign in London, or even a vegetable-oil driven bus-campaign by macaque-bottom across the US, frightening though both are, would simply be to surrender the very keystone of regional and world stability to Abu Musab al-Zarqawi and his merry men.

There is no choice here. Hey, you, macaque bottom, in the bus that smells like a chip van: can you not understand this? The world is at war, and the consequence of an insurgent victory in Iraq would be a geopolitical calamity that could exceed in all its abominable gravity the consequences of the Bolshevik Revolution, the mother of all catastrophes in the twentieth century.

[26 July 2005]

1.4. The Russian Sub

Forty years ago this week, a heroic Russian submariner named Arkhipov almost certainly saved the world from nuclear disaster. He was a senior officer on the Soviet 'Foxtrot' class submarine *B59* off the coast of Cuba. At the height of the 1962 missile crisis his boat was detected and depth charged by a US naval destroyer, USS *Reale*.

The *B59* was armed with nuclear-tipped torpedoes. Under attack, out of radio communication, and in the belief that war had begun, two of its executive officers wanted to retaliate; but they had no legal authority to fire without the specific assent of the third XO aboard, Arkhipov. They demanded he permit the return of fire; he refused, though he faced certain execution if his judgment were subsequently shown to be wrong. But had the *B59* fired its nuclear weapons, the third world war would have probably begun.

One night rather earlier that autumn, a group of pupils were gathered on the bell tower of Ratcliffe College, Leicestershire, while Brother Primavesi erected the astronomical society telescope, intending to find Saturn. But before we looked heavenwards, Brother Primavesi pointed the telescope horizontally over the darkling wolds of north Leicestershire and told us to take our minds over the horizon, above the fens of Lincolnshire, across the North Sea, to Holland, the plains of Low Germany, Poland and the vast Russian steppes beyond; and he announced, with that satisfaction which astronomers invariably exhibit when discussing the sheer banality of the world, that going east from our bell tower we would find nothing higher than us until we reached the Urals.

The Urals: the heart of Soviet darkness. That night we gazed into the light-less sky, and in our minds made that journey eastwards, before making that other journey into the sky, to the mysteries of Saturn and its rings.

When the crisis began to gather a couple of weeks later, we know little about the events in the western Atlantic, merely sensing the fears that were growing in the adult community that taught us. The daily prayers, suddenly and commandingly, included prayers for peace – for peace had ceased to be our condition and had become instead our objective. We began to understand the fate that was facing us.

For myself, the issue was clear enough. President John F. Kennedy was an Irish Catholic, and therefore I was his. It was simple. I owed him unutterable allegiance. On the other hand, there were the vile communists who had seized Cuba, and who threatened world peace. It wasn't complex stuff, merely the way boys put a moral shape on the world.

But I lived in England, and my moral shape was not that shared by my cousins in Ireland. Visible from the bell tower lay RAF *Cottesmore*, where nuclear V-bombers crouched, pointing towards the east and the Urals. More deadly still from our point of view, a US Thor missile base had recently been constructed nearby. Both places were therefore targets. This meant one thing: when war came, it could come here first. And we were old enough to know that whether or not this would be the last war mankind would fight, we could not survive its opening salvoes.

So hourly, the certainty of all-engulfing catastrophe grew closer and closer. We tuned into AFN, American Forces Network, following the news with avid pessimism, and abandoning pop music altogether. Each night the school was called to prayer, beneath the vast monuments to the boys who had perished in the two earlier world wars.

Then came the evening of decision. The entire school sat crouched around its various radios, and by bedtime, war seemed inescapable. There was no jingoism, no stuff about filthy communists, merely a ghastly certainty of what was to come. We went to bed, and praying, slept.

At 3 am we were awoken by the sirens of the fire alarm. 'Christ, it's war,' said a boy's voice in the dark. The lights came on, and we exchanged grey looks as we obeyed the fire drill, putting on our dressing-gowns and slippers and padding to the assembly hall outside. Through the black night, I remember looking east, towards RAF *Cottesmore*, towards the US Thor base, half expecting to see the impact of Soviet missiles from beyond the Urals, and realising that of course I would never see them, for my schoolboy knowledge told me that my eyes would be melted instantly by the thermonuclear flash.

Around me, believing that war had begun, hundreds of boys silently gathered in the assembly hall. One boy near me said the Rosary. I spoke no prayers that I now remember, for my mind was locked elsewhere, on my parents, and the certainty that I would never see them again. In the school hall, apparently out of habit, and in their clipped subaltern accents, prefects conducted stiff-upper-lip fire drill, name by name – Abbot? Here! Archer? Here! Ashe? Here! – while we all dutifully waited for death. I hoped to die outside rather than in the crowded assembly hall.

The slowly, incredibly, the word spread that that alarm had been caused by a real but small fire in the school. The fire drill was genuine after all. We trooped back through the silent, warless night towards our dormitories. Braced for death, and now disappointed, I looked east through the dark, still wondering if and when the holocaust would come.

One of the reasons that it didn't was the ice-cold courage that same night of a Russian sailor called Arkhipov, deep under the Atlantic ocean some 4000 miles away. He helped make the world what it is today. Wherever you are, Arky: thank you.

[25 October 2002]

I.5. Srebrenica

How apposite that the British commemorations to mark the end of the Second World War should fall on the tenth anniversary of the massacre of Srebrenica. That same day, Luxembourg voted NOT to reject the 200,000 pages (or so) of the European Constitution, a result hailed by its genial idiot of a Prime Minister Jean Claude Junkker, as proof that the Constitution was not dead. Indeed – and with as much logic, because a group of ancient communists in Kalingrad demand it, the Soviet Union is alive and well.

On 11 July 1995, the two international institutions that resulted from the genocide of the Second World War, the UN and the EU, allowed us to time-travel back to Eastern Europe in the early 1940s. On that day, over 8000 Bosnian Muslim men and boys were marched to their doom from the Bosnian town of Srebrenica by their Serb captors, aided by a compliant battalion of Dutch UN troops.

And so Srebrenica in its way characterises the vanity and the ineptitude of this project of a united Europe, which, the last time it was tried, was also the home of the Final Solution. Yet 50 years later, the armed might of democratic Europe proved utterly incapable of preventing another little exercise in genocide, though it had full warning – for those who had been there knew what was coming.

After several trips there in 1992–93, I said in this newspaper that unless Serbian nationalism was violently suppressed – and I specifically proposed the use of massive air power against the infrastructure of both the Bosnian-Serb regime and the Serb-dominated Yugoslav state – genocidal catastrophe was certain.

Of course, as we know, there were no such pre-emptive measures, for

Europe's elites had another project on their minds: the bureaucratic creation of a vast but toothless super pan-European welfare state. And throughout the melancholy and self-deluding process of creating a united Europe, there has been one great giveaway word that reveals how the Euro-elite regarded the peoples it was steering towards its chosen destiny. Whenever national authorisation was required – by parliamentary vote or referendum – the process was always called 'ratification'. Not consultation, not consideration, not authorisation, and certainly not veto-ification; instead, the plain people of Europe became the mere ratifiers of the Euro-elites' decisions and rubber-stampers of their paperwork.

Except, no longer; the Dutch and the French peoples have essentially ended the Euro-elite's project. Yet even the Euro-elites themselves have throughout the processes of unification continued to follow their own national interests. France is only a European Country until its glance reaches the Straits of Gibraltar, and then it reverts to its imperial mode. Even more fatuously, the various aerospace industries of Europe are spending billions producing three rival fighters – the Rafale, the Gripen and the Typhoon, thereby both triplicating research and development costs (making aircraft that are almost certainly inferior to Russian and American designs).

So the fantasy that is 'Europe' was not exploded in the Dutch and French referendums this year, but ten years ago in the hills around Srebrenica. And more than the death of a dream occurred as the Serbian Scorpion paramilitary gang began their butchery. The murders convulsed Europe's Muslims, and turned Omar Sheikh, a beer-drinking, womanising, rock-loving Englishman of Pakistani origin, into a Islamic fundamentalist. He finally expressed his new ardour by beheading the captured American journalist Daniel Pearl in Pakistan.

The irony here is perfectly terrible. For it was the US, acting almost unilaterally, which brought the agony of Bosnia to an end, and which similarly curtailed the pogroms of Albanian Muslims by Serbs in Kosovo. But this seems to have made little difference to the perception of the US amongst European Muslims. That 70 per cent of the population of Iraq turned out for the election there, despite murderous terrorist threats, has made little or no difference to anti-US Islamic opinion within Britain.

Moreover, for all the condemnations of last Thursday's atrocities in London from Islamic leaders, there have been few enough Muslim voices calling for their entire community to unconditionally assist the British security forces against the jihadists. No fatwa of the kind that sent Salman Rushdie into hiding for a decade has been issued against Thursday's bombers, or is even likely. However, one Muslim cleric in London last weekend declared that any future use of tracker dogs in London's underground to check travellers would be offensive to Muslims.

British politicians and clergy have been falling over one another to declare the innocence of the overwhelming majority of British Muslims. However right, proper and accurate that is, it is not of itself sufficient. We in this country have taken a similarly Rebecca-of-Sunnybrook-Farm approach in the past. For years, the voice of official Ireland declared that support for the IRA in the Republic was confined to a tiny and wholly unrepresentative minority: in the late John Kelly's lapidary words, to 'a few savage old hill-billies'. But we were telling ourselves lies. In fact, unspoken support for the IRA amongst Northern nationalists probably never fell below 40 per cent, and was powerful throughout large pockets in the Republic.

Similarly, an opinion poll in Britain after 9/11 showed that 40 per cent of British Muslims actually supported Al Qaeda in its campaign against the US – a figure that is so shocking that no one today mentions it. And across Britain now, I don't doubt that a great many ethnic Britons are contemplating the immigration policies of the past half-century and are asking: Oh my God: what have we done?

[12 July 2005]

I.6. RIP President Eyadema of Togo

This column is this morning in mourning for the great President Gnassingbe Eyadema of Togo, and grief bedecks my brows as tears short-circuit my crackling keyboard. Gnasheur – as he was known to his adoring, and now orphaned, broken people – was the epitome of the true African leader. Modest, retiring, and scrupulous at all times, his opponents regularly and devotedly committed suicide in the government cells to which they had besought admission. In the forty years since this former sergeant took control of his country, it grew mysteriously and catastrophically poorer, and he – inexplicably – proportionately richer. Economists are at a loss to explain it.

But let us rejoice! His son, he liveth! Yes, young Faure Essozimma Gnassingbe has succeeded to the presidency, and properly so. Did his father not appoint him Minister of Equipment, Mines, Posts and Telecommunications (and anything else that caught his eye) on merit only? And having nimbly clambered up the slippery pole of Togolese politics purely by talent, he is now at its pinnacle, where is able to savour the grief and the condolences of President Chirac, who sent the following communication: 'My thoughts turn towards the Togolese people. I am sure they will find themselves gathered together democratically in this ordeal.'

Quite so. The last time the Togolese people gathered together democratically was seven years ago, when Gnasheur discovered that his opponent, Gilchrist

Olympio – presumably is of Gaelic-Greek ancestry – was winning. Gnausher promptly called the election off, and very properly became President-for-Life. It will probably be a while before Togo dabbles again in that messy and inconclusive experiment called democracy. In the meantime, we can be sure that the Elysée will continue to give its full support to the boy-president, as it did to the da, and as it once did to the neighbouring Emperor Bokassa, who tackled the population problem in his country by eating some of its citizens. Pygmies are delicious when taken young, I'm told, their toes (once washed) in particular.

The question being asked in the chancelleries of the world is – how will Bébé Gnasheur conduct his country's relations with President Chirac? You will remember Chirac: he was the man Bono embraced because of his 'anti-war' stance. But of course, it all depends on which war. France recently destroyed the Ivory Coast's air force because of some local disagreement. I'm not sure if Togo has an air force: if it has, it had better stay on the right side of Chirac, whose taste in treachery is positively Mugabwean.

Togo's fellow West African states – Liberia, Sierre Leone and air forceless Ivory Coast – are now in anarchy. On the far side of Africa, so too is Somalia. Sudan has just announced that it will not hand over any of its policemen or soldiers for trial by the International Criminal Court on war crimes charges resulting from the current and heart-warming genocide in Darfur. Meanwhile, Zimbabwe is continuing about its sorry path towards calamity.

And still goody-goodies in the West continue to maintain that Africa's problem is essentially one of debt, and that all we need to do is to wave a magic vanishing wand, and whatever the Congo is called today – which is not the same as last week, nor the same as next Tuesday – will suddenly resemble Zurich.

Now, you can call the latest quick-fix for Africa debt relief, but really, it is simply aid by another name. And Africa knows all about aid. Between 1950 and 1995, it received $1 trillion's worth, in 1985 prices. One trillion. That's one, followed by twelve zeroes, 1985 values.

A recent study of thirty sub-Saharan African countries showed that between 1970-1996, their capital exports amounted to £187 billion. Their ruling elites meanwhile were shown to possess private, overseas assets that actually exceeded the public debts of the countries concerned by nearly 50 per cent. Moreover, the study revealed that roughly 80 per cent of every dollar borrowed by those countries was returned to the west in capital-flight *within the year.*

So waiving debts will not diminish the corruption of African regimes. Meanwhile, well-meaning Westerners continue to delude themselves with meaningless pieties: witness the idiotic cheers that greeted Nelson Mandela's statement at a recent rally in London: 'Like slavery and apartheid, poverty is not natural. It is man-made and can be overcome and eradicated.'

Such gibberish is the exact opposite of the truth: poverty is entirely natural. The whole history of civilisation is about mankind's attempt to escape our natural condition, in which we are unclothed and impoverished savages, prey to climate, hunger, wild animals and disease. The notion that poverty is not 'natural' ranks in idiocy with Rousseau's fatuous observation: 'Man is born free, and everywhere he is in chains.'

Man was born a naked, dependent, mewling, puking, incontinent infant, who without the attentions of his mother and society generally would be dead within hours. And that's freedom? Yet such meaningless aphorisms enter our political lexicons and stay lodged there, to be trotted out whenever we feel the need to expatiate upon the evils of the world, especially the Western world, and the US most of all.

Africa is not poor because of debt-repayment to the West, or because it has been confined to an 'unnatural' poverty. Africa is poor because it remains close to nature, and because its leaders gorge themselves like natural Serengeti predators at a kill. To be sure, despicable wretches like Chirac don't help: but this doesn't explain everything, for impoverished Sudan, Liberia, Somalia and Zimbabwe are Chirac-free zones. Fortunately, however, happy, happy Togo has President Faure Essozimma Gnassingbe to protect it from a comparable journey towards anarchic barbarism!

[9 February 2005]

1.7. The Wretched UN

One thing for certain is that we shall never know the full death toll of the St Stephen's Day tsunami. With equal certainty, we can say that that one victim that the catastrophe should have claimed will be leering back at us in the future, an unkillable vampire that ceaselessly stalks the world, regardless of how often the rising sun of revelation catches it away from its catafalque, or how frequently the wooden stake of reality is driven through its heart. No matter its egregious blunders, its vast corruption, its staggering ineptitude, its ghastly sanctimony and its blustering pomposity, the UN will survive its failures in the Pacific as it has survived all its failures everywhere.

The UN has such a powerful place in the Irish popular imagination that it is almost above criticism. In a way, this is understandable. The UN provided the forum in which this state was able to make its first major mark in the world, and it was in the service of the UN that the army learnt to respect itself. The ambush in Niemba in which so many brave soldiers died had a profoundly unifying influence on Irish life. Even more important to the morale of the Army was its victorious

assault on The Tunnel in Katanga, a military achievement that required a profes-
sionalism and a gallantry for untried forces against veterans that even now seem
quite extraordinary. It is rightly a matter of considerable pride for the army.

But that was then, and this is now. So go on. Wait for the UN to authorise
serious action to prevent the genocide in the Sudan; and in the meantime watch
as the polar ice-caps melt. We have already watched as the UN impotently and
wretchedly presided over the massacre at Srebenice, the consequences of which we
are living with today – for to the lively Islamic imagination, the failure to protect
the Muslims of Bosnia was the responsibility of 'the west': that is, the Americans.

It was of course the Americans – not the wretches of the UN – who ended
the war in Bosnia. It was also the Americans who saved the Muslims of Kosovo
from ethnic cleansing by Serb fascists. Wherever the US was not involved and
the UN was – the Congo, Rwanda, Bosnia – there were massacres and ceaseless
war, even as armies of UN officials with their sunglasses and their four-by-fours
sipped sundowners on their hotel terraces. If the UN were deplored in Stillorgan
in midwinter, they'd still have their Raybans and their Land-Cruisers.

The greatest single UN mission since the Congo in 1960 has been Iraq, over
the past fifteen years. For the first decade, the US allowed the UN to handle affairs,
and the result was calamity. During an unprecedented orgy of misgovernance
and corruption, UN officials helped rape a country and its people, even as they
bolstered the internal power of a genocidal tyrant.

The cost of that festival of corruption is literally uncountable. Perhaps as
much as $20 billion went missing during the oil-for-food scandal, much of it into
the pockets of UN officials, and many thousands of Iraqis perished because of the
manipulation of sanctions by Saddam and his UN cronies.

Now this wouldn't matter all that much if we in Ireland hadn't raised the
UN into being a secular religion, possessed of a divine moral authority: a Catholic
Church without the dog collars. Uncritical Irish UNophilia is now so entrenched
that we have created the extraordinary triple-lock to the use of our armed forces
aboard. We require the authorisation of UN before a single soldier steps onto
a single Hercules – albeit a foreign one, being too mean to buy any ourselves
– to protect either or own national interest, or to help enforce a moral order we
believe to be right.

You don't ever triple-lock a fire axe, even if the locks are well-oiled and
well-made. Yet we have tied the deployment of the Defence Forces to the rusting,
corrupt and corroded lock of the UN, as if it were some guarantor of moral
perfection. And if Rwanda, Iraq, Bosnia are your idea of the international community working in harmony, then clearly the UN is the organisation for you.

To wish for the consent of the UN is to seek the good opinion of an otiose,
indolent, corrupt and morally inert slug. The UN has appointed the regime of

Mummar Gaddafi – which amongst many other tasty delicacies, was behind the Lockberbie bombing – to be the defender of individual freedoms. That's right: Libya now holds the chair of the UN commission of human rights. So don't be all that surprised if next, Sudan chairs a UN commission on multicultural tolerance, and Zimbabwe is responsible for guarding minority rights. Ah, and here comes Burma, no doubt soon to be UN champion of open and transparent government.

Still, the UN could still be expected to come into its own after a natural disaster, surely? Quite the reverse. After the tsunami, Kofi Annan apparently went missing. No doubt he was still unwrapping his Christmas presents from Libya and Sudan, as the US, the Australians and the Japanese spontaneously stepped into the breach. Meanwhile, from the UN headquarters in New York, came the buzz-saw sound of snoring.

For the UN mixes sanctimony with theft, humbug with greed, all spiced with a hefty dollop of sloth. Look up – and the Airbus boring holes in the ozone layer overhead is laden with UN officials flying first class to the Seychelles to discuss global warming.

[11 January 2005]

I.8. Make Poverty History

I listen to the debate about debt relief to the third world, I observe the numerous concerts around the world, in which rock musicians call for governments to do more to be done for Africa, and I feel as if I have been inhaling best Moroccan gold. Because as far as I can see, there is no connection whatsoever between what the do-gooders in the West proclaim to be the reasons for the hunger, disease and premature death in Africa, and the actual reasons. Instead, we get self-serving sermonising which flatters egos, eases consciences and makes the participants feel infinitely better about themselves. But concerts, and assembling multitudes in Edinburgh, and bawling that constantly reiterated and witless refrain 'Make Poverty History' will make no difference whatever to Africans' lives.

What happens to people who say such things? The admirable John O'Shea of Goal has been pointing out the futility of pouring money into Africa for over a decade now. Well, if they're lucky, they're simply ignored. If they're unlucky, they'll probably be treated to some foam-flecked denunciations of their imperialism, colonialism, racism, capitalism, fascism, or whatever fashionable crime the bien-pensant witch-burners feel like accusing dissenters of.

This Western fever about Doing Something For Africa is not actually about Africa. It is about moral self-indulgence, about making people feel better about themselves: simply, it is a form of voodoo. For the credulous in our post-Christian world accept as a matter of faith that concerts in Hyde Park and elsewhere can change things in Africa – and is no more or less ridiculous than the belief by the gangs of Sierre Leone that juju will make them immune to bullets.

For this is the new and godless religion, in which the priests are pop stars, the liturgy is rock music, and the object of reverence is an abstract and imagined entity called Africa. The witch doctors of this religion tell us that if Africa is forgiven its debts, then in essence all will be well. These debts are seen to be the responsibility of evil things called banks, and if only the banks could be persuaded to lift the debts, Africa could rise from the misery and the torpor that is overwhelming it. This is not logic, but simply the reinvention of the medieval miracle and mystery play.

The simplified view of the world this play offers is only possible if the ordinary intellectual faculties of scepticism and doubt are suspended; and suspended they must have been for people to believe the kind of rubbish that is routinely recycled about Africa. Take, for example, the figures for HIV/AIDS in Uganda, which are said to have been more than halved by the government of Africa's latest President-for-Life, Yoweri Museveni.

Now how can anyone actually believe any figures about AIDS in a country for which not one single reliable statistic exists? After decades of conflict, Uganda is still wracked by an insane civil war and no government institution functions nationwide. Only a pious devotion to the mumbo-jumbo of pop-voodoo could cause observers to accept that Ugandan rates of HIV/AIDS are far less than those of its neighbours; that's right, and the Irish Sea is far lower off the Dublin coast than off Wicklow.

The most obvious actuarial laws are suspended when discussing Africa, especially if the name of the Catholic Church is invoked. Take, for example, the Church's hostility to condoms, and its policy that the only way to halt the AIDS epidemic is through fidelity and sexual continence. Critics of the Church reply that condoms work 90 per cent of the time – and incredibly, they actually think that's an argument.

If you were told that crossing the road was safe nine times out of ten, how would you feel on the tenth trip? Okay, you might not be hit for sure on that occasion, but you know, actuarially, you inevitably will be. Similarly, since young people will have sex perhaps several times a day, what use your 90 per cent safety then? And does it matter which sexual deed transmits the disease to you – the first, the tenth or the twentieth? Because with a 10-per-cent margin of infection, you will, with reasonable certainty, sooner or later contract it.

And only with the religion that is called Africa are the ordinary mathematics of life utterly abandoned. Through the voodoo of that religion, the condom which is known to be unsafe 10 per cent of the time – and all accept this – somehow achieves the 100-per-cent magical protection conferred by the bullet-proofing waters with which the warriors of Sierre Leone anoint themselves.

An extraordinary intellectual and moral inconsistency lies at the heart of this religion called Africa. Bono preaches at governments to spend more on aid to Africa, but admits to availing of the tax-exemption schemes available to artists. He personally could afford to eradicate malaria from an entire country, yet he chooses not to spend his vast wealth on such a project. He would, apparently, rather spend his money chasing a hat through the Dublin courts.

Yet this imbecilic and degrading inconsistency doesn't prevent him lecturing, posing and preaching. Nor does it prevent him from being accepted on his own estimate of himself. And in its way, this confirms that this new worldwide movement that has filled our airwaves in the past few days is a religion – for in matters of faith, we do not seek intellectual consistency. Bishops preach charity but practise self-indulgence: a Rome steeped in gold and opulence praises self-denial; the Poor Clares are certainly not poor – and nor, by God, are Sir Bob and St Bono.

[7 July 2005]

WORLD WAR I

I.9. Dulce et Decorum Est

With a spellbinding optimism, Eneclann, the Trinity publishers, planned to have the launch of the CD Rom publication of *Irelands' Memorial Records 1914–18* in the open air at the Memorial Gardens at Islandbridge. In Ireland. In January. So, with a gale dumping the Bermuda Triangle on our heads, the launch was rushed to the bottom of the park, to the Trinity Boat Club, home to rowers for the best part of 150 years.

The hallway of the club is lined with team photographs of oarsmen back to the latter decades of the nineteenth century. I searched out the picture for the rowers of 1905, a century ago. The team captain back then was E. Julian. Ah yes. This was a name I knew.

Ernest Julian subsequently became Reid Professor of Law at Trinity, a post held in later years by both Mary Robinson and Mary McAleese, who did so much to further commemoration of Ireland's dead from the Great War – and poignantly so. For their distant predecessor went on to become one of the first soldiers of the 10th Irish Division to be killed in action in Gallipoli, in August 1915, having abandoned the safety of academia to do his duty as he saw it. And but for the optimism of Eneclann, and the weather outside, I would not now have been looking at his face.

In the cosmos, cogs click; synchronous waves ripple through dark matter; events jostle to arrive at the same place at the same time. There are 49,400 men listed in Ireland's Memorial Records. The Eneclann press release, written long before our retreat to the boat-club, chose to cite the stories of three of them as samples of the real men whom the volumes commemorate. One was Ernest Julian.

What changes Ernest's earnest face has witnessed since it first arrived on those walls one hundred years ago. From being a mere rower he went on to become captain and coach, and then with so many of his class and caste, in August 1914, this young professor marched to Lansdowne Road and enlisted in D Company of the 7th Battalion, Royal Dublin Fusiliers. He was mortally wounded in Gallipoli during the advance on Chocolate Hill just a year later. Within a further year, the Easter Rising unleashed new forces on Irish life, creating new historical perspectives that were owned by those who were either ignorant of, or actively hostile to, the cause which Professor Julian had served.

So though the new state in time did permit the construction of a memorial park to those who had perished on the Allied side in the Great War, it did not permit its schools to teach a rounded history of that dark time, from 1914 to 1922. One single narrative emerged, which rigorously excluded the more than 200,000 Irishmen who followed the call of their elected leaders and their churchmen and enlisted in British or Allied colours.

As Taoiseach, De Valera refused the park a formal opening, and over the coming decades, from his celluloid vantage point in the hall of the Dublin University boating pavilion, Ernest Julian could observe that the fate of Islandbridge symbolised the eradication of his generation of soldiers from the popular memory. Officially under the state's care, the gardens were, with a brutal neglect, allowed to fall into a shameful desuetude. By 1985 they were a scandal: Lutyens' ornamental triumph had become a vast, rat-infested rubbish dump, his cupola walls mere granite pages for graffiti, and wild horses grazed where dead men should have been honoured.

Julian could not then have believed that then, galvanised by the splendid and now departed Campbell Heather, the state would finally intervene and rescue the gardens. The tens of thousands of dead Irishmen, and a good few Irishwomen, were thus almost overnight rescued from the dustbin of amnesia, and now there is hardly a soul who adheres to the single-thread version of Irish history.

The Memorial Records now available on CD Rom are by no means comprehensive nor entirely correct: some of the Irish dead (and presumably many British) seem to have been overlooked as the official bureaucracy of death failed to match the ruthless efficiency of the machinery of killing. The Records were therefore created from imperfect sources – how imperfect, only further research will tell. Moreover, many non-Irishmen who served in Irish regiments are wrongly counted as Irish. The true Irish death toll for the war was about 35,000.

That aside, the Records – assembled just after the war by Eva Barnard, daughter of the Church of Ireland archbishop of Dublin, and sumptuously decorated by the genius Harry Clarke – constitute a massive historical and genealogical resource, now for the first time, computer-accessible through this magnificent CD. Every single college and secondary school in the country, and indeed anyone interested in our history, should have a copy: it costs only €94.90 (see www.eneclann.ie).

The Minister, John O'Donoghue, gave a generous speech at the launch, observing – and fairly – that across the way, in Kilmainham Jail, another tradition, dear to his heart, was also commemorated.

Quite so. And without wishing to fetishise the dead, is it not right for this state finally to assemble an official list of the IRA/Free State dead of 1916 to 1922? Only bigots benefit from ignorance, and those men and women of that time did their duty as they saw it. They deserve better than an anonymity which the men of Islandbridge, and – in particular – Ernest Julian, oarsman, Reid Professor of Law, and 1st Lieutenant, Royal Dublin Fusiliers, know about, all too well.

[25 January 2005]

I.10. Remembering the Irish Guards

How many ghosts will finally re-assemble in the National Concert Hall next Saturday to celebrate a return to their native land? Sons of the gentry and sons of the soil, policemen, farm-labourers and titled earls have shared a common exile that comes to a long overdue and symbolic end this day week, when the Irish Guards Band will finally play alongside Army Number One Band – the first time that a British army band has played in independent Ireland since 1922.

And who will be there, this coming Saturday, in that silent pallid throng, gazing from the gods of the National Concert Hall? The Hon. G. Morris, perhaps, killed in action at Landrecies on September 1, 1914, leading his men into action on a white charger, his wife at home in Galway, pregnant with the child who would one day be Lord Killanin: and look, there is young 2nd Lt Andy Bain, who had only just joined the 1st Battalion, when he was killed by a stray mortar shell seven days before the Armistice in 1918. By then, thousands of men – most of them immediately Irish, and the vast majority of Irish extraction – had passed through the ranks of the Irish Guards.

The names, to be sure, speak of an officer corps that came from the ruling classes of the United Kingdom and beyond. What illustrious forebears in Imperial Russia had Lieutenant Rodakowski, killed in the mud of Flanders in the vile month of October 1917? And may we safely conclude that Major Hon. J.F. Hepburn-Stuart-Forbes-Trefusis was not one of the Forbes who ran the smithy in Stoneybatter? But not all the officers were by any means grandees. Lieutenant Daniel Joseph Hegarty, Lieutenant Patrick Redmond, Lieutetant Joseph Barry, Lieutenant Lawrence Murphy; their names suggest more modest origins. And one of the Irish Guards officers to survive the war, a youngster named Brady, joined the RIC, serving in Sligo. As District Inspector, he banned reprisals against Sinn Féin/IRA homes after attacks on policemen.

But his humanitarianism did not save his life; he was killed by dumdum bullets in an ambush on his car. His gravestone in Glasnevin Cemetery records that he was killed 'doing his duty'. As indeed he was, a duty with which I entirely identify, rather than with that of those who slew him.

Some Irish Guards' lives are traceable; most are not. Twenty-nine Kellys, twenty-seven Murphys, eleven O'Neills, twenty-two Byrnes, eighteen O'Briens, fill the rank and file of otherwise nameless soldiery, culled from glen and mud cabin and RIC barracks. Hundreds of policemen of 1914 were by 1915 in the uniforms of the Irish Guards. By 1919 the survivors were back in the police; and many of those who managed to survive that experience were either hunted down in their homes in a post-ceasefire orgy of killing of ex-soldiers or ex-policemen, for which they were of course doubly qualified, or were forced into exile.

The Irish Guards of 1939 was again a predominately southern Irish regiment, its rank and file overwhelming Catholic. It participated in the debacle of Norway, and fought a rearguard action at Boulogne, just over sixty years ago. It served in North Africa, Italy, Normandy, Belgium, Holland and Germany: hundreds of free men from both parts of Ireland freely joining in the war against Naziism. For years it was believed that one of these was Lance Corporal John Patrick Kenneally VC, whose exploits are even celebrated in a museum in his home town of Cashel.

Yes, John Patrick Kenneally was from Cashel; but he didn't win a VC. As Richard Doherty and David Truesdale describe in their book *Irish Winners of the Victoria Cross* (Four Courts Press, and quite invaluable for people interested in this subject). The real Kenneally met a Birmingham Jew named Leslie Robinson on a building site, and they swapped identities. The new Kenneally went on to win the VC with a spectacular display of bravery in Tunisia: but what happened, I wonder, to the new Leslie Robinson? Is he now Levi Rabin in a kibbutz, who makes sure he is never seen naked in the shower?

Who can say what Ireland lost in these engagements? One illustrious son was Major John Kennedy whose story is told in the privately printed account by Robert Jocelyn. With war's end a few weeks away, Kennedy, a much loved and fearless officer, was ordered on a unsupported clearing-out operation under the noses of German artillery. It was folly of prodigious proportions, which lost the Irish Guards, within spitting distance of peace, 175 casualties, including the life of the gallant John Kennedy MC of Bishopscourt, County Kildare.

In terms of public memory and official acknowledgment, these men were in a way banned from Ireland; next Saturday in the National Concert Hall the ban is formally lifted, as the Army's Number One Band, and the band of the Irish Guards, play together under the batons of Commandant John Ryan and Major Andrew Chatburn, all proceeds to charities aiding ex-servicemen from each tradition; and in some cases, and more than a few, that means both. Tickets for the parterre available from the NCH: but as for the grey and silent throng in the gods, why, they paid the price of entry years ago.

[17 June 2000]

I.11. An Absurdly Titled War?

Writing his European Diary selections from Flanders the other day, our Jamie Smyth said that the Great War was 'absurdly titled'. Well, no doubt the people who so absurdly titled it were not thinking of how we might in time come to change the meaning of the word 'great' so that it also would come to mean 'excellent', 'healthy', and 'in good form'. They used the word in exactly the same way that Cecil Woodham-Smith used it when she referred to 'The Great Hunger', and others used it to describe The Great Fire of London or The Great Plague, no one intending to imply any approval whatsoever of the disastrous phenomena the adjective was describing.

It's November. Might I suggest something to you? Drive out to the country, walk into a field and stand still there for ten minutes. That should do it. And then bear in mind that the men of the Great War would spend two weeks in the front line. Two weeks without heaters or fires or dry feet or proper, modern waterproof clothing: just wool and flannel and hobnailed leather and no exercise of any kind by which to stay warm. Two weeks almost without moving, as the wind blew down from the North Sea freighted with sleet or snow or rain, or endless, penetrating damp. Two weeks immersed in wet soil. Two weeks crouching. Two weeks without proper sleep. Year in and year out: for millions of men, millions and millions of them.

We do not do justice to the men of the Great War visiting our vocabularies and our twenty-first century standards on them. They were nineteenth-century men, with a largely unquestioning acceptance of what they must do, just as they had in civilian life at home. There is little evidence indeed that they felt it wrong that deserters should be shot. In as much as they had opinions on anything, they were probably more than touched by fatalism. They probably sensed that the short straw awaited them all, sooner or later: the best way of coping was by being true to their mates, never letting them down, covering for one another in front of the NCOs and the officers, and sharing whatever spoils came their way.

Lasting and poisonous mythological caricatures, aided by *Oh What a Lovely War!* and *Blackadder* have been created to describe this period. It suits both us and the Brtish to think that you had heroic soldiers, gallant if unimaginative junior officers, and blundering fools as generals: the lions led by donkeys of Ludendorff's famous quote. Except he never said it after all, why should he? Those lions led by donkeys beat the German Grand Army in the field.

Contrary to the myth that most people hold dear, General Haig was not a blundering butcher. He made many mistakes but which general did not, with the new technologies of tank, aircraft, massed machine-gun, artillery location and radio making their military debut? This was the first war in history in which generals could neither see the battle or issue instructions directly to the soldiers. They were blind, deaf, dumb. Ah, but were they not skulking in their chateaus deep behind their lines? Well, headquarters necessarily had to be out of range of enemy artillery: but skulk hardly does the men justice one hundred British generals were killed in action in the war.

An equal myth – perpetuated in part by the snobbish post-war poets – was that British officers were public school toffs. Really? In fact 200,000 officers of 1918 had been commissioned from the ranks. One of these was Freddie Plunkett from Tipperary, who began the war as a sergeant with the Royal Irish Regiment and four years later ended it as a Brigadier General with a DSO and bar, MC DCM and Croix de Guerre. Similar decorations were awarded to Brigadier General Jack Hunt, a Dublin working-class Catholic who at the outset of the war had been a mere drill-sergeant at Trinity College Dublin.

It is impossible to say who was the most promising of all the Irish soldiers who – unlike Hunt and Plunkett – did not make it back. But the most obvious of all was Alfred Durham Murphy. Survivors of his battalion. The 2nd Leinsters, would annually gather each January after the war for a mass to for the repose of his soul. I met one of them once, a Redmondite volunteer named Tierney, over twenty years ago, and when he spoke of his commanding officer all those over 50 years later, this ancient gentleman wept.

Alfred Murphy was a phenomenal soldier: brave, intelligent, resourceful, and ferociously loyal to his men. He was from Ballinamona House near Cashel,

County Tipperary, the scion of a Catholic gentry family. He was touched by charisma and humour, and contrary to another myth, like many of the gentry, he did not have an English accent. He had gone to France in September 1914, and in almost continuous action, had been awarded the Military Cross and the Distinguished Service Order, for gallantry in the field.

By January 1917 he was a 27-year-old Lt-Colonel of the 2nd Leinsters. He was inspecting his men in the trenches when a large German shell landed in the middle of them, killing seven enlisted men. Their commanding officer was also killed. One of those killed in the blast was his orderly whom he had known at home – William Corcoran, from Cashel, County Tipperary.

The Murphy family at home were devastated by the loss of this wonderful, talented man, and turned his bedroom into a shrine. His brother Eddie became a founder member of the IRA – the Irish Rainfall Association – and meteorologist, and thus could be said to have been the founder of the Irish meteorological service. An epileptic when the condition was surrounded by baseless superstition, he never married. His sister Kathleen was deeply attached to Piers McCan, who was elected Sinn Féin TD in 1918 while in Gloucester jail and who died there of flu shortly afterwards. She never married. Thus a 300-year line of Catholic gentry at Ballinamona finally came to an end. Nothing great about that, either.

[11 November 2005]

I.12. The Sinking of the Leinster

As the assistant purser of the *Leinster*, Bill Sweeney, drifted from his life in 1979, did he wonder how the fate that had befallen his vessel 61 years had been so totally forgotten in Ireland? To be sure, he had recently been interviewed by some young fellow – what was his name? Whelan, was it? – about the catastrophe, but otherwise, no one cared. Hundreds of people coldly massacred within sight of Kingstown, yet the country from which they had sailed had forgotten them.

The amnesia was total, perhaps because it was voluntary. It is possible to eradicate *public* recollection of an event either by massive coercion, such as that practised in the Soviet Union. This used terror to prevent people speaking of a famine or a massacre, yet still they whispered what they knew to their children by the fireside. The hearth became the guardian of the truth. There is another form of amnesia, which is consensual and altogether more compelling, and it was employed in Ireland. It used the social tools of schooling, disapproval and taboo to prevent anyone questioning the emerging national narrative. To remember, even privately, was to betray the new state.

Thus the sinking of the *Leinster*, one the cruellest and most needless acts of the First World War, was consigned to the historical waste bin. Irish history books ignored it. Germany – after all – had been the acclaimed 'gallant allies' of the Easter Proclamation. The act was forgotten, so were the dead, and so too were the survivors. Declan Whelan alone had thought to take down Bill Sweeney's recollections. The *Leinster* had gone from public memory, for all time.

Well, not quite. No doubt had it been left to various governments, all memory of everything not associated with the Golden Thread of history, linking the Fenians with today, would have been forgotten. But amongst those killed were postal workers in the mail room, and their union remembered them. And there were a few inconvenient individuals, who would consult old newspapers and would ask: How could such a monstrosity be forgotten? How could the sack of Cork and Balbriggan, in which deaths numbered perhaps three or four, become almost declarations of national martyrdom, to be recited by every child in the land, yet this cold-blooded and deliberate massacre of hundreds, could be totally eradicated from public memory?

Even today, when we profess to be able to take a broader view of our history than that created by three-quarters of a century of schooled-amnesia, there are those who find mitigation for the sinking of the *Leinster*, because it carried soldiers. But the U-boat skipper could not have known that – and no rules of war permitted the no-warning sinking of a civilian mail-ship containing large numbers of civilians. Had a brace of British torpedoes taken so many Irish lives, the east coat of Ireland would have developed a serious list with the memorials to the victims.

There is but one memorial in Dun Laoghaire, erected by the postal workers union, and now another, and perhaps more important one, has just appeared: Philip Lecane's account of the tragedy *Torpedoed! The RMS Leinster Disaster*. It is perhaps a melancholy reflection on Irish interest in the *Leinster* that Philip's book has not been produced by an Irish publisher, but by Periscope Publishing of Penzance in Cornwall.

There are tales here too terrible for contemplation, such as that of Essie Gould from Limerick, who boarded the *Leinster* with her entire family, en route to visit their father, a former soldier now working in a munitions factory in England. Possibly the good wages available in the industry enabled him to pay for the journey to their doom. His wife, Catherine Gould was accompanied by her children, Michael, Essie, Alice, Angela and Olive, aged between one year to twenty. All were lost, save Essie. How did she and her father console one another over the years ahead; and did they find anyone at home remotely interested in the unspeakable fate which war had reserved for them?

And how long before Tralee forgot its *Leinster* dead? Four girls from the town, Chrissie Murphy, Lizzie Healy, and sisters Lena and Norah Galvin, were lost in the mailboat: were they as swiftly abolished from the Kerry memory as the two Black and Tans who were thrown alive into the gas-making furnace in the town three years later? But no act of amnesia was required to abolish all memory of poor Robert Palmer. He was a cripple, a word no longer in vogue, but it probably adequately describes him. Disabled from infancy with a spinal injury, he was on his way from the Cripples' Home in Bray to Barnardo's in London, and never stood a chance. He is truly forgotten, for his name did not even appear on the official list of the dead.

And then there are John McCormack's nephews and nieces, ten of them: their parents Thomas and Charlotte were lost on the *Leinster*. What became of these ten orphans down the coming decades? And did the great Irish tenor help them financially?

It is not the narratives that a society tells which define it so much as the tales it does not tell. We have scuffed over the unmarked graves of history's inconvenient dead, and coughed to hide the sound of our shoes. Yet every now and then a torch shines in history's darkness and suddenly, in the dungeon of their exile, the serried eyes of the forgotten start up with gratitude. Philip has lit such a torch, and it is one to break your heart.

[25 May 2005]

WORLD WAR II

I.13. *Chamberlain or Churchill*

'Which do you want to be remembered as,' asked Jason Fitzharris of the Taoiseach last week: 'Chamberlain or Churchill?'

Well, I can't speak for Bertie – why, even he sometimes has trouble doing that – but speaking for myself, I think I'd rather be Neville Chamberlain. He recognised realities, and did not base his policies on dreams. Churchill both evolved policy and governed by fantasy, and moreover, thirsted for war, repeatedly, throughout the twentieth century. His belligerent dreams caused him to go charging off in all manner of direction, regardless of the conditions there. In the full measure of time, though not in my lifetime, Churchill will be seen as one of the great warmongers of the twentieth century, an abominable man with an insatiable appetite for conflict.

Neville Chamberlain acknowledged one central truth; the British people in the 1930s did not want to go to war. Warning them of the dangers of the

Third Reich, as Churchill was doing, did not incline them to seek a return to the breastworks of Flanders and the trenches of Picardy. Chamberlain knew that he could not induce those people to fight in a war that was not of their national interest, any more than Dev could have done here in 1939.

Chamberlain did all he could to prepare to protect the British national interest and prepare against war. The Spitfire, Hurricane, Mosquito, Manchester (the precursor of the Lancaster) were ordered when he was Prime Minister. So too were radar and the first jet engine. The British army was reorganised into becoming the first all-mechanised army in the world.

However, governments can mobilise technological change, but they cannot, in a democracy, change popular will. Chamberlain knew that the people of Britain, and therefore a popular army drawn from such a people, had no stomach for real war, as events were to testify. In essence, the British army cut and ran in May 1940, no less than the French, and but for the naval genius of Sir Bertram Ramsey – in every sense the match of Nelson, and more – it would have been left stranded in France, and Hitler's command would inevitably have soon reached to Slieve League and the Cliffs of Moher.

But by this time, Churchill was Prime Minister, and though his speeches of the summer and autumn of 1940 contain some of the greatest rhetorical flourishes in the English language, it was not he alone that caused the people of Britain to fight on. By this time, there could be no dealing with Hitler. After all, Poland had entered an alliance with Hitler in the dismemberment of Czechoslovakia, and its reward was the Nazi compact with Stalin, and its utter destruction.

National survival is one thing: assertion of national will abroad quite another. Just as the British army was no match for the Nazi armies in France in 1940, nor was it a match for the outgunned, outnumbered, under-equipped Afrika Korps from 1941 on. Organisationally, culturally, psychologically, the armies of the Third Reich were infinitely superior to those of the United Kingdom.

Chamberlain knew this in 1938; he knew that he could not induce the British people to fight for a country they could not find on a map. This is not the absurdity it is often held to be but an inviolable truth that holds today as much as it did then. Only a bellicose old fool like Churchill would maintain the opposite.

At the close of the nineteenth century, from Sudan to South Africa, he had sought bloodshed. In 1914, as first lord of the Admiralty, he conceived the folly of attacking Turkey, and using all his bullying and debating skills against the war cabinet whose members could not cope with his overbearing mendacity and ferocious willpower. The result was just about the greatest defeat of British arms in history, and it is why an uncomprehending generation of Irish children was raised to sing, 'It was better to die 'neath an Irish sky, than in Suvla or Sed el Barrh.'

Of course that wasn't his only contribution to Irish musicology. Where would all the ballads be without the Black and Tans that came into existence at Church-ill's behest, even as he levied a quite wicked war against the infant Turkish state?

His later tenure as Chancellor of the Exchequer proved to be disastrous, until the backwaters and the back benches very properly beckoned. From there he was rescued by war, and at the Admiralty again, he promptly repeated his Turkish folly, this time in Norway, his intention being to secure supply routes to help Finland against the Soviet Union. For, not content with taking on the Third Reich, he also wanted to fight the Reds too. In other words, a barking lunatic beyond remedial care, whom the British people properly dumped at the first chance in 1945, before he led them to war against India.

So Bertie, Neville Chamberlain was a good man who dreaded a repeat of the First World War, just as you have dreaded a repeat of the past thirty years. But he did prepare for the worst, even if his timing was poor (but how could it be better when faced with the monomaniacal genius of Hitler?) Nonetheless, it was he, not Churchill, who prepared the RAF for the battle of Britain and the British army for modern warfare. Moreover, he knew that when a peaceful man plays cards with a crook, the day will come when he must reach for his gun and come out fighting. That's a lesson always worth bearing in mind, Bertie, but especially now.

[2 March 2005]

I.14. D-Day

June 6, 1944, and at last the serious reckoning between freedom and tyranny was about to begin. Nor was the tyranny Nazi-alone. For the virus of Marxist totalitarianism that erupted in St Petersburg in 1917 proved to be the greatest human calamity since the Black Death. Within five years Soviet Communism had consumed the old Tsarist empire: within another ten years, the virus of state totalitarianism had spread to Germany, mutated, and produced the Third Reich. Borne on the wind of an alliance of convenience, and hybridised with indigenous strains of barbarism, the virus had then seized Japan. Italy, Spain and Portugal pro-duced their own peculiar forms of the disease. China, Korea, Vietnam were busy incubating fresh variants.

Thus sixty years ago, most of the Eurasian continent and its attendant islands, were in thrall to totalitarian dictatorships, run by secret police: the Gestapo, the NKVD, and across the Japanese empire, the Kempeitai. The scale of these con-joined empires of despotism was vast, their northern borders running from the North Cape of Norway along the Arctic Circle to the Bering Strait, while their southern meridian marched from the Bay of Biscay all the way to New Guinea and the Great Barrier Reef, upon Australia's northern shore.

Hopes for world freedom now resided in the peripheral, anglophone societies of the United Kingdom, its empire and commonwealth, and most of all, its former colony, the United States. In the history of humankind, there has never been such a contest between two sets of values: between common-law societies of the English-speaking peoples against an entire continent of totalitarian regimes and their hundreds of millions of slaves.

Yet in all truth, only the perspective of history allows us see the truth of that first week in June 1944 – that this contest was one of world freedom on the one hand and all the toxins of global totalitarianism on the other. For the concessions made by Churchill and Roosevelt at Teheran in 1943 had effectively ceded Eastern Europe to Stalin. No one then really suspected how dark the night would be that would soon fall on the countries east of the Oder and the Elbe, and for the decades ahead, because it was the immediate future which filled every waking and sleeping moment of the Allied commanders, 60 years ago.

The architect of the D-Day landings was Bernard Law Montgomery, a little bantam cock of a man, a pedantic master of detail, a man who engaged affection and fury in equal measure. Socially he was inept, almost autistic. When the Prime Minister's wife Clementine Churchill told Montgomery's aide that it was time to change for dinner, Montgomery interrupted her. 'That won't be necessary. I never dine with my ADC.' Lady Churchill, incredulous, replied with an icy anger: 'Who are you to tell me whom I entertain in my house! Captain Chevasse is my guest and will dine with us.'

His manners aside, Montgomery was the master of the set-piece battle, and D-Day turned out to be his greatest triumph. It was an encounter with his oldest adversary, Erwin Rommel, whom he had had frequently outgunned and out-fought, but had never before out-thought. But in Normandy, finally, he did.

Rommel assumed that the Allies would make their landings at high tide, to spare the advancing infantry prolonged exposure to defensive fire. So his primary beach defences would be underwater at high tide, and largely consisted of mines on frames, to blow the landing craft up before they could reach the shore. Montgomery's plan was to avoid these defences by landing at low tide, and push armour forward to deal with the defences before the infantry would follow, and advance inland.

Hindsight allows us to contemplate this project with equanimity. There was little enough in the souls of those who planned the assault. Churchill himself had been responsible for two calamitous landings, at Gallipoli in 1915 and Narvik in 1940, which had ended in evacuation and defeat. Two landings in Italy not long before, against largely unprepared defences at Salerno and Anzio, had been near-disasters. So, the auguries were not good, and were made worse as D-Day, June 5th, approached and the fine summer weather of recent days gave way for tempests and high seas. Suddenly, the landings were simply impossible. Eisenhower postponed them.

By this time colossal aerial efforts had gone into subduing the German defences, and at terrible cost: 2000 aircraft and 12,000 aircrew had been lost over France preparing for D-Day within the past two months alone. Now it seemed as if the invasion force of 6483 vessels and nearly 16,000 aircraft would have to be stood down for at least two weeks, playing havoc with morale, organisation and timetables. However, weather forecasters spotted a break in the bad weather, and while Eisenhower ordered the invasion to go ahead, one day late, Rommel, without proper forecasts of Atlantic weather systems, seized the chance to return home for his wife's 50th birthday. The greatest mistake of his life.

But of course, war favours the warrior who makes fewest mistakes. The decision to go was sounder than anyone who knew: the next possible day, and indeed by that time a mandatory date, June 19th, was to experience the worst storms in channel history, which would have destroyed the invasion fleet. There lies a sobering thought indeed. However, where the Allies did blunder was to focus too much on the landings, and not plan properly for what would follow. This not merely affected operations, almost fatally, but equally, has coloured much of popular perception thereafter – that somehow or other, the D-Day landings made victory inevitable, and fighting in France was quite different from that of the Great War.

Not so. Just as the planners for the Somme in 1916 gravely under-estimated the defensive qualities of the German barbed wire, the Allied planners in 1944 catastrophically failed to take into account the high Normandy hedgerows, the bocage. These restricted visibility enormously, effectively nullifying Allied superiority in materiel and in the air, and made fighting conditions almost totally unrelated to the training the invaders had undergone in Britain.

So, D-Day did not provide a First Day on the Somme, as Churchill had dreaded: instead of the 20,000 dead that he had at one time feared, British casualties – including wounded and missing – on the day totalled just 3000. But for each day thereafter, the fighting was every bit as intense and bloody as it had been in Picardy a generation before. Allied losses in the Battle for Normandy in the summer of 1944 were of Great War proportions – 425,000 killed, wounded and missing, roughly double the German losses in killed and injured.

Yet the events of the unfolding months do not detract from the heroic achievements of the soldiers, seamen and airmen of D-Day, but add to them. The men who on June 6th forced their way past the German defences on those now famous beaches, or who landed by glider and parachute in the orchards and the pastures beyond, were to spend the summer fighting there. There in that deadly bocage country, rifle companies that were built up over years were within a few days destroyed, and replacements would arrive from other units, would be re-badged, and sent into battle, often to die namelessly amongst complete strangers. It is a melancholy tale of dogged bravery as unrelenting as anything the Western front can show.

Moreover, perhaps 20,000 French civilians were killed by Allied bombers. After USAAF bombers blasted American positions, killing and wounding 500, the army protested. The air force rejected the complaints, insisting that the stray bombs that did the damage were within the normal expectancy of errors. In other words, buster, that's war.

That's war indeed. The 12th (Hitlerjugend) SS Division, made its entrance on the battlefield late on D-Day, and was a truly terrifying force, which routinely murdered its prisoners, usually Canadian, often tying them to trees and cutting their throats. Under the awesome General Klaus Meyer, at 34 the youngest German divisional commander of the war, an entirely new form of warfare made its debut, one which we have been made more familiar with of late: SS soldiers would strap on explosive charges and detonate themselves beside British tanks.

In all this slaughter, perhaps the key event, and a reminder of what this was all about, occurred at Caen prison the morning of June 6th: 87 suspected members of the Resistance were taken out and summarily shot, almost in retaliation for the landings. Thus June 6th lives on, and properly, in the imagination of the world as a symbol of freedom, when thousands of men closed with the Normandy coast, vomiting with seasickness and terror, not knowing how many minutes they had to live.

Opposite Omaha Beach, the special floating tanks designed to reduce the German concrete German fortifications were swamped by cross currents, and sank. What steel should have done would now have to be done with human flesh, and was, but at a cost of 5000 casualties. In some small towns in Pennsylvania, from which were recruited so many men of the 29th Division who had perished in the landings, almost every family lost a relative or friend on the narrow sands of Omaha.

In Ireland, too, over the coming days, sheepish telegram boys would be delivering the British War Office telegrams, though certain post offices delegated this dreadful duty to local clergymen. One hundred thousand Irishmen, from north and south, had joined the British army, including two-thirds of the Irish Army of 1939, and many participated in the landings. The Royal Ulster Rifles was the only British regiment that had two battalions in the landings, one glider-borne, one on the beaches, and the 9th Independent Parachute Battalion that landed early on D-Day morning was based largely on Irish volunteers.

The most significant Irish contribution on the day probably came from Captain Redmond Cunningham from Waterford. The son of John Redmond's election agent, he had volunteered as a dedicated anti-Nazi, and now led a troop of Royal Engineer tanks in the first-wave assault on German fortifications. Mines blew up two of his four vehicles. He needed a replacement tank. He went along the beach on foot, looking for one, while all around him mines were exploding, men were being killed, and mortar-bombs were landing. He returned to his own tank, and that too was blown up.

He then led the survivors of his men on foot to clear a dense minefield, with mines every eighteen inches. They spent four hours doing this, under fire. Then, equipped with fresh tanks, he led the remains of his troop forward against enemy positions, eventually causing the surrender of 900 Germans. That night he drove alone into Caen; and finding no Allied soldiers there, turned back. He was the last British soldier to enter Caen for more than a month, as the German garrison held firm.

Redmond Cunningham, the only Irishman to win an MC on D-Day, was thus a participant in the first day in a Eurasian land war that, hot and cold, was to last another forty-five years. Initially the foe was Nazism; yet its kindred-creed, communism, soon took its place in the totalitarian line-of-battle against freedom, this time from behind the Iron Curtain it erected in its newly gained territories. It was confronted remorselessly by the economic might and military deterrence of the US, until victory was finally won in 1989. Redmond Cunninham was alive to see it.

But the primary price in Normandy sixty years ago was paid by ordinary people, plain men drawn from their civilian lives to fight an evil whose depth was beyond all civilised imagining. Such plain men, volunteers all, were crew in a Royal Canadian Air Force Lancaster bomber on operations in support of Allied troops in Normandy, which was attacked and set on fire by a German fighter. The skipper gave the order to abandon ship.

As he was about to bail out of the doomed aircraft, Flying Officer Andrew Mynarski, in peacetime a furrier from Winnipeg, looked through the flames engulfing the fuselage and saw that the tail gunner, Patrick Brophy was trapped in his jammed gun-turret. Instead of jumping, Andrew Mynarski fought his way through the inferno, and desperately but unsuccessfully tried to swivel the turret to release the gunner. As he struggled, he caught fire. Finally, aflame from head to foot, he stood up, gave a warrior's farewell salute to Brophy, and jumped to his death.

Moments later, the Lancaster hit the ground and exploded, throwing young Brophy and the other crew-members clear. All, miraculously, survived. As an allegory for the fight to clear Eurasia of arbitrary murder and death camps, this tale of a Canadian-Pole nobly giving his life trying to save that of a Canadian-Irishman suffices. Now, sixty years on, the ancestral homelands of both men, Patrick Brophy and Andrew Mynarski VC, enjoy a common freedom and a common economic purpose, within a common European Union. If ever a date in world history is worth celebrating, it truly is June 6th, 1944.

[6 June 2004]

I.15. David Irving: The Holocaust & Auschwitz

Holocaust. From the Greek, *holos*, whole or entire, and *kaustos*, burnt: wholly consumed by fire. And David Irving was right. There was no holocaust. The genocide that consumed the Jewish and Romany peoples from 1941 onwards had none of the cleansing and singular purity of an all-consuming flame. That genocide was sprawling, brutal, bloody and largely done by human hand. Whether gas chambers were involved is irrelevant. Most of the victims of the Nazi genocide were probably shot or, worst of all, were worked to death.

The imprisonment of David Irving is the very quintessence of European hypocrisy towards Jews. The continent that hosted The Final Solution is also the primary subsidiser of the Palestinian Authority, which is also probably the greatest source of published anti-Semitism in the world. The PA churns out books and television programmes that present Jews as pigs and monkeys, and that extol the virtue of suicide bombers who kill Jews. Yet simultaneously, across almost the entire EU, it is illegal to say what I just said in my opening paragraph: that there was no holocaust.

As it happens, I have read most of David Irving's works. He is a brilliant researcher, is partly mad, and is clearly bad. But those who say that he denies the Nazi programme of genocide of Jews simply haven't read his writings. Page twelve, volume two of his extraordinary *Hitler's War*: 'Hitler had jeered in January 1939: "Today I am going to be a prophet again. If the international finance-Jewry inside and outside Europe manages just once more to precipitate the world war, the outcome will be, not the bolshevisation of the earth and the consequent triumph of Jewry, but the annihilation of the Jewish race on earth." '

The next paragraph, he quotes Hitler in November 8, 1942 referring to that prophecy: 'As a prophet, (the Jews) always laughed at me. But of those who laughed loudest then, countless laugh no longer today. Nor are those who are still laughing even now likely to laugh when their time comes.'

Page 15 talks of the 'demographic extermination' of unwanted elements in Poland, including the Jews. Irving refers to the 'murderous orders' of the SS chief Heydrich, and his project of 'liquidising the Jews'. The Nazi General Riechenau's statement is quoted. 'This is why the soldier must understand why we have to exact a harsh but just retribution from the Jewish sub-humans. This serves the added purpose of stifling at birth uprisings in the rear of the Wehrmacht, since experience shows these are always conceived by Jews.'

Irving quotes Hitler as saying the proclamation was 'excellent', and then himself goes on to refer to the 'barbarous massacres of Jews'. 'The ghastly secrets of the extermination programme were well kept.' 'Each day after July 22 a train-load of five thousand Jews left Warsaw for the extermination center at Treblinka.' 'By August 1942, the massacre machinery was gathering momentum.'

I say all this because I am sick of reading the misrepresentations of Irving's opinions; that he is a consistent denier of the Nazi programme of genocide. Moreover, I am inclined to share his distaste for the fashionable 'branding' of the fate of Europe's Jews by the term 'holocaust'. And I am emphatically with him when he rebuffed a challenge from a particularly stupid BBC reporter: 'Do you accept that six million Jews died in the Holocaust?'

Six millions Jews did not die in the 'Holocaust' and there was no singular 'holocaust', capital h or not. We don't know how many Jews died, but the Nazis were not so efficient as to ensure that it was precisely six million. There is a numerical purity about that number every bit as dogmatically insane as the Nazi notions of racial purity. We can never know how many Jews were murdered – but that they were murdered, in their millions, even David Irving did not deny in his trilogy, *Hitler's War*.

Irving's most contentious points are that Hitler did not know of the geno-cide of the Jews, which is simply silly, and that more people died at Chap-paquiddick than in the gas chambers of Auschwitz, which is unforgivable, but in a moral, not a historical or a criminal sense. It is disgusting to make such cheap gibes about Auschwitz, of which Irving himself wrote: 'But Himmler's ghastly secret was coming out, for two Slovak Jews had escaped from Auschwitz exter-mination camp ...'

But even that acknowledgment is irrelevant. Anyone has a right to have wrong opinions, free of the sanctimonious dogma of doctrinaire EU liberal secu-larism. Anyone should be able to declare that the Nazis didn't massacre Jews, or that no Armenians were murdered in 1915, or that Dresden was a legitimate target, or that it was right to bomb Hiroshima, or that Jesus was not the son of God or that Mohammed was not a prophet, without going to jail for doing so. In a free society, being able to be wrong is the very definition of freedom: otherwise we are ruled by thought police.

And paradoxically, the only countries in Europe that have made 'holocaust-denial' a crime are those that were once governed by Nazi thought police. But not Ireland, not Britain. The intellectual legacy of the Third Reich lives on wherever people today are not entitled to be wrong. For being wrong is not wrong. What is wrong in a free and civilised society is using one's opinions – right or wrong – to promote racial or religious hatred. That is what the Palestinian Authority does – and moreover, we in the EU pay it to do so.

[22 February 2006]

Some further reflections upon the disgraceful imprisonment by the Austrian authorities of the virtually friendless historian David Irving. The twenty-four hours that have elapsed since my last column on the subject have given me the chance to get angrier still. To be sure, that Irving might well be a thoroughly nasty piece of goods, with vile neo-Nazi views; but he is entitled to be unpleasant and to hold whatever unacceptable views he likes, not least because the definition of what is nasty, unpleasant and unacceptable today might not necessarily hold tomorrow, when any of us might find ourselves being so defined.

In 1989, Irving declared that Auschwitz concentration camp and its gas chambers were the holiest shrines of the new twentieth-century religion. I'm not quite sure by what he meant by this, but inadvertently or otherwise, he was right. Piety about Auschwitz is the great secular unifier of European culture. Before France and the Netherlands went to the polls to vote on the European Constitution, both the Dutch Prime Minister, Jan-Peter Balkenende, and Sweden's EU Commissioner, Margot Walstrom, declared that the consequence of not endorsing the European Union Constitution would be another Auschwitz. Yes, I know.

In the secular theology of the modern EU religion of Europhilia, no argument is free of its Auschwitz trump card, even if the electorates aren't necessarily buying it (as – happily – the Dutch and the French didn't). Auschwitz is invoked at every turn as a symbol of the evil past that we have left behind: never again, comes the querulous cry, never again.

Investing a single place with potent symbolism of being the embodiment of an extinct evil and present virtue is what a shrine is all about; and just as pilgrims go to Glendalough and Rome, so too do they go to Auschwitz. Thus this on the internet:

Visit Krakow and Auschwitz in March from £129* per person.
Price includes:
  2 nights in 3-star hotel with breakfast,
  return flight from London to Krakow
  Auschwitz Tour

*Hotel – we offer you accommodation in one of the 3-star hotels situated in Kaz-
imierz – the former Jewish district – only a few minutes walk from the Krakow's
Old Town (4-or 5-star hotels are also available).*

Being able to stay in the former Jewish district adds a certain piquancy to
genocide-chic that no satirist could devise. You get see where they lived and
where they died, and why, even the chimney they vanished up: and what more
could you want? Well, a five star hotel, actually. Okay. You can have that too. The
Final Solution, with room service.

So we pray at the shrine of Auschwitz, and swear that the EU will prevent any repetition. Never again, we intone. Yet since Auschwitz was liberated,
at least a million people have been killed in programmed massacres in each of
the following countries: the Soviet Union, Kampuchea, communist China on
three occasions, the Congo also on perhaps three occasions and Rwanda. Massacres in the hundreds of thousands have occurred in Yugoslavia, Algeria, Sudan,
Ethiopia, Afghanistan, Iraq, Angola, Mozambique, Zimbabwe, Liberia, Lebanon,
Sierre Leone, Burundi, Vietnam, Korea. The EU, the home of the 'Never Again'
antiphon, actually stood by for years and dithered while the Muslims of Bosnia
were being despatched. So much for 'never again'.

The invocation of 'Auschwitz' is merely a secular and inverse form of the
medieval invocation of the Holy Name, and to sacrifice a palpable heretic in its
name is the greatest act of public piety possible. Never mind that Irving's supposed
act of holocaust denial was seventeen years ago; never mind that he recanted his
heresy; never mind that the fatwa against Salman Rushdie was lifted after ten
years; never mind that Irving's three-year sentence is far longer than given to
those guilty of assault and robbery; never mind (as I was saying yesterday) that the
EU subsidises far worse acts of anti-Semitism by the Palestinian Authority than
anything Irving is guilty of. Our secular religion of Europhilia simply demands a
sacrificial scapegoat, and he is it: and as bad and unjust as the sentence has been
the palpable gloating in the media at seeing the unbeliever bite the dust.

That he is a deeply unpleasant man with appalling views and disgusting
associates is irrelevant. What if he is – only in part – speaking the truth? What, say,
if only two million Jews were killed by Hitler's goons? Is it good news that four
million Jews were not murdered? Nazis, of course, would say it was bad news:
but what about you? What would you prefer? Do you actually want six million
Jews to have been butchered by the Nazis? For surely, the fewer Jews who died
in Hitler's genocide, the better.

Yet grotesquely, we are stuck with the moral converse: to have had a holocaust of six million Jews is now the dogmatic piety at the heart of the political
and legal culture of Europe. And the cathedral to this holy number of six million,

the St Peter's Basilica of the Holocaust, is Auschwitz. One cannot question or doubt the number, any more than one could have safely challenged the Crucifixion and Resurrection of Our Lord five hundred years ago. We have replaced the death of one Jew with the deaths of six million, and laid their sacrifice down as the altar-stone of a post-Christian Eurofaith. They died that the great idea of Europe might live. And whoever publicly declares otherwise, goes to jail. Torquemada would have understood perfectly.

[23 February 2006]

I.16. Revisionism at Work

We so often follow the lead of the American and British in everything that it is probably inevitable that the campaign to transform the Holocaust into a historically sacrosanct law will spread here; and given our love of moral posturing, we no doubt can look forward to a real treat on this issue. The Germans already have a meaningless law that makes it a criminal offence to deny that six million Jews died in the Holocaust: does the figure of 5,999,999 suggest that the atrocity was any less atrocious for the one Jew saved?

It does not. No intellectual or moral cause is served by turning history into a moral and legal dogma; all that is served is a reactionary notion about the individual's intellect and the state. That kind of notion underpinned the united theological and criminal legal code that caused Aristotle's beliefs in the movement of the heavenly bodies to be eternal verities, the denial of which was punishable before the courts. The issue is not the rightness of what Aristotle thought, but whether or not his beliefs in the universe should be protected by the rigours of the law, even from the mad, the foolish or the bad.

The known historical record concerning the Holocaust, God knows, is clear enough – there was a concerted attempt to destroy the Jewish population of Europe. To my mind, and without exaggeration or melodrama, no more evil single enterprise has yet been attempted in human history. But the figures for the gassed do not reach the nice and handy six million; the total death toll was more probably four million, many of whom died of hunger and disease rather than gas poisoning.

Nor was the Holocaust the only, or the first, attempt to dispose of unwanted human beings; what distinguished it was its Germanic efficiency and the documentary zeal with which the Third Reich recorded this particular historical triumph for did not little Germans of the future need to be shown what great things grandpa and his generation did to cleanse the world of the Jewish threat?

Before the Holocaust there was the massacre of the Armenians in the Ottoman Empire, largely by Kurds rather than by the ethnic Turks who are now held responsible for the killings. Nobody can know how many Armenians died – less than the figure given by Armenians, more than the figure admitted by Ankara.

It had not the concerted and centralised purpose of what the Nazis were to do thirty years later, and much of it was caused by bizarre and spontaneous jacquerie lynch mobs – but it had some of the characteristics of genocide. It would be absurd to make the denial of the Armenian massacre a criminal offence in law – as it would to deny that the fates of the aboriginal peoples of the US and Australia could, by cumulative experience and final effect, be akin to the Holocaust planned, if not fully achieved, by the Third Reich.

The horrible truth about freedom is that we have to allow the bad the right to speech, even as we allow it to ourselves, provided that that speech does not incite others to harm the health and lives of others. Holocaust denial does no such thing; in fact, in its own funny little way, it is a moral reassurance from neo-Nazis that this was something so terrible that it would have been beyond their beloved Adolf to contemplate. If they find the idea of mass murder so repugnant, is that in itself not reassuring? Do we need to protect ourselves with the criminal legal code from the intellectual ramblings of such people?

And if we do, who else must be silenced that they might not harm some central historical tenets, which should therefore be guarded by the courts? In New York State, it is now the law that children be taught that the Famine was an attempt at genocide of the Irish by the British. If British politicians are seriously going to make it a criminal offence to deny the Holocaust and Tony Blair has come out in favour of it: no doubt he hopes to win the Jewish vote and conciliate the doctrinaire, Left-wing dogmatists who have little enough to cheer about from New Labour and Americans are by law decreeing the Famine to have been genocide, what other historical episodes might not be incorporated into the criminal legal code?

We can all play at this game; fatwas and the intellectual intolerance of the imams were once the preserve of others. Now they seem to the plaything of Western politicians too. Might the British not insist it be a criminal offence to deny the historical significance of the Battle of Britain? Might not the Germans introduce a law compelling children to be taught that Dresden was the equivalent of Auschwitz? The Americans have already grabbed our Famine – might we not insist that Irish children are taught by law, to be enforced by the courts of the land, that the American Civil War was a shameful and wickedly imperialist assault by the Washington government on seceding states?

I happen to believe in the right of peoples to depart from political unions with which they are no longer in sympathy. Is that not the story of the Irish within the United Kingdom? Was that not the aspiration of generations of Irish political leaders through generations? So why should different rules be applied to the peoples of Alabama and Virginia, the Carolinas and Tennessee? Did not the plain men of those states, with not a slave to their name, freely lay down their lives in the cause of the rights of those states?

But that does not mean my beliefs should be a matter for the law. Individuals must make their own minds up about the rights and wrongs of the war between the states; for having made up my mind freely in one direction, might I not, with that same freedom, change my mind in the other direction?

Not according to the new priesthood that the History As Law phenomenon suggests is coming into existence. No room for intellectual error exists within that Inquisition; and when there is no room for error, who dare inquire? The willingness to be wrong in the pursuit of right is the keystone to intellectual freedom. It is a keystone we should keep our eye on.

[1 February 1997]

I.17. War Criminals

The death last week of the Nazi-hunter Simon Weisenthal gave media commentators yet another opportunity to race around the rat-run of the morally trite. If I have to read one more sententious utterance about Eichmann and the 'banality of evil', the witless cliché every posey pseudo-intellectual unfailingly reaches for when discussing the Third Reich, I will not be held accountable for my actions.

There was nothing banal about Eichmann, and only Hanna Ardendt's cursory appearance at his trial allowed her to coin a phrase that has since entered the banality of academe. Eichmann was a sophisticated, dedicated and brilliant man: he is proof that evil at its apex is often complex – indeed, needs to be complex if it is to be successful. But Arendt reduced him to a two-dimensional, tiresome little universalised caricature, which lives on wherever people wish to sound profound. (The banality of evil: Ah yes, heads nodding gravely, how very true.)

What is truly banal is the way Western liberal society has turned Simon Wiesenthal into a secular saint and the lightning conductor for all our guilt about political mass murder in the twentieth century. His tireless investigations into Nazi war crimes are held as proof that Western democracies care: genocide will never go unpunished again! Murderers may never sleep safely in their beds, for fear of the international policeman's hand on the slumbering shoulder, the gun-barrel in the ear, the whispered words: 'You're under arrest.'

In fact, Simon Weisenthal's career proved the converse is true. In part, this was because he was a remorseless self-publicist, whose claims were often fantastic: indeed, the former head of Mossad Isser Harel complained that Wiesenthal had no role whatever in the capture of Eichmann. Whether he had or not, his single-minded pursuit of Nazi war criminals has created the fiction that war criminals can know no safe sanctuary, thereby blinding the world to the greater truth that the majority of genocidal operations of the twentieth century were not by 'fascist' regimes, but by communist ones; and communist murderers for the most part were – and still are – able to spend the rest of their lives sleeping soundly in their beds.

For the extermination of entire species of inconvenient human beings was not the invention of Hitler and the Third Reich. The first person in the twentieth century publicly to enunciate mass murder as policy was the Jewish Bolshevik Gregory Zinoviev, who in September 1918 declared: 'To overcome our enemies we must have our own socialist militarism. We must win over to our side ninety million out of the hundred millions of the inhabitants of Russia under the Soviets. As for the rest of them, we have nothing to say to them: they must be annihilated.'

The model-genocidalist of the twentieth century, the true proto-Eichmann, was the communist Lazar Moiseyevich Kaganovich. Just as on the one hand, Eichmann cannot alone be held responsible for the death of a single Jew – for that, after all is the nature of bureaucracy – on the other, it is impossible to say just how many people Kaganovich was complicit in murdering by execution, working to death and by deliberate famine. Some figures go as high as twenty million people, with maybe one million of them his fellow Jews – but who can say?

What is certain is that Kaganovich was uniquely central to the horrors of Soviet communism from 1917 to 1957. By the 1950s, he was the only Jew still in high office in the USSR, the rest having been murdered: and though his career ended with Stalin's death, his life did not. He died in his bed in 1991, nearly 30 years after his more notorious emulator, Adolf Eichmannn had been executed by the Israelis.

So Kaganovich represents all the other communist apparatchiks of the twentieth century who – provided that they survived the purges of their fellow communists – had nothing to fear from anyone else. For what fate befell the industrial-scale murderers of Mao's China, or Pol Pot's Kampuchea, or Ho Chi Minh's Vietnam or Kim Il Sung's North Korea? How many went to their end with their toes nicely curled up beneath starched and ironed sheets? Almost all of them.

The qualifications for being tried as a war criminal are as follows. You must come from a small unimportant nation that has been defeated politically or militarily – such as Serbia or Rwanda, or from a large nation which has been defeated unconditionally in world war, which can only mean Nazi Germany or Imperial Japan. As for the executioners and murderers of the other totalitarian regimes of the twentieth century – just about all of them communist – they can be sure they have escaped or will escape punishment.

Yet there no international outcry over this tolerance for socialist murderers, perhaps for the same reason that it was so chic for so long to be a communist fellow traveller in Irish life. A sizeable section of what is now the Labour Party were once members of Official Sinn Féin, the 'Stickies', who took their party line directly from the communist Party of the USSR, and no doubt would have vigorously opposed any attempt to bring Kaganovich to justice.

Yet people who had aligned themselves with Franco's Spain or Allende's Chile would never be allowed to enter the political life of Ireland without being mauled by the ex-Stickie left. So how is it that former Stalinists are unfailingly allowed to airbrush from history their own sleazy, slavish adherence to Moscow, and to the Gulag that was the model for The Final Solution?

[28 September 2005]

I.18. Dachau's Jewish Victims

April 1945 was one of the turning points in the history of mankind's under-standing of itself. That we are a despicable species has been known since Eden; no race anywhere is without a myth about a golden time before the Fall, for Fallen we certainly are. But our understanding of the scope of evil, and its spectacular depravity, could only be only understood when unmitigated evil had its unmiti-gated way.

It had its way in Bergen-Belsen, liberated by British soldiers on a Sunday morning sixty years ago today. Two days later US troops liberated Buchenwald. On Thursday, 19 April Churchill told a shocked House of Commons of what Allied soldiers had found. That night, government censors sitting in the three main newspaper offices in Dublin removed all references to Churchill's speech and the concentration camps from the next morning's editions.

Eleven days later, Hitler killed himself, and soon afterwards, Eamon de Valera, though fully aware of what Allied troops had found at Belsen and Buchenwald, offered his condolences to the German legate Herr Hempel. A few days later Lt Colonel Edward Sheils DSO and Bar, of Clonee, County Meath, was killed in the Reichswald Forest. Government censors in The Irish Times duly censored his death notice, removing all reference to the fact that this Irishman, who had freely gone to fight oppression and tyranny, was a British soldier who had served in North Africa, Sicily, Normandy, Belgium and Germany. Instead, that past was elided, and the death notice simply recorded that he had died – as indeed he had.

By this time, the world was learning an entirely new litany of names: Ravensbruck, Flossenberg, Sachsenhausen, Mauthausen, Belzec, Sobibor, Theresienstadt, Auschwitz and Dachau, each worse than the other. But nonetheless, Dachau was special unto itself. It was the first true concentration camp, and its slogan was uplifting and magnificent: 'There is only one Road to Freedom and its Milestones are Obedience, Zeal, Honesty, Order, Cleanliness, Temperance, Truth, Sense of Sacrifice and Love of Fatherland.'

It was opened on 20 March 1933, seven weeks after Hitler came to power, and from its earliest days, its Nazi commandants behaved with unspeakable savagery. Its inhabitants wore coloured triangles to identify them by their taint: red for political offenders, green for 'criminals', pink for homosexuals, brown for gypsies, and a yellow Star of David for Jews. Dachau thus became the template from which were shaped hundreds of other camps across the Reich.

Dachau was not an extermination camp, but a labour camp: people were usually worked to death, not murdered, though of course many were. It was here SS doctor and homicidal quack Sigmund Rash experimented on prisoners, exploring the consequences of immersing them in liquid oxygen. And each camp produced its own variant of the Dachau franchise. At Matthausen in Austria, the SS had the 'Staircase of Death', a 45-degree slope up which long columns of prisoners five wide were made to carry lumps of granite in hods on their back. Over the years, perhaps thousands perished on those evil steps, flogged to death or shot or crushed by toppling boulders from above.

It was in this camp in September 1944 that 47 captured Allied airman were sentenced to the worst punishment of all in the Third Reich: to be worked to death. It was here also also that the last commandant, SS-Obersturmbannfuhrer Zieries gave his son 50 Jews for target practice. Amongst the prisoners here were tens of thousands of Spanish republicans who had fled to France at the end of the Spanish civil war, and who were rounded up after the Nazi victory in 1940; only 3000 were still alive in January 1945, and of these, 2163 were killed over the coming months.

Such splendid detail! But of course, keeping meticulous records was something the Nazis did so well: Matthausen, for example, had 36,318 executions, and in Buchenwald, 8483 Soviet prisoners were murdered by being shot in the back of the neck (which was indeed the preferred method of the NKVD at home, and which it had employed on the thousands of Polish officers at Katyn).

When US soldiers of the 45th Infantry Division liberated Dachau, they were confronted by the naked bodies of tens of thousands of dead and dying prisoners, and by the sight of the camp guards surrendering under a white flag. Forty guards were promptly bludgeoned to death by prisoners, and 122 were shot out of hand by GIs.

The surviving 346 SS men were then lined up against a wall and systemati-cally machine-gunned to death, while Technician Fourth Class Arland Musser photographed the entire affair. Later, the US Army court-martialled eight officers and NCOs for their role in the killings. When General Patton, Military Governor of Bavaria, heard about the forthcoming courts martial, he sent for all the pros-ecution documentation and photographs, and burnt the lot in his waste paper basket. The accused men all walked free.

If you think there is rough justice of a sort here, you are wrong. Most of the SS guards who were murdered were newly arrived conscripts, while many of the worst and most brutal villains had already escaped. Thirty-six of these were later sentenced to death, but because of the massacre of guards, all sentences were commuted.

Dachau became a base for the US army, which handed it over to the Bavarian Interior Ministry for use as a police barracks. It was from here that in 1972, during the Munich Olympics, that the German police launched their abortive operation to free the Israeli Olympics team captured by PLO terrorists, and in which nine of the athletes were killed: twenty-seven years on, Dachau's final Jewish victims.

[15 April 2005]

I.19. *Loving the Land, USA*

How disappointing for our many American-hating fellow Europeans to see that people in New Orleans are now returning to most areas of the city. But even as the sound of sniggering still echoed over Europe's capitals, the US army corps of engineers were quietly plugging the supposedly unpluggable breaches in the levees, and simultaneously despatching a sullen Mississippi back to its riverbed.

Now, I like and respect John O'Shea of GOAL, but he was wholly wrong to have said we should not send anything to help disaster relief to the US. Even a single army engineer with a bucket would have been a symbol of the brother-hood of freedom, of blood and of history that binds us, and an acknowledgment of the unpayable debt that we owe to the USA.

The UK, without the US, could never have liberated Occupied Europe in 1944, or any other year. Worse, it is just remotely possible that the USSR, aided by that supreme bungler, Adolf Hitler himself, might have defeated the Nazis without the assistance of the USA – a glorious prospect indeed, with Stalin's tanks within viewing-distance of the White Cliffs of Dover. So democratic victory sixty years ago was a largely American achievement, and without ever becoming slaves either to America or to history, we should never forget that.

The debt does not stop there. For down the decades that followed, the forces of communist tyranny were halted on that line from Stettin to Trieste by the real curtain that descended across Europe immediately after the war and which was provided by the USA. This was the steel curtain of freedom, forged by American guts and American gold and American guns. This side of the curtain, in the greatest act of selflessness that European civilisation has ever known, our economies – even that of neutral Ireland – were brought from the abyss of war-time impoverishment by the Marshall Plan.

So we send our sapper with his bucket to the US in order to show that we will always remember what the US has done for us, and moreover, to remind our young people that there is a reason that we in Europe are free, and it is spelt with just three capital letters.

I had the privilege recently of dining with a group of Europe-based US Marines. When you meet such people, you understand why the US is the great power that it is. I was sitting next to Christopher, a black Floridian staff sergeant who would have been an officer in any other armed force – but the Marine Corps insists that only college graduates can receive commissions (to my mind, an unnecessary qualification, but it does say something about the intellectual expectations of the Corps).

What had struck him most about Europe here was Europeans' lack of patri-otism. He said, naturally and quite unaffectedly, that he loved his country above all else. He then corrected himself, and said, he loved his God first, his wife and family second, his country next, and the Corps fourth: but in reality, they were an indissoluble unit. He was in the Corps because he loved his country: this was a God-given duty, as was that towards his family.

Soon he would be returning to the US, and if service in Iraq followed, so be it. Of course, he didn't want to leave his family, but he had his duty to do for his country and the Corps, and he would uncomplainingly do it. May heaven guard him.

Does anyone in Europe – even religious people – ever say that they love God any more? Yet if you actually believe in God, it is a peculiarly otiose folly not to acknowledge your worship of him. For whose disapproval do European believers fear more: that of their sneering, atheistic contemporaries, or that of God, whom they believe to be the creator of heaven and earth, and all things in between, including those very contemporaries?

Moreover, does anyone in Europe even respect patriotism any more? I don't mean the often shrill, exclusive, hate-filled witch called nationalism, but rather that rounded, embracing quality of loving the land you come from, and the people who inhabit it, and honouring the duties that both demand. True patriotism – the sacrifice of your own self-interest in the interests of your country and its people

– is one of the great and most ennobling forces of the world. Americans have it in abundance. It is perhaps their greatest quality. It defines the US Marine Corps.

Patriotism does not mean conformism. It does not mean a single version of history. It doesn't mean that your country has always done right, and will never do wrong, but it does mean that your desire to serve your country is an abiding feature of your life. Europeans, however, have largely abandoned such notions as quaint and anachronistic, and worse, in this country a self-declared love of Ireland for decades nearly became the monopoly of murderous, blood-thirsty heathens.

Though most men and women who join our own Defence Forces do so for utterly patriotic reasons, they would probably be too embarrassed to tell a stranger, as Christopher did, that they did so out of love of country. Yet such emotional reticence is surely dysfunctional. For in an era of celebrity, a culture that does not make a virtue of esteeming itself and its values is one that sooner or later is doomed – or at the very least, one that is probably going to have to be saved, once again, by the marines, soldiers, sailors and airmen of the USA.

[20 September 2005]

II. Gender & Stuff

II.1. Portmarnock Golf Club

All right, why does Portmarnock Golf Club deny full membership to women? Yes, yes, yes, coming to this column to read about golf is like going to Crossmaglen Rangers to find out about cricket, but nonetheless, on this occasion I'll try valiantly to write about golf without vomiting. We intrepid journalists.

As usual with male-female issues in this country, the fury over Bord Failté giving money to help fund a golf thingummy at a club that doesn't allow women members has been richer in stereotype and rhetorical evasiveness than in intellect.

The most wearily predictable complaint was that if the term 'black' was substituted for 'women' in the Portmarnock ban, there would be outcry. This is the Cortina argument, and a tiresome commonplace in a discussion about any 'minority' group: for like the old Ford, it's a cheap and simple way of getting there, in this case relying on a reflex-guilt spasm over racism and slavery to achieve intellectual compliance.

Sorry, girls. Nothing doing. The state-supported National Women's Council of Ireland has fifteen members, all of them women. But that doesn't make it Thelma, Alabama, any more than a gathering of men that wants to remain all male is a Ku Klux Klan klynch mob. In creating clubs, you always have to prohibit, otherwise all you've got is a shopping mall. Sex is as bad or as good a reason for exclusion as any other. Ask any women's fitness class.

But there's a certain disingenuousness in the way that male golf clubs – *and excuse me while I just get sick over the side of the ship here: ah, that's better* – talk in public about their respect for female golfers. On the few occasions when I've found the iron resolution to cope with those dazzling male golf-sweaters and not quite so dazzling male golf-minds, I've been left with the firm impression that men golfers loathe golfers-with-ovaries for two reasons.

The first, is that golfing girls apparently think that the purpose of the game is a good long natter to be, very occasionally, interrupted by the odd half-hearted foozle at a ball; and the second, even with the wind behind them, women can't hit a ball farther than a ten-year-old boy buried up to his neck in sand can throw it with his teeth,

In reply: one, it sounds both plausible, and better still, admirable: if only all golfers were like this, ovaried or otherwise. In no time at all, golf-courts, or whatever they're called, would be so clogged up that the sport would be abandoned, and vast tracts of the countryside would once again be returned to civilisation.

Portmarnock members apparently don't wish this to happen to their golf-court: which is, alas, their right. It is also their right to exclude women, and no one would think twice about any women's society that sought to exclude men.

Is it right for the government, through Bord Failté, to offer funding to the Nissan Irish Open in Portmarnock? On the grounds of taste, culture, decency and all that's valuable in Irish life, no, absolutely not. One can hardly stick one's head up in the Irish countryside any more without revisiting sniper alley in Sarajevo, white balls whizzing around the place, and maimed farm workers dying intestate in the ditch. For the state to be subsidising this lethal delinquency at a time of critical labour shortages is perfectly inexcusable.

But on the matter of how Portmarnock GC organises its business, what is the problem? The state funds any number of all-female organisations, but I know of no male-only organisation that receives money. And it's not as if the government grants will go to Portmarnock golf club; they won't. They will go to the tournament itself . . .

– *Excuse me for a moment, while I stick my head out of this porthole for air. Only two-thirds of the way through this column about golf, and I feel as if I've swallowed a gallon of bilge water. Deep breath. Okay, I'm ready again –*

The Portmarnock affair simply proves that feminists want the weight of government to be brought negatively to bear on institutions whose general conduct they disapprove of. So where does it stop? If Portmarnock were by feminist fiat to be compelled today to admit women as full members, might not the GAA be tomorrow be made to spend equal amounts on sporting facilities for the two sexes, regardless of demand?

That would be a sad day indeed; but not as sad as this one, when I am reduced to writing about the most gruesome pastime – with necrophilia with one's grandpa a possible exception – that humankind ever invented. Frankly, I think women should be grateful there are men-only golf clubs. Like baseball hats, or those oh so funneee signs saying 'You don't have to be mad to work it here, but it helps', they serve as a health warning of serious personality deficiencies in the neighbourhood.

Listen girls: male-only clubs are sad, grisly places, and you should rejoice that its members are finally out of the cupboard or sock drawer or whatever it is, and have declared that they prefer the company of chaps. Let them. Instead of whinging, which you're rather too fond of doing, please join me in a prayer service as golfers and golf-fans gather by the thousand at Portmarnock for the Nissen Open. And so together, we may entreat the Lord to summon a vast tsunami: that it may, without compassion, drown the whole bloody lot of them.

[12 December 2002]

II.2. Feminist Censoriousness

As certain as the yoke in the egg is the price one pays for criticising any of the feminist quangos in this country – and if this does us any service, it is to remind us of the powerful current of intolerance that runs deep in Irish society. This was once rooted in Sinn Féin republicanism and the Catholic Church, and which is now most active in dogmatic feminism and doctrinaire liberalism. And though feminism uses different words and social tools than those deployed by the adherents of Rome and Tone, the intention is the same: conformity, acquiescence and abjection.

The latest display of this hysterical feminist intolerance of dissent was prompted by a recent column criticising the state-assisted Woman's Aid – there is of course no such thing as Mens' Aid – for its well-publicised march to commemorate the 108 women victims of violence in the past nine years. In fact, I hadn't been aware when I wrote my piece that Sinn Féin had participated in this grisly exercise in sexual apartheid – which makes the whole affair utterly surreal.

Was the ghost of Jean McConville, mother of ten, present for this jamboree? What about Caroline Moreland, mother of three, abducted and held for ten unspeakable days before being murdered by the IRA in July 1994? And was Sinn Féin allowed to be present merely because these women (and many others) had been murdered *before* the time span chosen by Women's Aid to select its victims? In that case, no doubt Rosemary West could have been present to deplore violence against women, perhaps carrying posthumous a letter of support from Fred West.

I expected an epistolary lynching for my column, and the sisters, in all their arrogant, blind stupidity, didn't let me down, God bless their little knickers. Moreover, there was a singular theme that united most letters and which ran: Why is *The Irish Times* printing such stuff? The writers were genuinely incredulous that *their* newspaper should carry opinions with which they so violently disagreed. Archbishop

John Charles McQuaid would have felt exactly the same if he had opened his copy of *The Irish Catholic* and found an article on the merits of vibrators.

Another common weapon of feminist censoriousness is to dismiss what the girls don't approve of with the R&D argument; that it is a mere rant or a diatribe – why, maybe even both. Such misogyny, they imply, doesn't deserve a cogent reply, but a metaphorical belt from a sisterly crozier instead. And this time round, the crozier was accompanied with the playground sneer: Why doesn't your columnist (na-na-na-naaah) look at male violence for a change?

Excuse me, but that – God help us – is what the sisters have been bloody well doing for decades: and with some justification. The streets of Dublin are not made dangerous by groups of drunken young women – though they are often disagreeable enough – but by young men. Males in early adulthood can be extremely lethal creatures, which is why I – me, rather than the letter-writing feminists with steam coming out of their nostrils, and probably every other orifice – have described testosterone as the 'plutonium of hormones'.

The need to take control of young men was why Jacob devised the patriarchy, not as an instrument of repression of women, but as a means of protecting them from male aggression and male desire. Only an utter cretin would maintain that men and women are equally violent or equally lustful.

Equally, only an utter cretin would maintain that what we see in our streets is a straightforward reflection of what we see in our homes. Domestic violence is radically different from public violence, as Erin Pizzey discovered over thirty years ago. She has often reiterated that only a small majority of domestic violence emanates from men. Roughly speaking, the responsibility for domestic violence is equally divided between the sexes.

But of course, in all their gnashing frenzy, the sisters decline to answer that unanswerable truth, and instead continue to portray victimhood as a one-way street, never acknowledging the men who are beaten and abused by their wives. They don't admit to Gary Cotter dead in his bed, cold-bloodedly shot by a wife who – almost typically – then walked free from a court after pleading guilty to manslaughter.

So, the Sisters of Erin trawl through the statistics and come up with whatever fantastical picture they want, without ever addressing the uncomfortable truth as revealed by Erin herself. That is such a monster that they simply ignore it. And when I repeated the figures of casualties from the North – that only one tenth of the victims of the Troubles were women – one sister sneered I had already pointed that out – so why did I bother repeating it?

Well, firstly, do not the sisters endlessly repeat their same refrains? And secondly, it tells us a central and irrefutable truth about Irish society – that even in civil war, terrorists generally refrain from violence against women. So when it occurs in the home it is a contradiction of an almost universal moral consensus. But the sisters, aided by a culture of cowardice in our political and legal classes, have distorted that benign consensus to create a wholly false picture of who is responsible for domestic violence.

That is bad enough. Yet almost worse, in a way, are their frenzied and vicious attempts to silence anyone who publicly dissents from their malignant, hysterical fantasies. And indeed, one day they might even succeed. But sorry, girls: not yet.

[16 December 2004]

II.3. Gender-Based Violence

We've all seen some pretty daft headlines in our time, but the one that appeared last week in this newspaper prend le bloody biscuit: 'We need strong voices to break the silence on gender-based violence.'

Now its shortbread-grabbing quality is not immediately obvious in those words. After all, there may be some form of gender-based violence which none of us have heard about – the violence of mothers against teenage boys, or girls against their fathers, or elderly grandmothers against middle-aged sons.

Let us read on.

'A cloak of silence covers one of the world's most widespread and persistent human rights abuses,' wrote ex-President Mary Robinson (for it was she). 'The perpetrators are seldom brought to justice … The abuse is gender-based violence. The victims are …' what? Elderly men being beaten by nurses? Baby boys being abused by kindergarten minders? Male babies being circumcised? No … 'mainly woman and children.'

Yes, women and children. We'll just remind ourselves of the opening paragraph. 'A cloak of silence covers one of the world's most widespread and persistent human rights abuses.'

Now, this is very probably the most idiotic and inaccurate opening paragraph it has ever been my misfortune to read. There is no more 'silence' on the issue of violence against women and children than there is about global warming or the war in Iraq. It has been in the forefront of media imagination for the past twenty years, at least.

You can do this yourself at home. Google 'violence against women'. I found 4,580,000 non-specific global items – and this on a theme of which our former President intones with querulous self-regard, as if she alone were speaking out, 'A cloak of silence covers one of the world's most widespread and persistent human rights abuses.' A Google of 'Violence against women in Pakistan' got 773,000 items. The same subject in Saudi Arabia drew 225,000 references. In Thailand, three million. In Russia 1,010,00. So much for the 'cloak of silence'.

Then, to put the Robinson allegations of 'silence' properly into perspective, Google a matter of national pride, which is put into the forefront of world attention at every opportunity: Ireland and horses. The response? Just 166,000 items. In other words, Robbo is talking rubbish, and in more ways than one.

'As part of the ongoing need for awareness-raising and education on gender-based violence, the UN special Rapporteur on violence against women Dr Yakin Erturk and Minister Conor Lenihan will launch a photographic exhibition ...' da dum da dum da dum. Who writes this stuff? The only place where people talk about 'ongoing needs' and 'awareness-raising' is in the Wonderland world of the UN.

But alas, there was more. She also declared that there were now 13 organisations working together to lead the global fight against gender-based violence. (So how they get recruited in the cloak of silence covering this issue? By sign-language?) She added: 'One of the newest members – I am proud to say – is the Defence Forces.'

Now don't give me that. You were commander-in-chief of the Defence Forces, the greatest honour of all that goes with being President. These are the best people in Ireland, bar none. You abdicated as their commander-in-chief to pursue a better job. There are not many people in this country one can readily identify as patriots, but the members of Defence Forces qualify. You, Robbo, do not.

Moreover, how do the Defence Forces appear in this thing 'the global fight against gender-based violence?' Are they not for the most part men, trained to kill? It is that not the skill which distinguishes them from post office workers, clerks, and gardeners, not to speak of ex-presidents? Is not violence – largely male-violence – their defining feature?

For the truth is that the proper term for 'gender-based violence' is 'male violence.' Men can form into hierarchies which are capable of the most appalling infamies – the atrocities in Darfur, the suicide bombings in Iraq, the 'honour killings' of rape victims in Muslim countries, the catastrophe of the Congo, and the joys of Yugoslavia: and I would love to hear GBV ideologues explain what happened at Srberenice. Unsocialised, this is what men do – but far more to other men, as it happens, than to women and children. We also paint the Cistine Chapel, put a man on the moon, create grand opera and invent antibiotics.

So the 'gender-based violence' is not explained away in the politically correct mumbo jumbo of UN-speak, or as Robbo put it: 'The root causes lie in the imbalance in power relations and gender equality.' Not true. The root causes are not institutional but hormonal. Long before the first king was crowned or the first law promulgated, man was violent towards other men and towards women. Men made institutions to control that violence. Who did? Men did. *Men*.

No one is defending rape. No one is defending violence against women. And no one denies that the authors of the most of the physical violence in this world, and all the sexual violence, are men.

But you have to admit, Robbo's got some nerve. How does she get away with lecturing us on anything? For she is our very own Edward VIII, her Mrs Wallis being her international career at the UN, which came before her duty to her country, the constitution and the people. Had Brian Lenihan won the presidential election and then been guilty of such betrayal, he at least, like the Duke of Windsor, would probably have had the decency then to spare us any self-righteous homilies. Not Robbo, by God, not Robbo.

[14 March 2006]

II.4. *Women in the Media*

God I hate this time of year, when the Leaving Cert results emerge and feminists start preening and sneering, meanwhile complaining about the relatively lower incomes of mature women, as if the adult world were decided by the exam results of 18 year olds. The debate – such as it is, though the na-na-na-naa superiority competition that we are obliged to witness every August hardly merits the term – is bad enough, but it usually passes, in time. All that is needed is for us chaps to keep our noses below the parapet, and our powder dry, and all should be well.

Michael Buerk, the BBC newsreader, did neither, and now he's allowed the 'debate' turn nastier than usual. I was hoping it would stay on the British side of the Irish Sea, but this being August, and with almost nothing to write about other than the patent academic superiority of girls over boys, I was hoping in vain: Brenda Power weighed into Michael Buerk last weekend in *The Sunday Times* with the usual combination of personal abuse and withering sarcasm that any man who does not accept the party line on feminism can faithfully expect.

The last well-known British journalist to attack the role of women and feminism in the media was Neil Lydon ten years ago. It was, in fact, a poor piece of journalism, both simplistic and exaggerated in its judgments, and badly researched. It was but one article, just one, and we are all entitled to have a bad day at the office. However, he was not given such indulgence; instead, he was promptly lynched in the media. Editors boycotted him, one by one his columns were dropped, and his income simply vanished. He had to sell his house, and he almost went bankrupt – all on the strength of one article.

Who would bother doing that sort of thing again? Well, actually the BBC newsreader Michael Buerk did: only sort of. He didn't actually write an article on the power of women in the media, but was being interviewed in the *Radio Times* – and as anyone who has done an interview knows, in print journalism, the interviewer is the one who decides what appears on the page. Moreover, few of us (especially journalists, who are usually on the other side of the process) are clever enough to construct sentences as we talk which are not open to misconstruction, or which fully convey what we are trying to say.

Even allowing for that, his arguments were weak. 'Almost all the big jobs in broadcasting were held by women – the controllers of BBC1 television and Radio 4 for example,' he is quoted as saying. Good. So what about BBC 2, BBC3, and BBC 5, or the various ITV networks, or Channel Four, or Radios One, Two and Three? Who controls them? Martians?

And then there was his attempt at humour – always a way of leaving open a flank for attack by the sisters. 'What are the men left with? All they are is sperm donors, and most women aren't going to want an unemployable sperm donor loafing around and making the house look untidy. They are choosing not to have a male in the household.'

Instead of this being taken for what it was, a piece of fun at men's expense, it was taken as a literal statement of what he believes. And so of course, he has been torn limb from limb, though his observations about the traditional qualities of maleness – reticence, stoicism, single-mindedness – are surely worth more than the shrieks of derision and misrepresentation that they have earned to date.

'Look at the changes in the workplace,' he added. 'There is no manufacturing industry any more; there are no mines; few vital jobs require physical strength. We have lots of jobs that require people skills and multitasking – which women are a lot better at.'

Brenda Power reduced that to: 'Buerk believes that women are stealthily and callously manipulating a society where physical force is being replaced by communication, empathy, initiative and tact.' Yet he didn't say this: is it any wonder a feminist can win an argument, using such intellectually worthless rhetorical methods? And what can one say to her argument, which actually cited the stoning to death of women in certain countries as ammunition against poor Michael Buerk?

Moreover, we have often seen feminists employing the kind language that is denied the rest of us. 'If men didn't want us to guess that they were useless, they should have made themselves more useful. Now they've been rumbled, all they can do is whinge,' is the observation of that intellectual she-bear of feminism, Germaine Greer. And maybe boys do whinge these days: but girls sneer, as in Brenda Power's description of Michael Buerk as 'a crotchety-looking newsreader'.

Does she want to know what I feel about her appearance? Does it matter? Does the look on her face make any difference to the argument she's making? Would a male writer be allowed to refer to the nature of a woman's face if he was disagreeing with what she was saying? And if he did, would he not be lynched for doing so?

Last weekend *The Sunday Times* illustrated the issue of female power in the media today by showing a picture of a confident young woman crushing two world globes, like testicles, in her hand. No doubt it was thought to be amusing. But what newspaper would dare to present the opposite imagery, in which male power is – rather 'entertainingly' – visually represented by a man violently and triumphantly abusing female genitalia?

[23 August 2005]

II.5. *Reforming UCD*

Hugh Brady's reform of University College Dublin continues: the term is, I believe, streamlining. The eleven existing faculties are to be reduced to five, and 90 separate academic departments will be replaced or amalgamated into 35. But why such a modest plan? Why not amalgamate the entire university into the already existing Faculty of Interdisciplinary Studies?

Let me say those words again. The Faculty of Interdisciplinary Studies. Does anyone really know what they mean? From his distant grave, comes the sound of the bones of its founder, John Henry Cardinal Newman, stirring restlessly. Why, I even saw the former President of UCD Paddy Masterson on the Luas the other day, looking distracted. Was he thinking about the rising imperial power of the Faculty of Interdisciplinary Studies? Was he inwardly cursing himself for allowing a one-roomed department of women's studies during his otherwise splendid tenure as President, which has since mushroomed into the only government-funded, academic unit with a clear political agenda in the largest university in Ireland?

Nestling somewhere within the bosom – if one can still say that word in mixed company – of FIS is WERRC: Women's Education, Research and Resource Centre. WERRC is currently advertising for students to apply for various postgraduate courses, all labelled 'women's studies'. One course is an MA, the other MLitt. Can these possibly be Master of Arts and Master of Literature? Girls, are you letting yourselves down by using the M-word of the chauvinistic patriarchy? Or have you in fact covertly inserted a politically correct, academic neologism into the titles, which in their longer form stand as Ms A and Ms Litt?

If you have, I don't blame you. The Irish academic world has laid down with supine abjection before the juggernaut of political correctness emanating from the US (where of course it is now just about dead, largely killed off not by men, the lilly-livered poltroons, but by intellectually rigorous women academics). Get what you can, while you can: this is lotus-eating time for those who talk the mumbo-jumbo of the sisterhood and of related movements.

WERRC recently announced a wide range of courses 'with particular strengths'. One of these is 'Lesbian and Queer Theory and Politics'. Ah. So suddenly homosexual males are included in a 'resource centre' dedicated to women's studies. Why? In what sense are homosexual men women? Who was consulted about this gender reassignment? Do the gay men of Ireland know that they have become honorary women in new UCD-speak?

So, who may enrol in this course? May male heterosexuals studying 'Lesbian and Queer Theory and Politics' start referring to male homosexuals as 'Queers', in a way that is forbidden to the rest of the population? And how does one pronounce it so as to differentiate the word from the perjorative 'queer'? Do such heterosexual students then become honorary 'Queers' for the duration of their course, so enabling them to use that word, which of course is only selectively authorised by the PC-lobby? But presumably, once away from the aura of liberation of WERRC, they forfeit the right to say Queer, which becomes taboo again.

Does no one in WERRC recognise how absurd such institutionalised linguistic apartheid actually is? You cannot have university courses using words which are only available to the politically indoctrinated, but not to the rest of the population. This is creating an academic priesthood, with its own arcane liturgy, containing a privileged vocabulary limited solely to those who have subordinated themselves to the gods of multiculturalism and interdisciplinary studies.

Another course WRRC is offering is 'Feminist Research Methodologies'. Have you any idea what that means? It suggests that feminists have invented some intellectual research tool that is not available to the rest of us. How very interesting. Is this methodology available to women only, or is it available to feminists only? And can feminological men engage in these forms of research, but not women who are not feminists?

Moreover, universities do not usually allow on its syllabus any other course that is so dedicated to achieving a political or ideological goal. Could secular UCD have a course promoting 'Catholic Research Methodologies'? No. Could politically neutral UCD have a course promoting 'Marxist Research Methodologies'? No. Could academically free UCD have a course promoting 'Islamic Fundamentalist Research Methodologies'? No.

But the sisters are different; and they are different because intellectual wooliness and academic cowardice have allowed them to be so, within the cosy world of interdisciplinary studies, of which, I confess, I know little. What are the courses available in this discipline called interdiscipline? Are there modules combining rites of Indonesian pearl-fishers, eighteenth-century English law on tort, and metallurgy in Jane Austen? Can one study Native American burial customs, Foucault's use of the past historic tense, and the feminist movement in Ireland during the Famine? Well, in a world that promotes 'Feminist Research Methodologies' and 'Lesbian and Queer Theory and Politics', I don't see why not.

For as we have seen, WERRC is unique among university departments. It has a political goal that it declares in its own advertisements. 'WERCC is one of the leading Women's Studies centres in Europe, with a commitment to making a difference through transformative feminist scholarship, research, teaching, outreach and networking activities.'

So the purpose of this gibberish is not academic, but to pursue a 'transformative' political agenda. And most reassuringly of all, this is not coming from some privately-funded madcap university in New Hampshire, but from the largest university in Ireland, state-funded throughout. So, gentle reader, it's all WERRC while we pay. Yes, John Henry, and well may you weep.

[22 March 2005]

II.6. Apologies for the Rapes

Some moments in court must remain unforgettable, and one such came the other day when the rapist Salman Aslam Dar told Mr Justice Paul Carney that he was sorry for what he had done, beseeching forgiveness, and declaring that he wanted to be a good man.

Prosecuting counsel Mary Ellen Ring SC then rose and asked him if that was the first time he had offered an apology, for *rapes*, mark you, that went back to February of last year. The wretch remained silent for several minutes, no doubt searching his abominable mind for a way of getting out of that one.

Then unable to concoct a reply, he then said, 'I am sorry.' Well, of course he was sorry then; why wouldn't he be? The gun of imprisonment was to his head, and he had much to be sorry about: namely the years in jail that lay ahead. He was sentenced to three terms of seven years by Mr Justice Paul Carney for the three rapes that he committed on the northside of Dublin over a few vicious, methodical months. However, the judge drew attention to the fact that the Court of Criminal Appeal reduced to 15 years the 21-year jail sentence he had passed on a taxi driver who raped three women in a single night. Not wanting his sentence on Dar to go the same way, he suspended two years of each of the seven sentences, in effect giving this triple rapist the same as the earlier one.

Well, it's understandable why Paul Carney felt his hands tied: no one likes the public rebuke of having one's judgment rejected. But this 15-year sentence cannot be right. Provided he is a good boy in jail, this Dar creature will be out in 10 years, when he will be just 33, and – one hopes – on the next plane back to poor bloody Pakistan. But at that same age, Peter Sutcliffe, the Yorkshire Ripper, was only halfway through his career as a serial killer.

To be sure, part of the reduced sentence reflects Dar's guilty plea. Courts often take this option in recognition of the trauma that raped women have to go through when giving evidence against a not guilty plea. However, there are clearly limits to the wisdom of a such a policy, as the case of Salman Aslam Dar illustrates, because in pleading guilty he was acting purely out of self-interest.

Two of the rape victims had picked him out in identity parades, and his DNA matched that found in the bodies of his victims; and, since they had been savagely attacked and beaten – he smashed one woman's head against a wall many times – a plea of consensual sex was not possible. In other words, in that curious expression one hears on television but nowhere else, he was bang to rights.

Here is the real paradox. The stronger the case against you in a rape case, the more likely that you will be able to avail of the rewards of a guilty plea. A not guilty plea is certain to fail, so the accused actually benefits from the spectacular flagrancy of his crime. This is surely wrong, yet it is a traditional practice of our courts. Thus a man who beats his victim senseless and savagely rapes her, leaving his semen inside her, can actually benefit from his ruthlessness. The less savage, possibly more ambiguous rape, leaves no such escape route.

Surely it is right for the judge to retain full discretionary powers over sentencing, regardless of whether or not a guilty plea has been entered. Discretion is discretion: the judge may take the guilty plea into account, but it cannot be right that a sentence reduction is now almost contractually written into court practice, when the guilty plea was simply cynical realism.

The deal should be the other way: not a lighter tariff for a guilty plea, but a heavier one for a tendentious not guilty one. The rapist who has made his victims go through the trauma of describing the most terrible ordeal of their lives should know that there is a price to pay for that: life meaning life. Maybe this will not deter rapists, but it will give a clear signal to women of how society regards the integrity of their bodies, their minds and their lives.

Perhaps the most astonishing item of all in this trial was that it was told by a psychologist who had interviewed Dar that Dar said the first victim had been racially abusive to him. Excuse me. But how is this relevant to a violent rape? Violent rape is without a context. It exists in a class of quite of its own; no mitigation, no provocation, no allurement, no enticement, no marital vow and no extenuating circumstances can relieve it of its utter and unspeakable awfulness.

Moreover, surely such evidence amounts to hearsay. And we no longer live in a world where hearsay can simply be dismissed as such. Quite the reverse. When *Newsweek* published a baseless rumour that the Koran was being flushed down the toilets of Guantanamo, 20 people died in the consequent riots in Pakistan and Afghanistan. An Irish court heard an allegation made by Dar that his first victim had been racially abusive to him. This is non-evidence, but to credulous minds, it could appear that the rapist had somehow been 'provoked', and was in fact the victim. Such evidence is legally permissible. But it would be better not dignified in the public forum of an Irish court, but instead in a judge's chambers.

[23 June 2005]

II.7. The Joy of Shopping

Men of a certain age, such as myself, usually harbour few ambitions, and those that we have are usually modest enough in scope: but none quite compares with my desperate and passionate yearning never to enter Dundrum Shopping Centre. This apparently irresistible, manic craving is so great as not to be in the usual range of human appetites: indeed, it is more akin to the rampant sexual lust of a stallion, but of course, in reverse.

I am a male. The title of this column probably gives that little secret away. And healthy men do not like shopping, unless it is for electric screwdrivers, books and possibly magazines containing pictures of naked woman. But we do not browse through heaps of underwear: we do not caress socks as if the sensation were sexually arousing; we do not hold shirts up to ourselves and ask: Does my bum look big in this? We prefer to buy a pair of shoes two sizes too small and cripple ourselves rather than linger for one hundredth the time that it takes so many women to decide that, no, they won't be buying any of the 240 pairs they have spent a most enjoyable weekend trying on.

Meanwhile, the poor despairing shop assistants are running around in small circles on their hands and knees, barking, and biting lumps out of the chair-leg. Then of course they remember that the next weekend the woman shopper will be back looking for a pair of runners, but will leave with eight pairs of shoes, half of which have heels you could knit a sweater with and which are so unstable that the woman wearing them has to be supported by scaffolding. Imelda Marcos bought so many shoes not because she was Imelda Marcos, but because a) she was a woman, and b) because she could.

Women enjoy shopping. Men do not. It's almost as simple as that. Possibly homosexual men do, but I doubt it. I say this with some authority, because last week I discovered I was homosexual. Scientists somewhere or other have discovered that homosexual men have a poor sense of direction, very like women. I have a dreadful sense of direction, which must mean either that I am homosexual, or that I am a woman. But I can't be the latter, because I don't like shopping. Therefore I'm homosexual and can use the word 'queer', and go cottaging and cruising and develop a taste in buns, though in my experiences most cottages have rising damp, I dislike boats, and buns were never the same once Bewleys dropped the almond of the species. I'm partial to scones though: does that count?

Sorry, sorry, sorry. A long way from my utterly pathological phobia about Dundrum. But news of the opening last week wrung the withers of my soul, not least for the pictures, which rather resembled the Oklahoma land-race, if, that is, that great contest for territory was between female hippopotamuses. Did the time of the opening coincide with a breakout from the hippo-house at Dublin Zoo? Or is that region of Dublin 14 so called because the bellies of the natives resemble Lambegs, and after people have had sex, they declare with some elephantine satisfaction – that they've just done drum?

Either way, I haven't seen as much avoirdupois on legs since I got stuck in the communal showers at the Tokyo Sumo All-Japanese Wrestling Contest, a tale which the world is not yet ready for – though I might throw in the observation here that these Sumo lads have got tiny, tiny … no, no, on second thoughts, perhaps not. One never quite knows when one is going to run into a posse of Japanese wrestlers. You never want to annoy fellows who travel cargo and wear double-H cups. They could create an unpleasant moment or two.

Anyway, the pictures provided hideous proof that we are producing females – I saw no males in the start-line for the shopping centre – that could flock unnoticed with sperm whales – and heavens, if they're very lucky might even get a done drum. Even more significant was the revelation that the opening was blessed by Church leaders. Maybe there was some confusion and they were there to bless mammoths rather than Mammon.

Certainly, the papes turned up, as did the Methodist Normans, probably singing their little Wesleyan heads off, and the burly Presbyterian Alistairs, all to perform the baptism of Europe's largest shopping centre: offhand I can't remember whether the Jews, Buddhists or Muslims were also there. The official justification for all this was that the Churches should be wherever people are. Really? As it happens, The Shangri-La Lap Dancer & Exotic Massage Parlour is looking for a chaplain. Perhaps the done drum crowd might suggest some dog-collared volunteers to spread their spiritual balm over Luscious Lucy and Gorgeous Georgia as they weave their manual magic. And those eager shoppers at the vibrator counter at Anne Summers could probably do with a quick blessing or two before they rush home.

The reality is that it's over. Just about every commentator has remarked on done drum being the cathedral of the new religion, and the cliché is true. We know that the next stop is the sabbatical shop-over: the super-sized family spending all Sunday waddling slowly around a shopping centre like pods of vast cetaceans browsing their way through a particularly rich pocket of plankton. The ecumenical presence was less a blessing than a handover. The baton has moved on. Goodbye, christianity.

[10 March 2005]

II.8. She-Butchers

Do we really need to ask about the uproar which would have resulted if a man hit his sleeping wife 26 times with a plumber's hammer and knifed her 21 times, and was only found guilty of manslaughter? We don't. We know that there are half a dozen state-subsidised feminist agencies that would have been shriekingly denouncing the legal system that had come to such a bizarre and grotesque conclusion.

But for poor Declan O'Neill, there is only silence. Slaughtered in his sleep in a savage and unprovoked assault by his wife, not a voice has been heard from Official Ireland to condemn the legal conclusion that his death was not murder. Indeed, if Official Ireland has its way, the name of Declan O'Neill will be soon forgotten – and who knows, maybe the sisters will start a campaign to free his killer, his poor, darling wife, Dolores O'Neill, for gallantly defending herself against a slumbering man.

However, if Declan O'Neill had knifed Dolores O'Neill 21 times in the neck, had beaten her 26 times with a plumber's hammer, and had been found guilty of mere manslaughter, the sisters would have been demanding to know is why the court didn't hear certain evidence. For the trial of Dolores O'Neill was not told of her own history of violence and abuse towards the victim. The jury was allowed to remain in complete ignorance of key evidence that might have helped convict Dolores O'Neill of murder.

That evidence was compiled by the victim, in diary selections selection notes and in conversations with his siblings. After the trial, Declan's brother Dermot gave details of Dolores O'Neill's many attacks on Declan. She had hit him over the head with a bottle on at least two occasions. She had broken an ashtray on his head, and beaten him with a mobile-phone charger. One diary selections selection note in March 2002 refers to his having been treated at Tallaght Hospital for abrasions after she drove her car into him. If this is so, Tallaght Hospital would have a record of these injuries. Why were such medical records not presented to the court?

However, although evidence which suggested that Dolores O'Neill was a violent and dangerous woman was not allowed before the court, she was nonetheless allowed to make terrible allegations against her dead husband, such as that he often got drunk and beat her. After the trial, his brothers said that that he was such a light drinker that he was always the nominated driver on family night out. John Harbison, the state pathologist, testified that from the condition of the body, Declan was clearly not a heavy drinker. Moreover, since there were no defensive-wound injuries on his body, he was probably asleep when he was killed.

It is almost beyond parody, but the she-butcher who did this to a sleeping man was an employee of the Equality Agency: no doubt it is even keeping her job open, possibly even planning a campaign to secure her release: Release The Knocklyon One! She only bumped a fellow off while he slept! Defend A Woman's Right To Kill Her Husband!

However, our courts had already effectively vindicated that right. Last January, Norma Cotter was allowed to walk free from court after pleading guilty to a charge of shot-gunning her husband in bed. Corporal Gary Cotter was a soldier of this Republic. Had he been shot dead on duty twelve hours earlier, he would have been a national hero. Instead, he was coldly and calculatedly butchered in bed by his wife, and was accordingly forthwith banished from public memory. His wife was convicted of manslaughter – and was instantly given her freedom.

So, this is the second time this year that our courts have concluded that for a woman to kill her helpless husband in bed is not murder. We know such clemency would never be shown to a man who so killed his wife, for there is an entire collection of state-subsidised agencies whose sole job is to put pressure on judges and national institutions to ensure a general enforcement of the feminist agenda. One key feature of this is that women – even when they hack husbands to death or blow them apart by repeated shotgun blasts in their beds – are always victims.

I have no idea why evidence which might have helped convict Dolores O'Neill of murder for the frenzied attack on her husband was kept from the court: I merely note the silence which has followed it, as there was after the brutal slaying of Corporal Cotter, soldier of this Republic. We know, however, that there would have been uproar if either of the victims had been a she.

I am long used to the cowardly political silence that follows any failure to protect male rights – not least of all, men's right to life. Now, I am inclined to gather from the many foam-flecked published letters that demand that Madam sack me, that readers of this newspaper are vaguely aware of what appears in this space. Yet not a single letter-writer backed me when I wrote about the scandalous freeing of Norma Cotter, cold-blooded husband-killer: and I expect a similarly craven silence this time also.

But most emphatically, now and forever: no more 'strictly private' letters of support to this column, on this or any other issue. I detest such craven, lilly-livered backing. If you agree with me, but haven't got the courage to say so publicly, oh please, once and for all, just shut the phuq up.

[5 November 2004]

II.9. Prostitution

Belinda Pereira, RIP. What was she? A whore, a trollop, a strumpet, a tart? Prostitutes are as universal as they are universally reviled, and they are the easiest and least regarded victims of any serial killer. The first non-prostitute victim of the Yorkshire Ripper was also the first to be declared 'innocent' by the police, the innocence of the others being apparently vitiated if not removed entirely by their profession, thereby speaking volumes for the culture that could even categorise women in such terms.

Yorkshire, why do we need to go to Yorkshire to find evidence of this phenomenon? We have it here at home, in Maire Geoghegan Quinn's infamous and disgraceful Criminal Law (Sexual Offences) Act of 1993, which re-emphasised the criminality of what a prostitute does for a living. At the time, the bill was dressed up for what it was not, as a liberalising measure, because it decriminalised an activity that was illegal only on the foot of an unenforced Victorian law – male homosexual acts.

But some bright spark in the Department of Justice thought it was high time to reinforce the vicious Victorian anti-prostitution laws, and so at the very time that a supposedly liberal (and in reality, irrelevant) pro-homosexual law was being introduced, to much applause, a new and draconian anti-female law made its appearance, in silence, with not a word of an outcry.

For prostitutes have no friends, even – or perhaps, especially – among feminists, for they are outside every pale of decency. They insist on performing acts with men which feminists find degrading – which actually says more about the sanctimonious prudishness of so much of the feminist canon than about the prostitutes themselves. For why is sex for money more degrading than journalism for money or coalmining for money or barristering for money? Sex for money is not in itself degrading, but we make it so with a priggish preciousness that we enshrine in law.

The criminalised world that prostitutes are forced to inhabit by the laws and the agents of the State is one in which the working girl has no protection. Their male pimps are normally scum, and many of their clients are sexually dysfunctional and pathetic men, who hate themselves and the prostitutes they employ, for their weaknesses. Nobody speaks out for these girls; nobody – as nobody spoke out when Maire Geoghegan Quinn introduced her vicious anti-prostitute laws of four years ago. Male homosexuals were cool, right-on, hip and politically well-organised hookers were not.

And fresh laws came into existence that made the life of the prostitute even more difficult. They are worthless laws, and in that sense are perfectly consistent with virtually everything else emanating from the Department of Justice; but they are not without effect. Prostitutes live in fear of them – for if they were to be enforced, they are very wicked laws indeed. First offence, £250; second offence, £500; £500 and a month in jail for a third offence.

For what? For soliciting for sex. Why? What other private activity attracts such vengeful attentions of the state? None. These women – undereducated for the most part, usually poor, often mentally unbalanced – scare us in some way. We cannot trust ourselves to admit them openly to society, and certainly cannot leave them alone. Even with laws that seem intended to intimidate more than be applied, we make legal and moral lepers of them.

And not just them; we do the same to those who organise them too, so that the world of the entrepreneur is also criminalised.

Or should I say, entrepreneuse? My Irishwoman of the decade remains Marion Murphy, the woman found guilty of running a brothel in, Mountjoy Square a couple old years ago. The house was organised, the girls worked to a strictly adhered-to tariff, and the neighbours and the clientele had no complaints – but she was prosecuted, brought to the courts and fined, and had to pay huge legal costs. This was a truly contemptible prosecution, initiated not by the unfortunate gardaí responsible for policing that part of Dublin.

When I last spoke to Marion Murphy – alas, only by phone – she was still in the same line of work; I have not had the pleasure of meeting her or any of her girls, but I greatly look forward to doing so. It would be an honour to be in the company of such an honest woman, who manages to run a thriving business in such difficult circumstances. If Veuve Clicquot had any sense, they would make her their Businesswoman of the Year.

The truth is that prostitution, like any business, needs to be organised; to criminalise that organisation does not eliminate it but passes it into the hands of violent and exploitative men who are quite unlike my chum Marion. More than that. It causes the entire trade of commercial sex to operate within an underworld.

Do not rail against prostitution. You might not like it, as I do not – nor indeed am I all that fond of financial trading, coalmining or deep-sea welding – but our opinions are irrelevant.

Prostitution is a form of commercial activity found in all societies everywhere. It is intellectually and morally primitive to turn its practitioners into criminals or 'vice girls' who are residents of a lesser moral world. Belinda Pereira was not some resident of a lesser moral world. She inhabited my world and yours; in life, in death, she deserved as much respect as the rest of us, and she did not get it.

We can expect one certain response to her wicked murder; it will not be to undo the contemptible aspects of the Criminal Law (Sexual Offences) Act, one of the most heinous laws any European democracy has passed in living memory. What we will get, for sure, for certain and odiously hypocritical sure, is a crackdown on brothel keeping and on prostitutes, and on magazines like *In Dublin* that carry their advertisements. It will make the lives of prostitutes harder; and make the rest of us feel that much more saintly.

Bah.

[3 January 1997]

II.10. Medical Schools

Do we have medical schools in order to provide extremely expensive proof of the academic superiority of teenage girls over teenage boys? Or do we invest in our medical schools to provide our society with doctors for the 40 or so years after they qualify? There is a difference, you know.

The *Irish Medical Journal* recently published a paper by two doctors, Davida De La Harpe and Fiona Graham, on the future of Irish women GPs. And frankly, if things are as bad as they seem, we might as well start interviewing the undergraduates of African and Indian medical schools right now. That way, we might just get the pick of the crop in a few years' time, when the she-doctors decide a full working day is far too much – what? work nights? weekends? you must be joking! – and opt either for the occasional bout of daytime chest-tapping, or even get out of medicine altogether.

The authors sent questionnaires to 200 women who graduated from GP training courses, 1995–2001, and 134 (67 per cent) replied. Of those, 13 per cent were no longer GPing: so, 16 graduates who had taken incredibly precious places in medical school had abandoned general practice relatively soon after graduating. A further one-third had already ceased full-time work. Over 40 per cent said in future they probably wouldn't work out-of-office hours, and nearly one in 10 declared they would never work non-social hours, come what may. Over 80 per cent declined to work as a single GP in the country, and worst of all, only 10 per cent declared they wanted to remain full-time GPs. To round off the pretty picture, 75 per cent of all GP trainees in Ireland are now women.

All in all, a very promising future for the sick of Ireland – provided they don't live in the country, get ill only during office hours, have no heart attacks at night, and most of all, give several months' notice of their intention of being unwell so that they get on the waiting list of the shrinking band of working she-doctors nice and early.

Look, it might actually be far worse. These figures are for only two-thirds of the GP trainees. The other third didn't even reply. Why was that? Was it because they're already out of the profession, and felt guilty? Because if that's so, we're looking at a short-term medical catastrophe. It would mean, for example, that of the 200 trainees, 40 per cent were already, within the time span of a studentship, no longer working as GPs – apart, perhaps, from when the theatre manager makes his plaintive little plea.

That is speculation, of course; what is not are the intentions of the two-thirds who answered the questionnaire. I repeat: only 10 per cent intend to have a full-time career, available all-hours, and fully two-thirds expect to be working only part-time.

But hold on. These are the people who have taken rare, much-prized and socially vital places in medical college. We can't whisk replacements out of a hat the moment they decide to work only when there is an 'r' in the month and maybe every second Tuesday. So, we're going to have to find ways of curbing the attrition of these vital young sawbones so soon after they leave college. One is by intervention at the very start of their putative careers, by interviewing applicants for those precious medical places in college, and asking them: well, what do you intend to do with your medical career when you start a family? But of course, that kind of question is almost certainly illegal under our insane equality laws, and so, we're trapped in the nets of dogmatic nonsense of the gender-equality ideolo-gists. We are thus creating an entirely unsustainable medical system that will, of itself, fall apart within a decade or so.

So how are we to replace the armies of women doctors who leave? Why, by plundering the Third World, of course. So, just in the nick of time, over the horizon thunder the black and tan warriors of the Hippocratic Light Horse, drawn from the medical schools of Africa and India – which of course have no inhibitions about asking applicants for their incredibly precious places in medical school about their long-term commitment to the profession.

The authors of the IMJ paper are clearly true doctors: their naïevety is quite bewitching in its unworldliness. So, stars glittering in their eyes, they suggest that the career preferences of women GPs should be taken into account in 'the plan-ning and implementation of primary care', and since part-time partnerships are women's career choice, this work practice needs to be 'expanded and supported'.

Expanded and supported? God almighty, expanded and supported by what and by whom? There aren't enough doctors as it is. And how can you plan your primary care when the primary carers are back at home, caring primarily for their families? These are hole-in-the-bucket solutions to hole-in-the-bucket problems. We should be trying to prevent the hole in the first place, which is what you'd do if you chose your students as much by commitment as by points.

Intellectually, medical students are absurdly over-endowed for a career that involves 90 per cent mucous, 9 per cent self-pity, and 1 per cent genuine illness. It's a fair swap, surely, if the graduate intake has to drop a few trivial points in academic excellence in exchange for brio, enthusiasm and long-term commitment.

But, no. We prefer the futile myths of the equality agenda, and we will have to be bailed out of the resulting disaster by luring doctors from wretched, AIDS-wracked, medically deprived Third World countries.

Sheer folly; and wicked, moreover.

[21 May 2004]

II. 11. *Taboos*

Perhaps had Mary Harney had warning of the question, she would have phrased herself differently when asked about the sexually active eleven-year-old girl. It makes little difference. We all know there's no right answer to the question of how to cope with a child whose precocious sexual instincts are beyond the power of her immature personality to control. Thus this totemic girl is a perfect example of what happens when we throw taboos about sexual conduct out of the window, without knowing what we are going to replace them with.

For in liberal, post-Christian Ireland, we have destigmatised sex, and no longer declare any personal behaviour to be intrinsically wrong. The possession of a personal moral order is virtually unacceptable: we certainly would not dare tell an eleven-year-old girl that it is 'sinful' to have sex, even if we thought it might prevent her from having intercourse. It is an interesting sense of priority – for in effect, we prefer her to be pregnant than to have a troubled conscience.

In Britain, where intolerant and dogmatic liberalism has long been the Established Church, Victoria Gillick became a figure of official hilarity for attempting to prevent the state's provision of abortion and contraceptives to girls without parental knowledge. The state had become mother, counsellor, condom-supplier, pill-dispenser, and when all that failed, abortionist, to under-age teenagers.

And Britain probably prides itself on being a post-taboo society. It is not of course, for taboos exist in all societies, for originally useful if later forgotten reasons. They often then survived, wholly irrational in form and cruel in application. The taboo on sexual activity by the unmarried was created to ensure social and economic harmony in all European societies. But it reached a truly deviant, vicious form in this country, almost becoming a defining characteristic of Irishness. We didn't literally kill our unmarried mothers, but we did metaphorically: we created cruel rituals of exclusion and punishment that placed them beyond the Pale of ordinary humanity.

The pathological Irish terror of the carnal was certainly a legacy of the Famine, and it is one we seem finally to have banished. However, we have apparently replaced that taboo with at least one other, one which protects the feminist agenda. Who would publicly dare to declare that stay-at-home mothers are better mothers than working mothers? The point is not the rightness of the argument, but whether one may even publicly make it.

It was ever thus. Synge was attempting to explore the shallowness of the peasant taboo on murder amongst the Irish peasantry in *The Playboy of the Western World*. Unintentionally, however, he touched upon the real taboo of Irish life with his use of the word 'shift', triggering Abbey riots every night. Moreover, we know that if the hero had been playboy enough to get Pegeen Mike pregnant, the truly prevalent taboo would have prevented the play from ever being staged.

In my distant, more liberal days, I believed that if young people had proper sex education, all would be well: they would learn to have sex in a proper and mature way, and in due course would grow into enlightened, sexually responsible adults. But of course, this is utter rubbish. If youngsters are indifferent to learning generally, why should they be interested in sex education? They might be interested in sex, but that's a different matter entirely. You can take a bunch of thirteen-year-old boys and give them computer games, and they will play with them avidly: try to teach the boys about electronics, and pretty soon you're talking to a bunch of comatose youngsters.

Equally, the details of sex, like any other 'interesting' subject, are actually quite boring: fallopian tubes, monthly cycles, testes, ovulation, yawn yawn, go on Miss, get onto the good bit, sexual intercourse, orgasms, and so on. But sex is not the possession of just a few travellers flying first class who don't need to fly the plane; most people can fly first class sexually, and the consequences of indulging in it during your teenage years can cause you to fly the aircraft of your life into the ground.

We now all know about the sexualisation of childhood, although we might retain some perspective about how 'new' it supposedly is. At primary school, I used to wonder what one girl named Patricia was so obsessively doing at the back of the class, her hand between her legs. Now I know. When I was eleven, two of my classmates boastfully lost their virginities to one another. So sex has always been a feature of *some* children's childhood. The difference today is that *sexuality* is everywhere, and is part of the unwritten, unauthorised – but nonetheless authorising – taboo-free consensus that governs modern childhood.

Yet we still have taboos – witness our abysmal failure to deal with the self-inflicted realities of Traveller life or to question the triumphalist feminist agenda. For taboos are the G-spots of societal anxiety: press them, and you have an explosion of emotion beyond all logic. And you cannot consciously create a taboo; it is the product of the unconscious group-mind, and it is protected both by a vehement denial that it exists and by a perfectly lethal irrationality if you touch it.

Today the very concept of 'sin' is taboo. Post-Christian Christianity obsessively shies away from discussing it. Is it therefore so surprising that, with conscience excluded as a moral guide to sexual conduct, there are consequences that leave us dumbfounded and desperately reaching for the Dane: taboo, or not taboo? That is the question.

[10 August 2005]

III. Ireland

THE STATE OF THE STATE

III.1. *Ireland Is Anglicised*

It was, I suppose, to want too much to hope that Pat Rabbitte would simply condemn the Taoiseach's unilateral decision to revive the commemorations for the Easter Rising, on the grounds that it was a ghastly and anti-democratic abomination. Instead, he wrote approvingly of James Connolly: 'Connolly's rising was a strike, not against Britain, but against British imperialism, and the social conditions it generated in Ireland.'

That the Rising is a central feature in our history cannot be denied, in much the same way that the Famine is. But it is a horror: an unspeakable horror in which unspeakable deeds were done to living human beings, just as they were in Flanders and Picardy at the same time, and no one in his right mind today would dream of celebrating the contemporaneous events in those places.

What was the moral pretext for the violence of 1916? What justified the taking of human lives, the vast majority of them Irish, both then and the years to come? Well, consider the police raid one month before the Rising, on the shop beside Liberty Hall, which itself had secretly been turned into an arsenal and arms factory for James Connolly's Irish Citizens Army.

When Connolly saw a policemen looking through some documents in the shop, he drew his pistol and said: 'Drop those or I'll drop you.' The officer put the papers down and explained he had come to confiscate some outlawed publications. Connolly asked him for his warrant, and he replied that he didn't have one.

Connolly ordered him out and he obligingly withdrew. Later an Inspector Bannon arrived with four men and a warrant, which Connolly made him read out aloud. Connolly said the warrant did not apply to the Hall, so the officers again left.

Now was this in any sense a tyranny that justified homicide? Moreover, would it have been so terrible if Inspector Bannon had arrested Connolly for drawing a gun on a police officer, then forced his way into Liberty Hall and found the munitions hidden behind firebricks in a fireplace, thereby forestalling the Rising? Of course we cannot say how a what-if history might have been: but we can say that Inspector Bannon and his meticulous adherence to the rule of law was infinitely preferable to what happened in Dublin four weeks later, when hundreds of innocent people were killed by men who had never sought a national mandate of any kind.

To be sure, Connolly had run twice for Dublin Corporation for Wood Quay, but the electors were not fools – they rejected the ambitions of a Marxist lunatic who yearned for bloody class war. In 1915, Connolly wrote approvingly of the consequences of a future Rising; 'Starting thus, Ireland may yet set the torch to a European conflagration that will not burn out until the last throne and the last capitalist bond and debenture will be shrivelled on the funeral pyre of the last warlord.'

In other words, Connolly was a warmongering totalitarian-in-waiting, a proto-Lenin: not surprisingly, the Kaiser supported them both. And in return, the leaders of the 1916 Rising acclaimed the butchers of Belgium as 'gallant allies'. However, the Irish Transport and General Workers' Union certainly did not approve of Connolly's antics. Ten days before the Rising, it effectively evicted him and his Irish Citizen Army from Liberty Hall, extracting from him an undertaking never to return.

So contrary to almost everything taught as a matter of doctrine today, Connolly in no sense had the consent of the trade union or labour movements when he deployed the armed and largely illiterate lads of the ICA against the wholly unarmed colleagues of Inspector Bannon. However, this profoundly immoral use of impressionable youngsters was matched by Pearse when he sent his pupils of St Enda's to war.

So in 1916, it was Bannon and his men who held the banner of civilisation, not James Connolly, who at one stage during Easter week ordered his men to shoot looters. Very socialist indeed. Clearly, the Rising was utterly unconnected with improving the conditions of the poor (unless one includes killing them – including at least 28 children – in very large numbers, and thereby putting them all out of their misery).

Almost no intended goal has resulted from the Rising. Ireland is not Gaelic, not united and not constitutionally a republic. Ours is the most anglicised non-British country in the world, one which rebroadcasts all major British television services throughout its entire jurisdiction, and which has native editions of every major British newspaper. Our national media even report on English cricket. And by God, we are certainly not socialist, which explains our popularity with people from Eastern Europe, who know a thing or two about true socialism.

Contrary to Pat Rabbitte's contention that British imperialism made Ireland poor, the reverse was true. In 1910, emigration nothwithstanding, Ireland was one of the richest countries in a desperately poor world, and was more prosperous than, for example, Norway, Sweden, Italy and Finland. By 1970, self-governing Ireland, though untouched by the Second World War, had become just about the poorest country in Europe.

In other words, 1916 propelled this country into a catastrophic trajectory from which one of its participants, the great Sean Lemass, finally strove to free us. In 1966 he signed a free trade treaty with Britain, symbolically undoing the central purpose of the Rising half a century before. Yet now, 90 years onward, once again, we are about to 'celebrate' one of the most abysmal and politically dysfunctional episodes of blood-letting in Irish history.

[17 January 2006]

III.2. The Smoking Ban

Have we gone off our collective trolleys? Two pub owners, Ronan Lawless and Kieran Levanzin on Monday were fined a total of €6400, with another €3000 in costs, for both smoking on their premises, and allowing others to smoke there. That's not a large fine; that's whopping, state-of-the-art, come here Mr Bourke and let me feel your collar kind of a fine.

What were these two reprobates doing? Engaging in the kind of activity that is legal at home, in hotel rooms, and across every other country within the EU, and indeed, the entire world. True, in Afghanistan, they wouldn't have fined the lads for smoking but would have shot them for selling alcohol. Perhaps much the same in Basra.

But they were not convicted and found guilty of behaving as Sharon Shannon was, of being three times over the drink limit when her car went into a parked car just over a year ago. Her defence was that she was not driving at the time.

Judge Mary Fahy said the accused and her friends had told blatant and out-right lies to the court before convicting her, fining her €800, and disqualifying her from driving for two years. But Sharon Shannon was freed on appeal: why? Oh you'll love this – because her summons had been served on the day after its six-month expiry date.

(A brief interpolation here before we return to the main thrust of this column. Who was responsible for yet *another* failure to activate a summons on time? Why did it happen? And to what lofty rank has the wretch been promoted? For I take it from the frequency with which this sort of thing occurs that promotion is the usual outcome for such ineptitude, stupidity or malfeasance. If certain demotion or dismissal were the result, it would surely never happen.)

But back to the Shannon trial. Here we have a judge who was sure she was being lied to by a defendant facing a terribly serious charge. If the accused was driving – and Judge Fahy thought she was – considering how drunk she was, it was by luck alone that she killed no one when her car crashed into another vehicle. Yet she was fined a mere €800. To be sure, she lost her licence for two years as well, but she is a rich woman, and can afford a driver.

On the other hand, a court this week in effect fined two men nearly €5000 each for merely smoking cigarettes on their own premises. Well, you might say, two different judges work in quite different ways – which would be a fair point if there were two different judges, but there weren't. There was the one. Judge Mary Fahy.

All, right, we've established that in terms of financial penalties, it is (effectively) six times more serious for two consenting adults to smoke in their own pub than it is (theoretically) for an adult to get leglessly drunk in that same pub, get into a car, smash into another car, and then lie through her teeth about the entire affair in court. Smoking kills, et cetera. Of course it does – but not as swiftly and as certainly as drunk-drivers.

But the state now has a policy to eliminate smoking. Which is good. So what happened to the owner of a Cavan garage that sold cigarettes to a 13-year-old girl? Well, Thomas Cassidy was fined €250 for selling a tobacco product to an underage girl, and also ordered to pay €500 costs. We'll call it a €750 fine – about *one seventh* of the monstrous fine inflicted on each of our two publicans.

Maybe the fine was so small because he was a contrite and apologetic about his deeds? Well, when accused of selling cigarettes to the 13-year-old, he replied: 'I have no intention of ever complying with the health board. Business is business and that's how I run mine … I don't care if I'm caught. I will have no problem paying the f-ing fines anyway.'

This time the judge was not Mary Fahy but Judge David Maughan.

One of the recent catch-cries of recent years is how liberal and tolerant we have become, compared to the bigoted, Catholic-dominated Ireland that we left behind. Remember how condoms were banned by law? Remember the intrepid Dublin garda in 1991 who bought a condom from Virgin Megastore? He then prosecuted the shop and it was fined £400. It appealed, of course – and the appeal judge, a creature called O'Hanrahan – increased the fine to £500, observing that he was letting Virgin off lightly. As the law stood, each further condom sale could lead to a £5000 fine, with an additional fine of £250 for each single day condoms remained on sale, with possible imprisonment for the evil wrongdoers as well. The author of this law was that legendarily ascetic celibate, Charles Haughey.

Plus ca change. Condoms one year; smoking in pubs another. We have exchanged one busybody intolerant orthodoxy for another, meanwhile allowing grotesque anomalies – the drunk-driver, the man who boastfully sells cigarettes to minors – slip by relatively unpunished. We are using law not to protect the rights of adults to make adult decisions about their lives, but to erect legal totems, before which we prostrate ourselves, in the belief that we are morally superior to other people. But we're actually making asses of ourselves.

Footnote: The smoking ban will prove unworkable this winter, and pubs will covertly allocate rooms to smokers, just as supermarkets are now covertly giving people plastic bags.

[7 October 2004]

III.3. Suer Rats

To whom does one's heart go out more: to Simon McGinley, of Ballyfree halting site, Sligo, or Josie Murphy, the barge, the Grand Canal, Kildare town? On balance, I'd say Simon McGinley. Poor Simon had his disability payments, which he has been claiming for ten years, cut by the heartless ladies and gentlemen of the Criminal Assets Bureau after investigating officers discovered – shock, horror – £91,000 worth of bank draughts hidden at his halting site. Simon – he of the disability – explained the money away by saying that he earned between £60–70,000 buying and selling scrap. Furthermore he has had the misfortune of – along with his wife Kathleen – having been involved in no less than three motor accidents.

Three motor accidents? What beastly bad luck. It is of course of scant consolation that these accidents have netted him and Kathleen a mere £20,500 in compensation.

To which I say: not enough.

Why? Look at Josey Murphy. She didn't need to have nasty great car crashes for her to win a great hefty dollop of compensation. She found a caterpillar in her broccoli in her works canteen, and last week the Circuit Court ruled that she should receive £14,000 in compensation for the nasty shock she'd received. Nasty it might have been; but not as nasty as that experienced by Campbell Catering or their insurers or whoever it was who has to fork out the loot for the baby butterfly sharing Josie's veggies.

The Judge, no less than the eminent Circuit Court President, Mr Justice Smyth – so he must know his onions, not so speak of his Italian brassica – remarked that it was obvious that mention of the caterpillar, even in court, brought on a dramatic reaction in the plaintiff. When she found the beast in her broccoli, she told the court that the blood drained from her face. She had to leave work and was unable to work the final five weeks of her eleven-week contract. She wept as she described how her doctor had sent her to a psychiatrist, how she had lost weight, and was unable to eat out.

Which rather sounds as if not merely she should have been suing the caterers, but so should every restaurant she would normally have given her business to. As should the restaurant suppliers, and the farmers growing the food and makers of the fertilisers who couldn't sell the fertiliser to the farmers who couldn't sell the food to the restaurants and so on and so forth until the circle finally encompassed Simon McGinley up there in Sligo, who probably sues reluctantly, but no doubt could be prevailed on to do so, if only not to let the side down.

And the poor fellow clearly has to top up his earnings one way or another. After all, three car crashes only netted him twenty grand; what he needs is a grub in his grub – perhaps Campbell Catering would oblige? Though on reflection, that would hardly be necessary. For a consideration, I'd be prepared to help out myself. I couldn't count the number of times I've served myself greenfly in my salad. I once ate nearly a pound of cherries before noticing that every remaining cherry – and presumably every one I had already consumed – had a wormhole in it. I have very probably gorged myself many times on caterpillars camouflaged as broccoli – as Campbell pointed out in court, caterpillars sometimes burrow deep and unseeably into broccoli – and I am probably the better for it. Pre-school insects look like broccoli, their consistency is like slightly overcooked broccoli, and by jove they certainly taste like broccoli

And not just brocolli. In Australia once I was contentedly chewing a piece of cold steak until I noticed something about the bit remaining. Do you want to know how quickly you can empty your mouth of its contents? Discover that you're eating meat that is teeming with maggots, and believe me, you'll find you can spit out what you're eating faster than a nuclear bomb explodes. That's the funny thing about steak-eating maggots; they taste just like steak. Maybe that's why I've never sued anybody for these inadvertent gastronomic adventures into vivivorousness.

So I didn't take the Bosnian Serb who sold me the cherries to court, but then one tends not to in that part of the world. Even here in Litigiland, I've never sued the supermarkets for selling unsolicited greenfly in my lettuce, or unsought worms in my peas or legless little things with tiny black noses making free with the apples I've bought. I didn't even sue my Ossie friend Keith for leaving steak in the open overnight. Lord above, what a fortune I'm missing out on.

Though if I were as prone to distress as Josie Murphy, a lifetime of restaurant-salads might seem a sound career move. For if one dead caterpillar can net a person £15,000, what would the consequence be if it had been alive and doing press-ups on her plate? What if it had been a lesbian caterpillar and had made a pass at her? The insurance company hasn't been made which could survive that lawsuit.

And I must wonder: how does she like life on a canal in which rodents nightly perform the breaststroke all around her boat? Ah well, they're probably drawn to litigious folk: you see, they're suer-rats.

[ND]

III.4. The 'Slab' Moment

Is it intrinsic to our legal system that those involved in it seem utterly incapable of having a shared sense of time? A court last year released Judge Patrick Curtin because the warrant to search his house had expired before child pornography was found on his computer. He is now a free man, still drawing his salary for doing nothing. Good. So a lesson is learnt? Well what do you think?

Three men – Wayne Harte, Dwayne Foster and Jeffrey Finnegan – were arrested at 10.55pm, Sunday, March 5, on suspicion of the brutal and random murder of Donna Cleary the morning before. The next day, at 10.55 pm, Monday March 6, Garda Chief Superintendent Peter Maguire authorised the continued detention of the suspects. That night, Dwayne Foster died in custody, probably of some drugs-related condition.

So then there were two.

The next day, at 8.00 pm, Tuesday, March 7, those two were scheduled to appear in court to permit gardaí to continue interrogating them. Chief Superintendent Maguire, an outstanding policeman – a former head of Special Branch, a trained barrister and one of the most gallant defenders of freedom against Provisional IRA fascism this state has known – had made sure to allow enough court-time before the lawful custody had expired at 10.55 pm. Or so he'd thought.

But what did he run into? Lawyers, actually, who – apparently – live in different time zones, and so the hearing did not get under way until 8.30. The problems were compounded when Finnegan's counsel, Yvonne Bambury, declined to permit evidence for the remand proceedings to be heard together. Wayne Harte's case was heard first. At its conclusion, Chief Superintendent Maguire warned the judge that they were approaching their prisoners' release time. Judge McDonnell pooh-poohed him, and said not to worry about the clock. He then heard Finnegan's remand application, and at 11.20 ordered his continued detention.

The next day, Judge Iafhlaith O'Neill ruled that that detention was illegal because it had been imposed 25 minutes after the initial lawful detention had expired. This was precisely what Chief Superintendent Maguire had, in effect, predicted. Finnegan was thus released.

And then there was one.

Wayne Harte was released at 11.55 pm, March 8.

And then there was none.

How is this possible, and on so many grounds? The Curtin court ruled that a search warrant became invalid the very moment stated for its conclusion. Yet the Finnegan court apparently could ignore the warnings of an impeccable witness – a heroic counter-terrorist of our state – that this might happen.

Equally, the Finnegan appeal ruled that the gentleman in question had been in garda custody from the time the Bridewell hearing began the day before, when he had clearly not: he had been in the custody of the court, not the gardaí, for the final three hours of his detention.

But most of all: is the lifespan of a warrant not conclusively sorted out in law school? Or is our legal culture so diseased and precious that it regards itself as being above the ordinary temporal rules that the rest of us have to live by? So GAA has throw-in times, rugby kick-off times, but courts invoke Einstein's Law on Relativity? And is there intense lawyerly satisfaction at outcomes such as that described above? Inscrutable lawyer lore, triumphing once again.

Moreover, there was a bewitching symmetry between this ludicrous farce and events on the Border, as army and police of both jurisdictions finally closed in on the very man who has been the legal and moral inspiration for criminals for over 30 years: Thomas Slab Murphy. But why now? Why not 20 years ago? For now, it is too late.

In 1986 British soldiers in South Armagh saw a red car departing from the firing place of a mortar-bomb attack on a military base. The car entered Murphy's farm, this side of the Border. A British troop-carrying army helicopter landed nearby, but in Northern Ireland territory. Immediately, the soldiers were illuminated by arc-lights. Nonetheless, they started to search through outbuildings on the northern side. A Lance Corporal Robinson saw a figure lurking beside a shed, and ran forward and into the Irish Republic, where two men grabbed him and wrestled him to the ground.

However, help was to hand, as gardaí arrived. What did they do? Search the Murphy property for possible evidence of terrorist activity? Bring in dogs to search for any freshly arrived Libyan Semtex? Arrest the men who had assaulted and apprehended L/C Robinson? No. They arrested the soldier, for being in unlawful possession of a weapon, took him to Dundalk Garda Station and held him for six and a half hours.

That was the Slab Moment. That was the tipping point, when the Provisionals knew that this state truly lacked the will to confront and see off the IRA. Already powerful, the IRA in South Armagh grew more arrogant still. Eamon Collins gave evidence against Slab Murphy in *The Sunday Times* libel trial – and the IRA then brutally and ritually murdered him. The consequences for Sinn Féin? Why, its delegates didn't even get one biscuit less the next time they visited the Taoiseach's office or Downing Street.

Slab is not married but he has hundreds of children, truly chips off the old block. The Slabette generation now ruling our housing estates knows how to kill, how to terrorise, how to resist interrogation, and most of all, how to manipulate both the law and its conceited handmaidens, lawyers. Our bed is made. Let us now lie in it.

[15 March 2006]

III.5. The Shell Pipeline

How do people who assemble signatories for public letters choose their guest list? What central principle unites an artist, Bobby Ballagh, a columnist for this newspaper, Fintan O'Toole, and that scrupulous observer of the drink-driving laws, Eamon Dunphy? Why did the letter-organiser choose four members of the IRA army council – Pat Doherty, Martin McGuinness, Gerry Adams and Martin Ferris – one arms smuggler, Arthur Morgan, and a quartet of professional warblers, Frances Black, Luka Bloom, Christy Moore and Leo Moran? How did he or she choose a gay rights activist, David Norris, a Colombia Three Groupie with a few slates loose, Senator Mary White, and the only two public figures in Ireland who have actually participated in a rally supporting the Islamo-fascist terrorist insurgency in Iraq, Trevor Sargent and Mick O'Reilly?

However it came about, all the above signed a letter last week supporting the Rossport Five.

So, why was I not also asked to put my name to a document which concluded: 'We demand the immediate release of Philip McGrath, Brendan Philbin, Vincent McGrath, Willie Corduff and Micheal O Seighin from their unjust incarceration'? Was it possibly because (a) I wouldn't get into a lifeboat in shark-infested waters with some of the above, (b) I don't sign political petitions, or (c) I believe in the rule of law?

The law: ah yes, that strange concept, the law. So how many people were jailed for their opposition to the Shell pipeline in Mayo? Five? Wrong. The correct answer is none. Who made release of The Rossport Five possible? The protesters themselves? No. The answer is Shell, which applied in the High Court for the lifting of the temporary injunction restraining the men from interfering with the pipeline.

The Rossport Five were jailed not for their opinions, but because as men of principle they refused to give false undertakings before the court not to interfere with the Shell pipeline passing through their lands. So, contrary to what the letter-writers declared, by very deliberately defying the court, the Rossport Five themselves chose jail: and a court which does not protect its own authority is as worthless as a bank with no safe.

Moreover, the very name 'Shell' seems to cause reason to fly out of the window. Shell corrupts governments all over the world, Shell poisons democracy, Shell buys politicians, and judicially executes those its cannot buy, most famously such as Ken Saro Wiwa: or so Conchaphobes would have you believe. Yet Wiwa was executed not for his opposition to Shell operations in Nigeria, but for his part in the brutal murder of rival Ogoni elders. And though Shell actually tried to stop the execution, this hasn't prevent Rossport Five supporters from enlisting the support of his brother Owens in their campaign, as if the two sets of events were comparable.

Admittedly the original government deal with Shell was done with that fragrant creature Raphael Burke, and anything touched by that creature must have the raw tang of rat manure about it. But the Rossport Five are complaining less about the nature of that deal than the issue of safety: and if the pipeline is not safe, it's not safe, regardless of whether or not Shell pays royalties to the state.

Gerry Crowley TD – one of the signatories to the letter which I was so *scandalously* not asked to sign – claims that houses within 170 metres of the pipeline are within the kill-zone in the event of an explosion. I don't know where he gets his figures from – but what precisely is the kill-zone for the natural-gas pipelines that run under the streets of Cork and Dublin today? What is the kill-zone for gas leaking in a kitchen? Is either an argument against using gas anywhere? If so, it's equally an argument against petrol pumps, power stations, aeroplanes or technology of any kind.

Shell has been sinking wells around the Irish coast for twenty years: none had yielded anything until the Mayo find eight years ago. Other drilling goes on. Four years ago, Shell drilled an exploratory well 125 kilometres off the northwest coast. At 1600 metres, it was the deepest water well ever drilled in Europe. Nothing was found, and it was capped and abandoned. Shell recently sank a well over 4000 metres deep in the Dooish area, then drilled sideways and then sank another well to meet this offshoot, 4471 metres down. We await the outcome.

And without such spectacularly costly operations, 'our' gas reserves would remain exactly where they've spent the past 237 million years. Do you actually think Shell shareholders invest without expectation of return? Since you're *Irish Times* readers, you possibly do: unless, that is, you have a pension fund which has invested in Shell.

To be sure, the original Burke–Shell deal might stink to high heaven – but it is nonetheless a legally binding contract, with no get-out clause for subsequent governments that no longer like Ray Burke. So either the state buys its way out of that contract – including reimbursing Shell for the ten zillion the company has spent drilling holes to nowhere miles beneath the sea – or it enforces the rule of law, both on Shell for any unauthorised pipe-laying, and on landowners through which the gas pipeline must pass.

The central issue in this dispute is not Burke or Shell or the Rossport Five, but the rule of law and the authority of our courts – something that our letter-writers are apparently not too keen on. And when you consider some of their backgrounds, perhaps that's not so very surprising.

[19 April 2005]

THE CHURCH

III.6. Beatification & Pope John Paul II

What an interesting Pope this Karol Wojtyla fellow is turning out to be. He has beatified 1340 people and made 464 saints. That's an awful lot of superior saints swanking around in heaven, getting the best restaurant tables and flying first class. I know we're supposed to be equal in heaven, but frankly I don't believe it. What's the point in being canonised unless you can throw your weight around in the hereafter?

St Teresa of Avila seems to have hit on the most congenial form of saint-hood yet discovered. There she was, knees clasped tightly together, praying alone when she was visited by an angel bearing a spear. The angel then stuck the spear through the very pit of her stomach, and a most curious thing happened: her body was infused with an amazing sensation that lay somewhere between agony and ecstasy, and as the angel continued to penetrate her, she felt her innards convulse with a strange hot fire, so pleasurable that she swooned.

Yes, I think I know what that is. I just didn't know they were handing out sainthoods for it, and I'm only sorry I didn't find out sooner. Ah well, that's the way of these things. Like the supermarkets, you only hear about these special offers after they've closed. So Teresa's certainly seems to be the kind of sainthood for me – much better than what St Sebastian had to endure. After all, he got sim-ilar treatment to Teresa, but didn't enjoy it one bit. Which is perhaps why though there is no religious order named after him, there is one named after her. I bet morning prayers are a riot in that convent. I wonder: do they let people watch?

So, that's the truth about sainthood: it is delivered for all sorts of reasons. But there can hardly be a saint to match Karl, last Emperor of the Hapsburg empire, whom the Pope now intends to beatify. Emperor Karl I was the architect for the battle of Caporetto in October 1917. He was thus the inspiration for Hem-mingway's *A Farwell to Arms*, which contains the definitive account of a military disaster. It was also a landmark in the career of one Erwin Rommel, who took the surrender of an entire battalion of 1500 Italians, so to speak, single-handedly. St Teresa would have been very impressed.

Two reasons to remember Emperor Karl. Here's a third. Ten thousand Ital-ians were killed, another 30,000 wounded, with 300,000 prisoners and 400,000 deserters. (Rather Italian figures, those.) The Italian lines were finally held after mass executions of fleeing troops. But the rout was perhaps understandable: the Austrians and Germans were using phosgene gas for the first time, which a satis-fied Emperor Karl later reported had been very effective.

And the man who brought this about is being beatified – though at least, not for that. One justification of his beatification is that he fought for peace. But that's only partly true. After he came to power in December 1916, he certainly tried to negotiate a separate peace with the allies, but only on condition that he be allowed to keep to keep his empire intact. It's a pity he wasn't: the destruction of the Habsburg empire was one of the greatest follies in European history. But his primary motivation was his desire to be emperor, not to be a peacemaker. He even sought to create a new state of Poland and Galicia, under Austrian control, and you don't get made saint for that.

Emperor Karl abdicated his throne in November 1918, but retained some of the titles: Emperor of Austria; King of Hungary, of Bohemia, of Dalmatia, Croatia, Slovenia, Lodomeria, Galicia and Illyria; Grand Duke of Tuscany and Krako[e-acute]w; Duke of Lothringia, of Salzburg, Styria, Carinthia, Carniola and Buko-vina; Grand Duke of Transylvania and Margrave of Moravia, and many, many more, the most presciently sinister being Duke of Auschwitz and Sator.

He died of flu in Madeira in 1922, and his wife Zita started the Kaiser Karl Prayer League soon afterwards, though history doesn't relate whether praying did for her what it did for Teresa of Avila. But it certainly didn't do her any harm: she died in 1989, after sixty-seven years of widowhood, prayer (with or without the Avila effect) and ceaseless campaigning to get her husband beatified.

Of course, for a beatification to proceed, a miracle-healing has to be shown, and in 1960, one was duly found. A nun in Poland declared that Kaiser Karl had cured her varicose veins. To which I can only say, come back Lazarus. Miracles aren't what they used to be, especially since the nun was also receiving conventional medical treatment.

Now if varicose veins are a suitable locus for miraculous intervention worthy of a beatification, where does the process stop? Is a miracle cure for dandruff a reason to begin to process of canonisation? What about acne? Or baldness? Or athlete's foot? Failure to achieve sexual gratification might also be a cause for prayer to a holy person as yet unbeatified or canonised. However, I suspect there already exists a saint who is particularly qualified in that regard, to whom I would heartily recommend a frustrated supplicant to direct her prayers.

So why is the Pope beatifying a man who seems to have done so little to have deserved it and so much – 10,000 dead Italians – to disqualify him? Is it perhaps because Karl was once titular Grand Duke of Cracow, and His Holiness was once Archbishop and Grand Metropolitan of the same city? Or is it simply because the time has finally come for the grand old man to retire?

[6 October 2004]

III. 7. The 'O' Word

The one form of intolerance that is fashionable and almost universal these days is of the Catholic Church, especially in its European, white male manifestations.

The appalling headlines which greeted the election of Pope Benedict XVI – 'The Vatican Rottweiller' – would never have found any such equivalent if the Pope had been African. And no newspaper anywhere would have spoken of an Islamic leader in such tones, not least because editors probably nurture fond ambitions to remain alive.

Self-hatred is now a defining feature of West European culture. An Italian politician states that he accepts the traditional Catholic teaching about homosexuality, and he is hounded from office. Can you imagine a Muslim MP in Britain suffering from the same fate for declaring his allegiance to the teachings of the Prophet? I've been here before, but I revisit this territory again, in part because of the continuing correspondence in this newspaper, but also because a visceral loathing of Catholicism is almost de rigueur in salon society. It is as if people across Europe wish the Catholic Church to cease to be the Catholic Church and instead become the Gay and Lesbian Rights Action Front, with the Pope its leader.

Áilín Doyle the other day repeated Brenda O'Hanrahan's quotations from the former Cardinal Ratzinger: 'It is deplorable that homosexual persons have been and are the subject of violent malice in speech or in action.' But, she added, the cardinal then continued: 'When such a claim is made [that the homosexual condition is not disordered] and homosexual activity is consequently condoned, or when civil legislation is introduced to protect behaviour to which no one has any conceivable right, neither the Church nor society at large should be surprised when other distorted notions and practices gain ground, and irrational and violent reactions increase.'

Áilín Doyle declared of this: 'It would be difficult to think of a more offensive statement.' No, it wouldn't. It would be one the easiest things in the world. Death to all Fenians. Women are bitches.

You want I should go on? That she and I might disagree with the Cardinal doesn't mean that what he says is 'offensive'. Moreover, can anyone seriously believe that a prelate of the Holy Roman Catholic and Apostolic Church is going to actually approve of acts of sodomy? You don't really expect the Catholic Church to say that deed is as acceptable in the eyes of the Lord as the act of intercourse within the sacrament of marriage, do you?

The year is 2005, and the divisions between church and state are universal across Europe. Those divisions entitle churches to hold opinions which are not held by liberal secularists. They also entitle churches to ask of legislatures the politically impossible, and for law-making bodies simply to decline the request. But we live in a world of such moral complexity that it should be possible for people to state their opinions, especially when they are entirely free of hatred of any kind, without being accused of being 'offensive'. However, any conversation about the reality of homosexuality is now virtually impossible without the 'o' argument rearing its head.

Few right-minded people would agree with Cardinal Ratzinger's opposition to laws permitting male homosexual acts. I emphatically would not. Yet nonetheless, is it not probable that the AIDS epidemic that all but wiped out an entire generation of homosexual males in the US could not have occurred on the scale it did if the legal prohibition on sodomy had remained in place? The price of homosexual freedom can thus be measured in the tragedy of hundreds of thousands of lost lives, and the grief of millions.

That these are difficult questions, ones which are likely to trigger a generous use of the 'o' word, should not prevent us from considering them. For the sexual revolution of the 1960s has left us with so many complex, perhaps insoluble problems.

In Britain teachers have reported an epidemic of 'daisy-chaining', where children in their early teens retire to a room and have serial, unprotected sex with one another. In Ireland we recently heard of the practice of 'snowballing', in which a girl will pretend to kiss a boy, but instead blows the sperm she has collected orally from another boy into the mouth of her victim. 'Felching', performed by homosexual males, involves the use of a straw and is too disgusting to elaborate on.

Shocked? Of course you are. Which brings us back with a jolt to the kernel of Cardinal Ratzinger's concern: 'neither the Church nor society at large should be surprised when other distorted notions and practices gain ground, and irrational and violent reactions increase'.

In other words, where does it all end? We know that the legal prohibition on sodomy did not work, was cruel and led to all manner of hypocrisy and misery. But the virtual removal of all sexual taboos has not just eliminated them from predictable practices, but from entirely unexpected ones also, such as daisy-chaining and felching.

The sexual revolution was predicated on the myth that, with full sex education and the elimination of obsolete and neurotic restrictions on sexual indulgences, human beings – even teenagers – would be unfailingly rational and wise in the way they pursued sexual pleasure: a simply preposterous belief.

But if it offensive for even the Pope to remind us of this, then who in the name of God is to do so?

[12 May 2005]

III.8. Heaven in 11

The cause for the canonisation of John Henry, Cardinal Newman, has been furthered by the apparent recovery from spinal disease of a deacon in Boston. This is a long wait for the requisite miracle from a man who died in 1890. 'I had to tell John Paul that the English are not very good at miracles,' explained Cardinal Cormac Murphy O'Connor. 'It's not that we are not pious, but the English tend to think of God as a gentleman who should not be bullied.'

As it happens, the Vatican didn't need the Boston miracle, because the Cardinal was miraculously writing to this very newspaper, on the very same day, in a letter infused with tractarian piety.

'Madam,' it began, 'I note in your edition of October 17th that Dublin City Council is proposing to abolish the public right-of-way in the laneway Faith Avenue and Hope Avenue, Dublin. Could the council, in this case, be accused of a lack of charity? – Yours, etc, JOHN NEWMAN, Dublin 11.'

No, I'm not making this up. On 19 October, the very day of the Boston revelation, that letter appeared in *The Irish Times*. And remember – Dublin 11 is the home of Glasvenin Cemetery. Now it could be that John Henry is a Cockney, and speaks in elaborate rhyming slang. Eleven. Glasnevin. Heaven. However, there is little evidence of rhyming slang in *Apologia pro Vita Sua*.

So it seems that God has actually chosen to locate heaven in Dublin 11. Until this revelation, you always thought you'd take wing to somewhere special once you get buried in Glasnevin, when in fact, the entire saved world – Michelangelo, Mother Teresa, even John Henry himself – is destined to shuffle in to join you there, and spend the rest of eternity in that divine purlieu between Phibsboro and Finglas.

I used to live around there. It was nice enough – but I never thought it was close to heaven. Which only goes to show that you don't know what you've got till you've gone. And it also puts the northside jokes in their place: the residents of Sandycove and Foxrock and Stillorgan and Dalkey, no matter their riches, are going to have to make it past the pearly gates on the threshold of Glasnevin. It is clearly no coincidence that the Catholic church in Phibsboro is St Peter's.

So all those southsiders who have been preening themselves on their ignorance of the far side of the Liffey will spend the rest of eternity with cheerful northsiders drinking bottles of stout, smoking untipped cigarettes and ruthlessly being characters. So heaven is like being trapped in a Roddy Doyle novel, with a chip van, and horses ascending in lifts, incompetent robbers and people hilariously bawling FUQ! – and not for 190 pages, but for all time. How utterly spiffing.

So where is hell? And what does it consist of? Dalkey. Bono.

However, if another clerical John, namely Magee, Bishop of Cloyne, wants to find out all about hell, he should continue with his proposals to wreck St Colman's Cathedral in Cobh. It almost passes belief that 40 years after Vatican II, with its many virtues and its equal number of infamies, that any senior churchman, would want to continue with the programme of architectural conformism which has such a catastrophic consequences for Catholic building projects around the world. What you might call the V 2 effect.

Subsequent church buildings have resembled tepees, igloos, sheds, garages, hangars, slaughter-houses, theatres-in-the round – anything but the cruciform constructions which defined Christian architecture for a millennium and a half.

St Colman's is one of the most noble and inspiring Catholic churches in Ireland. It was designed by Sir Edward Pugin, the finest British architect of the ninteenth century, and – after John Henry – perhaps the greatest English Catholic of the time. He did other work in Ireland – notably Killarney Cathedral, which was a temple to magnificent, wedding-cake, neo-Gothic plasterwork. This was all but destroyed by that lying humbug and posturing wretch, Casey, who stripped the Cathedral's foundation rubble-stone of its gorgeous, irreplaceable plaster, in order to turn what was a Victorian work of art into a pastiche of a medieval abbey.

Most of us thought that with the Catholic Church now holed up in its last redoubt that it would not attempt to alienate public opinion any further. Quite the reverse – hence the modernist mumbo-jumbo to justify the proposed destruction of St Colman's sanctuary: 'What we have at the moment is a signifi-cant spacial separation between the priest and all the people in the Church.'

This is Californian cant. Of course, there's 'a significant spacial separation' – otherwise known as 'distance' – between priest and people. The Holy Roman, Apostolic Church is a hierarchical institution, which is why the Pope doesn't live in a caravan in a halting site outside Drogheda, and why, incidentally, Bishop John Magee goes around with a colossal decorated acorn on his head, otherwise known as a mitre.

Now if the episcopal Cobh cove wants to cosy up to the people, aided by a few chords on his guitar, and whining some profound Bob Dylan song, well, he can do that in the Queenstown Mission Hall, strum strum strum: 'The Church it is a-changing.' But it is not necessary to wreck Ludwig Oppenheimer's mag-nificent mosaic floor, or smash the altar rail, or the episcopal side chapel, as the Cloyne diocese intends. The liturgical mood of today is not that of tomorrow, and the Gentleman in charge in Dublin 11 will not lightly forgive those who irreversibly violate Pugin's Irish masterwork.

[21 October 2005]

III.9. Clonfert or California

In retrospect, the real turning point in the conduct of public affairs in Ireland came when government minister Frank Stagg neither resigned nor was sacked after being found approaching rent boys in Phoenix Park. This moral supinity was then compounded by the general approval bestowed on it liberal Ireland, freshly triumphant that it had another representative in the Park, but about somewhat different business: President Mary Robinson. One of those participating in the cretinous applause was this columnist, then a card-carrying member of the Lib-eral Ireland Club.

But it is now clear: this was utterly absurd. You cannot have government ministers consorting with teenage male prostitutes yet still being allowed to keep their jobs, no matter how personally painful dismissal is for their families.

Next, we had a Taoiseach who arrived in other countries on official visits with a woman who was not his wife, yet nonetheless expecting them to treat her as if she was. He had one wife in Ireland, the mother of his children, and another more exotic wife for foreign travel. How very Polynesian.

Now not even French presidents, who have mistresses because the French Constitution apparently insists they do, expect foreign governments to treat their extramarital consorts as Mrs President. But in Ireland we had two Mrs Taoiseach.

Then one day we woke up, and Celia Larkin was no longer the foreign Mrs Taoi-seach. Suddenly, the country which had once constitutionally banned divorce now had the swiftest divorce laws in the world.

Sooner or later it was inevitable that the Catholic Church would start emu-lating Liberal Ireland, and sure enough, in the affair of Mossie Dillane, it has. Thus Bishop Kirby on a 73-year-old cleric fathering a child by a parishioner 42 years younger than him: 'I hope that the priest, who has ceased to work in the diocese, the mother and all those involved, will be given appropriate time and space to plan for their respective futures. I consider this to be a private matter, and as such, I will make no further comment.'

'Appropriate time and space'? Where is this – Clonfert or California? And what's this about it being 'a private matter'? A priest violates his oath of celibacy and fathers a child by a parishioner, possibly an impressionable one, and certainly young enough to be his granddaughter, and it is not on the main order of the local bishop's business?

Let's restate the obvious here, because it clearly is no longer obvious. The Irish Catholic Church is the Irish Catholic Church. It's not wrong for it to have rules, nor is it wrong to proclaim them (if it can remember them, which nowa-days seems unlikely) especially when they have been flagrantly violated by one of its trusted lieutenants. Having sex with one of your parishioners is not an optional extra of the priesthood, not least because of the extraordinary role of the confessional in the ministry. That Mossie Dillane encouraged general confession does not mean that he did not give private confessions: and moreover, he stood towards his young parishioners just as a psychiatrist stands towards his patients.

Now you can say that the Church's attitude towards a celibate priesthood is outmoded and absurd and unreasonable. A perfectly reasonable stand to take. However, the church is not run by opinion polls, but its own rules, and unless it enforces those rules, it is not a religion but a football-crowd going home.

Commitment is the antithesis of freedom. You cannot be a carnivorous vegan. You cannot drink vodka at AA meetings. You cannot have the bereaved lap-dancing at a funeral. You cannot be all things to all AA vegan lap-dancing widows – unless, that is, you're the Irish Catholic Church of 2006. In which case, you can apparently apply whatever definitions of Catholicism you like, because far from anyone in the hierarchy objecting, they will instead urge people to give you time and space. You think atheist she-popes should be allowed to canonise their lesbian lovers, mid-orgasm? Sure, no problem. You want to ordain your wooden horse? Well, why not?

In all the catalogue of sexual abuse by clergy of the past decade, there was this single, consoling feature: that the Catholic Church had all along known the difference between right and wrong, which is why it tried to hush up and conceal the visibly, palpably evil. But nowadays, does it have any moral opinions for public pronouncement? Does it openly condemn aberrant behaviour and acclaim the virtuous? Or is it all a matter of individual choice, so that a priest's particular interpretation of his vow of chastity is pretty much up to him?

The Catholic Church is not alone in losing moral perspectives. It is symptomatic of our time that in the Dillane case, both the names of the mother and the child have been published. That a mere baby might be made famous simply because his father is a septuagenarian Catholic priest is the quintessential barbarity of this new value-free Ireland.

The Sunday Independent – which perpetrated this infamy – last week also conducted a poll asking people whether they condemned or condoned the priest. Nearly 80 per cent of its respondents did not think it wrong for an elderly Catholic priest to violate his solemn oath of celibacy and have full sexual intercourse with a parishioner two score years younger than him. Which is only what you might expect in this utterly unprincipled, liberal ethos.

So henceforth, you may drive on whatever side of the motorway you like. It's up to you. Okay?

[26 January 2006]

OURSELVES ALONE

III. 10. The Language We Speak

It was about ten years ago that the Hiberno-English word 'crack' began to appear in its Irish form in written English in Ireland. In its pretentiousness, in its witless posturing that somehow it is Gaelic and that we are preserving something uniquely Irish by spelling it in a supposedly Irish way, it sums up perfectly the ambiguities and the hypocrisy surrounding the Irish language. Spell an English word with a fada, and suddenly we're a nation of Irish speakers.

I have written on this before, and no doubt will write about it again, since I seem to be one of the few people in the Irish media who are prepared to take a hostile line towards the national fantasies over the Irish language. The unique and fraudulent position of the 'language' in our political life is sustained by chronic denial, stupidity and state-coercion. The predictable response to anything said here will either be the ranting frothing denunciations from Seamus MacGiolla Fada and Anguosa Mac Craic, or a studied neglect, so that no one need pay any attention to the rude little boy declaring that the emperor has no clothes.

He has no clothes: none. How many TDs opposed Éamon Ó Cúiv's preposterous piece of Stalinist linguistic engineering which made it illegal for any official
document in this state, whether from local council, semi-state to government,
to appear in English alone? None. Thou art a shower of cretins and cowards, all
cringing in terror that somehow you might be considered less Irish if you stood up
and accepted the reality that the Irish language project is dead. Finished. Over.

The confirmation of its death is the epidemic of the *gaelscoileanna*, which
provide an assured middle-class route to post-primary education, free of charge.
(The exception is the *Gaelscoil* in Ballyfermot, which is the 'proof', cited *ad nau-
seam*, about how proletarian these schools really are.) The gaelscoil is a middle
class option that will do nothing whatever to save Irish as a living language; Irish
is becoming merely the modern Greek, proof of the high social status of those
who can quote from *The Midnight Court* or the Caoineadh Airt Uí Laoghaire
over the port and nuts.

The O Cuiv proposals actually made it illegal to have any signs in English
in Gaeltacht areas – though not, needless to say, defining what an English word
is. 'Stop' is an English word today: it wasn't once upon a time. Words enter and
leave languages the whole time: who is to say that 'danger' is not an Irish word?
And who will feel all the better for it because some French tourists don't know
the current Irish word for danger – I'm sorry: nor do I, and nor do most of you
– and drive over a cliff? Maybe the apology will be written in Irish also.

One of the more hilarious O Cuiv proposals to rescue the language recently
is to designate Achill a Gaeltacht. Indeed, why not? Why not solve Albania's
poverty by redesignating it as Kuwait, and solve California's problem with the
San Andreas fault by redesignating it as Kansas? I've always had a problem with
Meath's flatness: henceforth it shall be known as Nepal.

Language policy throughout the history of the state has been shaped by an
alchemist's mad desire to turn lead into gold, combined with an abject political
refusal to accept lingual realities. The education of thousands of socially backward
children continues to be blighted by the vast amount of time learning Irish, as
word games are played to pretend more people speak Irish than actually do.

These games would be almost enchanting if they were not the peak of a very
large iceberg of stupidity. Bus Lána is mildly entertaining; and by happy chance, it
gets round the O Cuiv language rule because 'bus' is not really an English word,
but a Latin word of French deployment, 'voiture omnibus', which passed through
English to arrive in Irish. But what about the ridiculous confection that has been
devised for Luas: 'Lána tram'? No doubt it complies with the O Cuiv rule of
linguistic political correctness, that both words are now in Irish dictionaries: but
we cannot pretend other than 'Lána Tram' is a cumbrous and thoroughly uncon-
vincing attempt to gaelicise what is a very Anglo-Saxon term.

As a matter of interest: are the training manuals to Luas in Irish? This is a state body, so it is clearly in violation of the law if the manuals are in English only. I hope our language police are onto this one; also the manuals, timetables, trade-union agreements, contracts et cetera, for DART, Bus Éireann, Aer Lingus, Bord failte, and so on. Is *Ireland of the Welcomes*, which is published by a government body, now also bound to be published in Irish also?

But maybe the word 'lána' has the key. It was an English word that had a little clay-pipe shoved in its mouth, a cawbeen on its head, and a pair of buckled shoes on its feet. If we throw in a few Irish case-endings and litter our fadas all over the place on English words, we can convince ourselves that the language we are speaking is Irish.

It is not. We can be as winsome as we like about our attachment to the Irish language, and can warble, witter and flute at one another about the craic agus ceoil on the Luas as we came in from Ranelagh along the lána tram. The language we speak is not Irish. It is pious, cupla focail gibberish.

[10 September 2004]

III. 11. ... *and the Gardaí*

It is in the unconscious things we say that we give ourselves away – thus the headlines last week about changing the rules to allow 'non-nationals' to join An Garda Síochána. But what, please, is a 'non-national'? It is not, so far as I know, in use anywhere else in the English language, save Ireland. Is it another word for foreigner, only we're too polite to say the f-word? Or is it an Irish person who isn't quite foreign, but on the other hand, isn't quite national enough either, as in Peter Robinson?

More to the point, what is a national? Am I a national? I was born in England, but have spent most of my life in Ireland. I have but a single passport, Irish, but anyone who speaks to me will know instantly did I did not spend my childhood in Dingle, or Daingean as we are now obliged to say. So, do I qualify for the term 'national'? Come to that, was the American-born Eddie Coll a 'national' before or after he reinvented himself as Eamon de Valera? And would James Connolly have qualified for the term 'national'? He had, after all, only been living in Ireland a few years when he decided he had the right to kill people in Ireland's name – so did *that* qualify him as a 'national'? Sean Mac Stiofain, a founder of the Provisional IRA, had never been to Ireland before he joined the IRA, and his ancestral link to this country was thoroughly tenuous: a single grandmother – who happened to be unionist. Was he a 'national'?

Now there is no formal bar on 'non-nationals' joining An Garda Síochána; but the issue is not whether one is a 'national', whatever the f-word that is, but whether one speaks Irish, which of course is a mandatory qualification (ha ha ha) for membership of the force. So the Minister for Justice apparently intends to permit foreigners to enter the force, provided that they speak either English or Irish in addition to their own native language. And who is being asked to supervise the proposed changes in the law, but the caped crusader of the Irish language, yes, Eddie Coll's great grandson and look-alike, Éamon Ó Cúiv himself!

You really don't have to very linguistically sensitive nostrils to detect the familiar stench of first national language humbug here. Just how many Urdu- or Ibo- or Bengali-speakers will be able to address the Minister for Community, Rural and Gaeltacht and (now Policing) Affairs in Irish? And the rules which Michael McDowell has outlined – with the caped crusader at his shoulder – will mean that anyone whose first language is non-English, but also who speaks English, will be able to join An Garda Síochána without having to pass the Irish qualification.

But applicants whose first language is English will have to learn Irish (or that curious doggerel which passes for Irish in An Teampall Móa Gaeltacht) to qualify for membership of the Irish police force. Why? Well, primarily to keep the caped crusader, and all those snarling, fire-breathing Gaeilgeoirí zealots happy.

Yet this is almost certainly illegal, for it discriminates against those whose first language is English. It is probably in contravention of the European Convention on Human Rights. It is absolutely in contravention of the spirit but also probably the letter of the Belfast Agreement: (I would require a Senior Council's opinion on that, Minister, if you would be so good). For it places upon both both Irish and British people of indigenous Anglo-Celtic or Caribbean stock a requirement to leap through a few meaningless linguistic hoops which is not expected of recruits of Nigerian, Chinese, Japanese or Bangla Deshi origin.

Why do we continue with the farcical pretence that we need an Irish-speaking police force to enforce the law through Irish? Is this one of those questions that we simply conveniently ignore, just as we do the issue of what is a 'national' and what is not? And is the begging of such questions actually part of the condition that qualifies one for being a 'national'?

Moreover, we all know that the Irish language qualification for membership of An Garda Síochána is as rigorous as the Osama bin Laden Flying School's programme for landing airliners. It is a farce and an insult to the language: yet we must presume that we prefer the institutional denigration of Irish, merely that we be seen to be doing something about it, no matter how useless. And maybe this too enables one to be a 'national'.

We should not contaminate our policing policies with more witless rodomontade about the Irish language. It is right, in itself, that foreigners become

members of An Garda Síochána. To impose the Gaeilgeoirí agenda on the selection process is not merely risible and tendentious, but could sooner or later invite
a legal challenge from one of our Northern non-national brethren that 'Lallans'
is not English, and therefore the Irish-speaking requirement does not apply to
Ulster folk. Such idiocy is the inevitable result of our cloud cuckoo-land policies,
unrelated to linguistic reality.

Nor is it important, as Michael McDowell professes, that gardaí 'reflect' the
people they serve. Neither Shrewsbury Road nor Tallaght are policed by gardaí
who in accent, class, ambition or attitude reflect the local ethos. Policing has ever
been thus, and it is worse than wishful piety to pretend otherwise. It is to declare
Sikhs must police Sikhs, and Punjabis Punjabis. Otherwise we are creating a new
apartheid state.

[13 September 2005]

III.12. English Ignorance

The blurb by Bibliophile Books in London for Tim Pat Coogan's *Eamon de Valera;
The Man Who Was Ireland* runs as follows. 'Born in Manhattan, de Valera was raised
in Ireland and enrolled in the newly formed Ulster Volunteers after the failure of
the Home Rule movement. Tried for his life after the failure of the Easter Rising,
he narrowly escaped execution when Prime Minister Asquith gave orders to go
easy on capital punishment with an election in view. Dev was next on the list.
Sprung from jail in 1919 by his rival Michael Collins, he was elected First Minister
of the Dail and departed to raise consciousness and money in America, founding
The Irish Times, a medium for republican politics on both sides of the Atlantic.'

This, not from 14-year-old hoodie in Barnsley but from a reputable publisher. And though Tim Pat Coogan and I might concur on few enough things,
we can certainly agree that he never wrote anything like that Perhaps Irish historians have been getting it wrong all these years. Maybe the real Irish history
lies somewhere within the bookshelves of Bibliophile Books. Ah yes: and here is
Bibliophile's brief account of Cecil Woodham Smith's *The Great Hunger*.

'The Confederation of Kilkenny led to a rupture between the tea-growing
southern states under General Cromwell and the north, under President Sarswell.
Their forces met at the Battle of the Boil, and the defeat of the southerners there
began a tragic epoch for the South. Protestants who had been slaves in the old
days were now put in charge of the tea plantations. They were known as the
Tannin Blacks, perhaps because of the kind of strong dark tea-leaf they favoured.
Soon they formed a secret society called the Orange Pekoe Order, which led to

the 1798 Rising. The failure of the tea-crop in 1745 at Glencoe was to spell ruin for the great tea-planters, who departed for exile in an event that is still lamented by the Pearly Queens of Dublin as the "Flight of the Earl Greys". They were so named after the rebel leader who stood on the stern of his boat and watched his colleagues switch off their electric tea-heaters on a piece of rigging. "The amps are going out all over your rope," he declared.'

The sad truth is that you could probably pass that off as Irish history in many circles in Britain; indeed, I am coming to the lamentable conclusion that a total ignorance of Irish history is almost a defining quality of Englishness — and I do mean Englishness. The Welsh and the Scots do not seem so pathologically averse to grasping a few fundamentals about life on this island as do the English.

In part it comes down to the Arthur Conan Doyle's observation: 'How often have I said to you that when you have eliminated the impossible, whatever remains, *however improbable*, must be the truth?' The British people have had Ireland in the forefront of their television news for nearly forty years now, yet if you asked most English people whether Dublin was in Northern Ireland, most would either not know, or say that it was. Indeed, there is almost no concoction about Ireland that is too fanciful to be accepted by most English people.

But this is not ignorance based on an absence of newspaper and television coverage, or a failure to engage academically. But it is as if the media, academic and journalistic, are speaking in Hebrew for all that they are understood by the plain people of England. If you are the exhausted host of a dinner party in London, and you want your guests to leave, merely mention the subject of Northern Ireland, and they will flee, shrieking, out of the unopened windows of your first-floor dining room.

If the subject of Ireland — and more especially the North — resembled Mongolian philately, or lichens of Antarctica, merely a tiresome subject in which they had no material or national interest, this aversion would make sense of a kind. But it is not. The people of England have a profound national interest in this country. A prosperous, peaceful Ireland is good for them, and an Ireland at war perfectly ruinous. The Northern Troubles have cost them billions, and — if you include accidents and stress-related suicides while on active service — the lives of one thousand British soldiers. This is about as many who were killed in the airborne assault at Arnhem in 1944.

Yet the overwhelming majority of English people would rather be operated on for piles, without anaesthetic, on live television, than have a single intricacy of Irish life explained to them. Perhaps this is why British government after British government has pursued insane policy after insane policy towards Northern Ireland. It is because virtually all British politicians have lacked the real emotional and intellectual knowledge about the province which they should have acquired as a matter of course long before they were passed the poisoned chalice marked 'Northern Ireland Secretary'.

You can have no moral feelings whatever about something you have chosen to be totally ignorant of. And since Tony Blair has absolutely no moral feelings about anything whatever, it is easy to see how an English consensual attitude towards Ireland – uninformed by either knowledge or morality – is so easily formed. The ferocious obstinacy of Irish tribalism has been one reason for the enduring nature of the Troubles: but another, and every bit as potent, has been the conceited pertinacity of English ignorance.

[19 May 2005]

III.13. Blair, Come to Ireland

If identity were a purchasable commodity, if loyalty could be suborned by eco-nomic success, the Northern Ireland Troubles would now be over. Unionists would be so anxious to enter a united Ireland that we could charge admission, order in the queue please, here you, Paisley get to the back, and if I see pushing again, I'll banish you to the Siberia of Westminster, where you can break rocks. And Robinson, you can bawl Amhráin na bhFiann as much as you want, you can wait your turn, same as every one else. Take that Easter lily out of your lapel, Taylor: it won't get you an Irish passport any sooner your place deserves.

Of course, it's not like that. But still, let's dream of what might be possible if devotion to a flag could be won by argument, as we might have done last Wednesday after going to bed. That day, while the people of the Irish Republic saw taxes fall, yet again, both directly and indirectly, with more money for the poor, the old, the disabled, for children and most importantly of all, for me, under a decent government composed of decent men and women, the people of Northern Ireland had to endure another display of three-card trickery from the knaves who govern them from London.

Look. I'm not often right. In fact, I'm more often wrong. But I got that Labour Party right from the moment that charlatan Blair became leader. He is a spiv, an unpricipled conman, a ridiculous mountebank who stands for nothing and believes in nothing except the pursuit and retention of power, spinnning words and striking whatever poses he thinks will woo his audience, most con-temptibly and abjectly so when he he read the lesson at Princess Diana's funeral: the little sobs so bravely stifled, the lowered inflexion, the sincere and lingering looks at the congregation, the sad silences between sentences. He is the Hughie Green of British politics.

In Britain, taxes are rising, the railway network is in chaos as railways sleepers are examined one by one, this morning's 8.08 am from Nottingham to London Paddington will arive in August, once it's been recovered from the sidings in Aberdeen where it was mislaid in March, the Millennium Dome echoes to the feet of its single visitor, a Buddhist hermit looking for complete isolation – and by Jove finding it – even as the Blair's goons wreck London Underground in their disgraceful vendetta against Ken Livingstone.

Was government ever so bereft of ideas, and so driven by populist image-making? A problem with drunken yobs in public places? Why, take 'em by the collar to a cash-point and fine 'em on the spot. Teenage gangs on the street? Clamp down on 'em with night-time curfews. This bilge, short-cutting the entire process of the rule of law, wasn't uttered by some redneck taxi driver who also thinks Pakis should be sent back 'ome where they come from, but by the first minister of the land.

It is obvious that Blair has no moral centre. This absent of an ethical compass to guide him through the jungle of politics also allows his ministers to wander off course. Peter Mandelson once sneered on RTÉ – no doubt hoping to appeal to what he imagines were the prejudices of his audience – at the chinless wonders on Horse Guards' Parade. Those chinless wonders were willing enough to lay down their lives for their country and for freedom; and did so.

Listen, unionists. We're not perfect down here, but we know the meaning of loyalty. No Dublin minister would ever run down his country, or disparage our security forces abroad, and no such hypothetical minister would survive politically if he tried it.

What is Blair's great initiative to win the next election, as health queues grow, and motorways become carparks? To ban foxhunting. Upon reading those words out loud in Parliament, how close Queen Elizabeth must have been to having the Brigade of Guards chuck Blair and his cronies into the Tower, snarling: off with their heads! But unlike her first minister, she is aware of the limits of her powers, which is a frightful shame.

So. Let's ask the unionists a couple of questions in this hypothetical dreamworld where loyalties are exchangeable. Why stay attached to a country which certainly doesn't love you, which is governed by men and women with no abiding principle other than the acquisition and retention of the levers of power, where intrusive bossiness has taken the place of social policy, where words are spun as webs are woven, covering all meaning with a gossamer sheen of vacuity?

Come and live with us in an Ireland where we get an awful lot wrong; but it is a better place to be than a United Kingdom which regards you as a historic encumbrance. Our government is not perfect, but it's not at all bad, and it's led by an honest man. Moreover, we have a splendid head of state, one you'll come to respect and admire, as I have.

You think we can't accommodate you and your traditions? Really? You might just try us. This is the deal. You can fly what flags you want, march in July, remember your war dead – why, we'll even join you – keep your British passports, and retain your loyalty to the Queen. Most important of all, you can hunt foxes. And when she visits – which I suspect will be rather often – so can she.

What do you say?

[9 December 2004]

III.14. Irish Nationalism & 1916

Mary McAleese's triumphalist address at UCC last weekend also probably ranks as amongst the most imbecilic ever by any president, ever. It's as if we hadn't experienced a quarter century of catastrophic, 1916-inspired violence. Two things happened at Easter 1916. There was a proclamation of the Republic by Patrick Pearse, and there was an armed uprising by an unrepresentative group of men, most of whom were utterly ignorant of the proclamation and its contents. It is historically wrong to suggest that the two were inextricably related. Until the last minute (when it became too late for most of them to back out, though some did) most of the insurgents thought they were going on yet further manoeuvres, as they had done every previous Sunday.

The proclamation declared: 'The Republic guarantees the religious and civil liberty, equal rights and equal opportunities to all its citizens.' It might more honestly have then added – 'unless they are Dublin Metropolitan Policemen', as the unarmed Constable James O'Brien discovered when he was shot dead by Sean Connolly outside Dublin Castle minutes after Pearse had finished his GPO speech. The similarly unarmed Constable Michael Lahiff in St Stephen's Green made the same discovery some time later when Countess Markievicz gunned him down. Constable William Frith perceived his rights in this new Republic when he was later murdered in the bedroom of Store Street police station.

At Mount Street Bridge, the harmless, armless old buffers of the Georgius Rex ex-servicemen's association discovered how the new Republic cherished them when they were massacred on their regular route march to Ticknock. Five were killed, and seven more were injured.

Nor did his new Republic's guarantees of rights and liberties extend to Irish soldiers of the crown, 36 of whom were killed, with another 118 injured. Nor were equal rights, opportunities (et cetera) extended to the RIC, fourteen of whom were killed, and another 23 injured.

From the moment of its inception, these Irishmen were intentionally excluded from the 'equal' citizenship of the Republic (though the equal citizenship of the graveyard lay ahead). Hundreds of Irish civilians found their citizenship of the new Republic permanently terminated during Easter Week, and the President last week called their killers 'heroes'.

There are few accounts of how such victims died. Martin Walton, a 16-year-old Volunteer, provided one. 'When I arrived then at Jacob's, the place was surrounded by a howling mob roaring at the Volunteers inside, "Come out to France and fight, you lot of so-and-so slackers." And I shouted up to the balustrade, let me in, let me in. And then I remember the very first blood I ever saw. There was a big, very big tall woman with something heavy in her hand and she came across and lifted her hand to make a bang at me. One of the Volunteers upstairs saw this and fired and I just remember seeing her face and head disappear as she went down like a sack.'

Scratch one more citizen. My – it's all go round here, isn't it? Well it was certainly all go for hundreds of innocent Dubliners, at least 32 of whom went to their graves unidentified.

Now, I know this 'Republic' that was declared in 1916 very well indeed. It is not a Republic at all, but the formal inauguration of a political cult of necrophilia whose most devoted adherents over the past 36 years have been the Provisional IRA. Each year during the 25 years of the Troubles they rededicated themselves to this same Republic that 'guarantees the religious and civil liberty, equal rights and equal opportunities to all its citizens.' And each year, like Aztecs placating their heathen gods, they went out and killed more of its citizens.

If Pearse had simply read out his proclamation, and declared it to be his election manifesto, that would have been one thing. So too would it have been if he had declared the Volunteers would use arms to prevent conscription. Can't argue with that. But to have made his proclamation and then immediately to have violated its central claim – its guarantee of equal rights to all its citizens – means that it was worthless. It comes down to this, always, always, always. How do you judge a man: by his words or his deeds?

Naturally, those sick 1916–ophiles never dwell upon actual events. They intellectualise upon various pious abstractions of the Rising, with the Proclamation as the focus, as if the entire affair had been a poetry festival, allowing indefinite scope for pious, murder-free exegesis. This is where the President – naturally – focussed her address. However, once one starts discussing the sheer murderousness of the Rising, it gets rather messy: for 1916 was a triumph of proto-Provoism.

I've written often enough about this – and do you know, no one ever answers the same few questions that I always ask. Such as: what right had the 1916 insurgents to start killing innocent Irish people in Dublin? What right? (No, no, no: don't ask What Right had the British to rule Ireland? That's quite another question, to which, of course, the poor victims of the 1916 insurgents had no answer.)

Next question. Why had none of the signatories of the Proclamation, not one of them, ever stood for parliament? No answer? So here's another question. How could they possibly call the butchers of Belgium 'gallant allies'? Silence, again, eh? Okay, stay mum for this final one: how can supposedly civilised people today 'celebrate' an orgy of violence in which hundreds of innocent Irish people died?

[31 January 2006]

III. 15. Surnames

The Times of London last week celebrated to the 200th anniversary of the battle of Trafalgar with a republication of the original issues reporting the victory. The edition also contained the contributions from villages in Nottinghamshire to a fund for the families of dead and injured seamen. Some of the village names – Bridgeford, Rempstone, Wilford, Sneinton, Gedling, Bunny, Tithby, Calverton, Beeston, Willoughby, Gotham, Granby – were strangely familiar to me, but not all as places, but some as people: they were the names of families which I knew in nearby Leicester in my childhood, or of boys who attended Wyggeston grammar school where I studied for two years.

Now all my other education was at Catholic schools, where most pupils were of Irish extraction, and often of Irish appearance. Not so Wyggeston. It was emphatically English and Protestant, and the boys tended to have sallower skin, straighter hair, browner eyes than those at Catholic schools, clearly owing more to the gene pool of Gary Lineker than of Garryowen. And furthermore, many had retained in their family names the hamlets from which their ancestors had come in the Middle Ages.

And that is one of the extraordinary differences between England and Ireland. Almost no Irish surnames are toponymics: Kilkenny and Monaghan almost alone spring to mind, for Galway, as in the player of the flute, is probably a corruption of the Scottish 'Galloway'.

Otherwise, Irish surnames, and certainly Gaelic surnames, have little or no sense of place. They do have, of course, a sense of family – hence the plethora of Macs and the O's, though these do not suggest the easy stability and respect for origin that is conferred by a toponymic.

Edward MacLsyaght's *Surnames of Ireland* tells us that the most common name in Ireland, Murphy, comes from Ó *Murchadha*, which means 'sea-warrior', i.e. pirate. Kelly, it suggests, comes via Ó *Ceallaigh*, which probably derives from *ceallagh*, 'strife'. In other words, the two most common names in Ireland both have

their origins in conflict, which perhaps tell us something about the conditions in Ireland when surnames were being doled out.

The third most common name, O'Sullivan, is based on the Irish *súil*, 'eye', and is probably an insult. O'Doherty certainly is: MacLysaght says it comes from the Irish *dochartach*, 'hurtful'. In other words, we clearly have a tradition of giving people insulting surnames. Why does this not surprise me?

Probably the fourth most common name, Gallagher, in all its two dozen forms, helps explain the absence of toponymics in Gaelic Ireland; *gall* simply means foreigner. And where strangers had a dark complexion, they were *dubh gall* – hence Doyle, Mac Dowell, and the many variants thereof. Just to complete the picture of how outsiders were regarded in medieval Ireland, we come to the name Walsh, as in 'Welsh'. But the 'Wal' of Wales is simply an anglicised form of the universal – and usually unflattering – European term for foreigner, *gall* again.

In other words, ancient Irish society apparently did not do outsiders the courtesy of discovering where they were from and calling them by that name, but instead simply blanket-labelled them as foreigners. Céad Míle Fáilte, *gall*.

It is more than a matter of good manners, for what a cultural loss was thus incurred. For who would not be proud to be called Mountmellick, Mooncoin or Moville? How mellifluous it would be to able to introduce oneself as Simon Ennistymon or Cormac Rathccormack. Skibbereen, Parknasilla, Creeslough, Kilcrohane, Loughinisland, Lemanaghan, Delphi, Cushendall, Emo, Gweebarra, all beg to accompanied by a first name. Who could fail to radiate majesty if their surname alone were Grianan of Aileach? ('Good morning, noble lady, my name is the Lord Arkwright of Accrington, peer of the realm: whom, pray, do I have the honour of addressing?' 'Eilis Grianan of Aileach,' she replies, 'charwoman.')

To be sure, some places would make unpromising family names. Tommy Termonfeckin would probably have had a hard time at school, and Denis Dunsink would probably yearn to be called Gallagher or Murphy. It's hard to imagine anyone yearning to be called Bruff or Ullard or Two Mile Borris or Horse and Jockey or Sluggary Crossroads or Hackballscross (which in wiser, happier days was known as Myers' Cross). It is doubtful whether the boy could make it to adulthood with a name like Stillorgan, and all those places called Kill would take a decidedly Anglo-Saxon meaning when turned into a family name, as would their apparent victim, Slane.

The copy of *The Times* that prompted these musings also referred to Lord Nelson by one of his more forgotten titles, namely Duke of Bronté. This title apparently prompted the loyal Irish clergyman Patrick Prunty to change his name to Bronte. Nelson's career might had many consequences, and he might indeed have saved the United Kingdom from Napoleonic tyranny: but without him, the most famous literary family in the world would probably known today as the

Prunty sisters. This would have been appropriate indeed, for this little known Ulster name comes from the Gaelic Ó Proinntigh which, is unusually flattering for an Irish name, apparently meaning 'generous person'.

Were there ever more sublimely generous sisters in the history of the novel than Anne Prunty, creator of *Agnes Grey* and *The Tenant of Wildfell Hall*, dead at 29: or Charlotte Prunty, author of *Jane Eyre* dead at 39, and Emily Prunty, begetter of *Wuthering Heights*, dead at the age of 30? But how much grander still would they have sounded if they had borne an Irish toponymic and were known as, say, the Cahirciveen, Lisdoonvarna or even Mostrim sisters?

[26 October 2005]

III. 15. *Travellers*

Why did Dublin City Council erect a concrete barrier at Dunsink? Was it to stop the Canadian Navy from dumping four somewhat used submarines there? That would have been a good reason. Another reason is that probably their equivalent in scrap is dumped there every year, and the Council has a right to stop it. Well, what about the Travellers who are resident there? What about them? Most of them are there illegally. No one makes them stay there. If the blocks make life inconvenient for them, then they should move on.

Of course, they logically should have done that years ago, because Dunsink Lane has been an 'uninhabitable' cesspit for at least a decade. Had the people squatting there not been called 'Travellers', and had not their preference for living amid such squalor not been dignified with the word 'culture', then their children would have been put into care, and they would have been served with eviction notices, to be followed in short order by the bailiffs.

Dunsink has less to do with concrete blocks than the existence of a system of apartheid that creates a category of people called Travellers who are immune to some of the laws that apply to the rest of the Irish people. Dunsink for years has been a centre of organised theft and diesel-laundering. Many Traveller vehicles are either UK-registered, uninsured or untaxed. The state has created laws that impose duties upon local councils towards Travellers that have no equivalent for the larger community. Furthermore, Travellers have been indulged with the creation of a legal status and legal protection, but without a legally binding definition of what a Traveller is – the true hallmark of the fuzzy thinking and unprincipled cowardice with which we have *not* been facing up to the Traveller issue.

We have created a dependent community within the Irish state, which has now become pathologically dysfunctional. Nearly three-quarters of Traveller men are officially unemployed: yet Dublin has imported 30,000 Chinese people in the past five years, not one of whom, I bet, is on the dole.

Bishop Willie Walsh in Killaloe a couple of years ago allowed Travellers to park their caravans on his palace land – temporarily, or so he thought. Once there, they refused to go, despite his increasingly desperate requests that the lack of toilets had disagreeable consequences for everyone. Finally, he persuaded the families to move – but they went directly into the car park of the newly opened headquarters of Clare County Council. After a while, they were evicted, and where did they go? Why, back to the poor bishop's lawns.

Some time later, County Clare opened up a small show-estate for travellers, with halting sites and €300,000 houses. Two families on the bishop's land were offered the new homes and left, but then decided they didn't like their new traveller neighbours. Bishop Walsh sought to bring peace between the families, but unavailingly. The newly housed family then abandoned the house they had just been allocated, and departed in their caravan: where to? Back once again to Willie Walsh's gardens, of course.

The crowning moment of Clare Traveller policy came last year, as the County Council was preparing to host a reception in Ennis to welcome the Russian competitors in the Special Olympics for mentally handicapped athletes. No sooner had the council gates opened than a convoy of traveller-caravans occupied the car park, and the welcoming reception for these wretchedly unfortunate Russians had to be cancelled.

The Travellers' perception of the world has been shaped by a state which does not insist upon their having any concept of duties, and which tolerates every other social deviancy which in any other community would be a cause of opprobrium. Traveller society is caste-based, dirty, unhealthy, highly alcoholic, illiterate, often violently misogynistic and low-achieving – two-thirds of traveller children have abandoned all education by the age of 15. Most of all, Travellers are cursed with a life expectancy at least ten years shorter than that of the rest of the population.

The Irish media have invariably treated stories of Traveller excess – the savage faction fights, the drunkenness, the endless trespasses – with a querulous indifference bordering on outright neglect. Traveller expectations are thus always about the conduct of others, not of themselves – and these expectations have been ruinously fuelled by the workings of the Equality Agency, which has created the expectation that there is only Traveller victimhood, but never Traveller liability.

The state has taken upon itself the duty of protecting the Traveller way of life, when it sees no duty to protect any other way of life. Every local council in the land has a legal duty to house homeless citizens, and as citizens, homeless Travellers can avail of that system. But thousands of Travellers prefer to remain on illegal halting sites, or wait their turn for their special Traveller privileges, from a state towards which so few of them make any contribution whatsoever.

Travellers remain in squalor because they actually choose to. The escape routes exist: they merely have to avail of them. Economically and socially, the travelling tradition is over, just as Irish shipyard and jute traditions are over, just as forty-shilling freeholders are over, just as the feudal system is over. Only political weak-mindedness and fear of being labelled 'racist' causes the state to continue to prop up an obsolete, economically parasitical, and personally destructive tradition with grants, special laws or even no laws at all. And what we have got in return for such misdirected, and utterly destructive kindness? Why, petrol bombs and gardaí in riot gear at Dunsink.

[13 October 2004]

ARCHITECTURE

III. 17. The Buildings of Dublin

I was writing yesterday about the colossal and irrevocable changes in Ireland today. Many of these are attitudinal – and few things seem as comical as yesterday's passionately held but now abandoned opinions. Yet the most obvious and measurable changes are in the fabric of Irish life; in the motorways that cross our countryside, in the bungalows that by Martin Cullen's diseased imprimatur are spreading across the countryside like a plague of fungal concrete, and most of all, in the transformation of Dublin.

The capital that many of us knew in our youth is dead: that was the Dublin of a handful of restaurants, of little and limited nightlife, of a streetscape which was laid down in the 18th century, added onto by the Victorians, celebrated by Joyce, and then, after a lunatic period of destruction between 1916 and 1922, almost untouched by independent Ireland. The city was largely left to the falling rain, the soot and the rising damp, and for most of the twentieth century, virtually nothing new was built – and that which was usually was horrifying.

All changed. A parallel city, entirely new in vision and in dynamism, a mini-Singapore, is now seeping out of the edges of old Dublin. Docklands double in size and prosperity every year. Huge quayside apartment blocks have made the Liffey waterfront, unfashionable for two centuries, now profoundly chic indeed. Industrial suburbs have sprouted where a decade ago cows browsed, awaiting the CAP payments. A Castleknock Rip van Winkle who went to sleep in 1996 would think today that he had awoken in Johannesburg. We are still mid-flux; and possibly we shall always be. Maybe the convention that Dublin regularly enters a condition of stasis is now gone forever: Dublin know no stability, only change – which makes the arrival of Christine Casey's *The Buildings of Dublin* (Yale) all the more timely.

The book is slightly misnamed – for though it is a celebration of the many fine buildings of the capital, it is also a rich smorgasbord of urban culture and history. Thus we learn that the tollbooths on the North Circular Road from the Phoenix Park (at Aughrim Street, Phibsborough, and Dorset Street) were calculated by horsepower: a penny ha'penny for one horse, a shilling for six (some equipage, that), with tolls being doubled on Sundays – which was no doubt the real reason for the Phoenix Park murders.

The Dublin that was created in the hundred years after the eighteenth century Wide Streets Commission was built by an ethos that has since vanished. Twentieth-century Catholic nationalist Ireland simply washed over the Protestant community that had largely (but not exclusively) been the authors of the city. Consider Merrion Hall, raised in the 1860s to house 2000 Plymouth Brethren, the largest place of worship in Dublin. Now it is the Davenport Hotel.

It is not alone. Christine names so many Protestant churches, with the melancholy (*former*) providing a parenthetic gravestone to an entire and extinct urban culture. What has become of the (*former*) Wesleyan Methodist Chapel in Langrishe Place, off the North Circular Road? The (*former*) Wesleyan Methodist Chapel of Great Charles Street is now the home of Pavee Point. The (*former*) Presbyterian Church on Sean McDermot Street is now a grainstore. The (*former*) Welsh Orthodox Church in Talbot Street is now an amusement arcade, thus home to the abominable vice of gambling – the equivalent to the Catholic mind of the (*former*) Loretto on the Green becoming a pole-dancing club, or the (*former*) Pro-Cathedral being turned into a school for suicide bombers.

Over the past decade, Dublin has embarked upon the greatest and most challenging period of development in its history. Hedged in by hills and sea, dramatic vertical growth is now unavoidable – and alas, not always fair, for soon towers will cast long shadows over streets that for two centuries have enjoyed daylong sunlight. But the only way of not having vertical growth is by allowing endless sprawl on the southern, northern and north-western axes, covering several counties, leading to unmanageable traffic congestion, insupportably high land prices, and insufferable social alienation in a ring of festering, vicious conurbations reaching into the Midlands.

So the city's traditional skyline is changing for ever, just as the culture of Catholic Dublin is now vanishing as totally as that of Protestant Dublin before it. Tall towers will overlook seashores and empty, priestless Catholic churches will find new purposes, as a newly godless people learn to live without religion, and in stacks, as their fellows do everywhere. These very transformations oblige us to preserve as much as we can of the founding Protestant civilisation and its Catholic successors, just as Rome preserves its (admittedly) slightly more majestic pagan and renaissance legacies.

Books about Dublin were once ten-a-penny, and full of tired old clichés about a rare-ould-times city that never existed. The truth is that the poverty that characterised old Dublin in both Protestant and Catholic epochs generated more vice than virtue: it caused emigration, crime, prostitution, disease and premature death, and the legendary goodness found amongst those who lived in tenements was largely strategic; whomever we help today will be obliged to return the favour tomorrow. And that's all there is to it.

However, and happily, Christine does not peddle any of the dreary sentimentality about Dublin as it once was. Instead, in a seriously good book, she has lovingly painted a quite wonderful architectural and historical portrait of our capital, at the very moment that it embarks upon the greatest adventure in its history. All those unspent Christmas book tokens now have a home.

[6 January 2006]

III.18. Liberty Hall

The debate is underway: what to do about Liberty Hall? It is an important building in Dublin, for though it might not be of much architectural merit, it tells a real truth about 1960s Ireland. Why? Because buildings in a city make the truest statement of where power lies. The cathedrals of Christ Church and St Patrick's in Dublin, St Canice's in Kilkenny, St Mel's in Longford, were built on hills, from which they overlooked the entire community.

The great constructions raised by Georgian Dublin: the Customs House, the GPO, the Four Courts, the House of Parliament, had the same purpose: they were the most imposing buildings in the city, and were architectural assertions of authority by the major institutions of the Anglo-Irish state.

From independence on, virtually no buildings were erected in Dublin. However, one curious feature endured – despite the massive oversupply of workers in the Irish labour market, which logically should have crippled trade unionism, the reverse was true. Trade unions were still able to control labour supply, and access to jobs. When the Lemass-Whittaker economic revolution began in the late 1950s, trade union membership rocketed. Workers were obliged to buy the indulgence which allowed them to work: and with this mandatory Peter's pence, the unions built a cathedral in their own honour: Liberty Hall.

At fifteen storeys, it was easily the tallest building in Dublin, towering over everything and visible from everywhere. It was brash and modish, and shimmering with arriviste vulgarity. Some innocent Dubliners even called it 'the skyscraper'.

Liberty Hall; what a misnomer. This was the headquarters of organisations that ruthlessly promoted the closed shop, which actually obstructed people from working if they did not belong to a trade union, using coercion, boycott and the strike. Some trade unions centred there actively prevented women from entering some areas of the workforce, such as driving buses or being conductors; others vigorously defended different pay rates for women, and the ban on married women working in the public service.

So Liberty Hall was not a cathedral to freedom, but like any medieval church, was an architectural statement of authority. The trade union movement was the most powerful force in Irish life, after the Catholic Church, its authority everywhere.

Banks closed at lunch because the unions insisted on it. But hold on: lunchtime was the only available time for many people to go to the bank, so how could they ever get to the bank? Well, they couldn't. For banks were not there for their customers but for their staff and their shareholders. They were sources of employment and dividends, not of service to the public.

Large semi-state organisations like RTÉ, the ESB, CIÉ, the Department of Posts and Telegraphs, were trade union paradises, where management was not about managing the company but managing rival trade unions. RTÉ had about twenty unions, including the Seamen's Union, for the two men who climbed the mast, but the good old ESB did better, with some two dozen. Trade unions in the one company warred with one another over parity, differential and demarcation disputes. Truly wise men became monks and contemplated the sea; ambitious fools set out to run the major state enterprises of Ireland and ended up contemplating the four walls of John of Gods or St Patrick's.

Yet all this trade union power didn't help working-class people get richer, but instead, made the unions and their leaders exceptionally powerful: and in the manner in which they inhibited flexibility both of labour and of work practice, they actively restricted the creation of wealth. Workplaces were not wealth-creation zones, but areas of a myriad of endless boundaries where one worker's duty ended and another began. Here in *The Irish Times*, in the days of paper copy, one put one's work in a tray marked 'chief sub', which would be collected by a messenger who would carry it the ten feet to the chief sub's desk. If for the sake of speed you decided to hand the copy directly to the chief sub, it was a potentially strike-causing deed.

Thus trade union idiocy governed the everyday lives of ordinary people through countless and uncountable rules, most of them kept solely in people's heads. Working relationships were based on an intricate local folklore of who might do what and how, and all maintained by a mandatory system of union dues which kept a parasitic caste of bureaucratic drones in permanent employment in the Vatican that was Liberty Hall.

Now only fools would say there is no place for trade unions at all. Human nature is too inclined to bully when in power, and collectively workers can oppose a tyrannical employer in a way no individual can. But conversely, trade unions often used their power for non-economic reasons. Bricklayers' unions were as much about keeping hod-carriers in their place as they were in increasing brick-layers' pay; and the union to which I have the melancholy honour of belonging often seems more interested in enforcing the ideologies of political correctness than in journalistic freedom of speech.

When I see 'Liberty' Hall, what do I see? Do I see a building that symbolises freedom? Does it stand for my right to work for this newspaper without being obliged to be a member of the National Unionist of Journalists? It does not. For Liberty Hall is not about liberty, but trade union power. It tells us as much about Ireland of the 1960s as Christ Church does about Ireland in the Middle Ages, the difference being, Christ Church is worth preserving, Liberty Hall is not.

[1 September 2005]

III.19. Emo Court

Emo Court is one of the most exquisite architectural jewels in Ireland: it is Gandon at his most perfect, though also his most deferred. The building was commissioned in 1790 but only completed 80 years later, which even by the leisurely standards of Irish builders cannot be called impetuous. The finest part of the house, the rotunda, erected long after Gandon had departed for the great Customs House in the sky, was completed under the supervision of Thomas Caldbeck.

This is what makes Emo so wonderful, for it is, quite simply, architectural perfection, and one that was both vandalised and preserved by the Jesuits. Indeed, there are few examples in Ireland of the Jesuits' extraordinary sense of history to compare with their time at Emo Court.

Gandon had designed the house for John Dawson, later the Earl of Portar-lington, a scion of a banking family of Dublin, whose name lives on in Dawson Street. Emo Court is not large – not nearly as big as Castletown – and it was set in spectacular parkland. The driveway was one and a half miles long, which the postman and the milkman must have just loved, and was planted during the 19th century with sequoia Wellingtonia. Most of the drive is gone now, but the lines of trees are protected, and they still stand like soldiers across the lovely Laois landscape.

Like so many landed families, the Dawsons grew exhausted with life in Ireland, and chose to leave 85 years ago. The Land Commission took over Emo, and in 1920, the family auctioned off the house's contents. That, now, is a sobering thought: for just who would turn up for an auction in that year? Half the gentry of Ireland were skulking in London, while the other half sleeping in the kitchen with a shotgun across their laps, as the night sky glowed with burning big houses. Who was going to turn up for a sale of the contents of a Gandon House, when the fate of Gandon's other buildings across the island was being decided by Messrs Maguire, Patterson, and Par Aífinn?

Nonetheless, just about everything was sold, apart from a couple of lanterns, though God alone knows for what pitiful price, and the Dawsons left. Emo House was then put in the hands of those gods of sloth, inertia and demolition, the Land Commission. Yet miraculously, the house remained intact for another ten years, when the Jesuits bought it for a novitiate.

No space in the building suited as a chapel, so the J's demolished a wall between the magnificent rotunda and the dining-room next door. This was a perfectly shocking act, because the rotunda possessed an almost perfect geometric integrity. Moreover, the lower walls of the rotunda consisted of elaborate stone archways, and the cupola was 'supported' by ornamental Siena marble columns. There was no way to unite the dining room with the rotunda without removing these columns and archways.

Yet the Jesuits, whose spiritual tempo is measured in hundreds of years, clearly knew theirs was a temporary stewardship, for unlike almost anyone else at that time – and indeed for decades to come – they didn't smash the archways, but stored them in the cellars. And so Emo became the training ground for generations of young Jesuits. The great Father Browne, photographer and war hero lived here, and no doubt recorded what the seminary was like: his pictures would make a fascinating contrast with the house today.

In 1969, once again with extraordinary foresight, the Jesuits realised that their days of large-scale recruitment were over. They put Emo onto the market, so prompting the arrival of the true hero of Emo, the greatest in its history since Gandon: an Englishman, Major C. D. Chomeley-Harrison.

Deirdre O'Brien, our splendid tour guide, told us of this gentleman, and not taking notes, I now have a lingering suspicion that Chomelely occurs more than once in his name; that like Featherstonehaugh or ffoliot, Chomelely always occurs in pairs. For all I know, today he goes today by the abbreviated version of his name, and that his baptismal certificate consists of rolling foothills of hyphenated Chomeleys, clustering around one another like Chilterns.

No matter. This splendid man – we'll call him Chum – found Emo, and in Chum, Emo found its rescuer: and unlike any other great Georgian house in Ireland, it only found true glory in modern times. For our Chum has a truly magnificent eye both for furniture and a bargain, and he has made it his life's business to bring life and style to Emo. He has succeeded triumphantly.

He restored the stone archways to the rotunda. Two Siena marble columns had vanished completely so he went to Italy and found samples that matched the marble used in Emo. He reconstructed the rotunda with a matchless aesthetic: it emanates an extraordinary sense of artistic achievement, as if pure intent had been matched by perfect outcome, conveying a sensation which I once received in the Taj Mahal, but in few other places. It is a deeply, deeply satisfying room.

Moreover, there is something almost Wodehousian about Chum's simple enthusiasms: one photograph that has pride of place in Emo is of his headmaster at Stowe public school eighty years ago. Such a culture of lifelong, unwavering respect was born of the empire, and perished with it also.

Chum made Emo over to the state ten years ago, on condition that he be allowed end his days there. He still lives there yet, a truly great and noble Englishman in poor health, and if anyone deserves to be an honorary citizen of Ireland, he most assuredly does. As Cicero would have said: *Emo amo.*

[11 August 2005]

III.20. The Big House

One curious inversion of reality in Irish life is that the inhabitant of the Big House is somehow to be envied. Rubbish. If heard that I'd inherited such a property, I'd promptly go out and buy a box of matches and a can of paraffin. Big Houses are hell. Proof of that is that virtually without exception, somewhere within all those draughts, there is the equivalent of a Rathfarnham semi-detached, a little living area that precisely replicates a suburban home's dimensions and character.

The Big House burns money. It leaks. It is freezing. Most of all, the Big House is lonely: for when you stand at your front door beneath your leaking gutters you see no people, only hundreds of trees requiring a tree surgeon, and a mile of drive in need of relaying.

Perhaps Sir Josslyn Gore-Booth, ninth baronet, often felt like that as he peered out of Lissadell during his few gallant years in the house. There is no point in calling him Anglo-Irish. He was English, and it is enormously to his credit that he returned to the family home after his aunt Aideen died in 1994. But in time, he proved unequal to the struggle – and who can blame him? What friendships, what congenial company are possible when you are an Englishman marooned at the end of a long, dripping driveway in Sligo?

And so the link between the family and the house finally ended, as chronicled by Dermot James in his splendid *The Gore-Booths of Lissadell* (Woodfield Press). No family has a natural right to live in a particular house for ever, and I feel no emotion whatever that destiny had drawn the two apart: it is the working of that destiny that is so interesting, and which makes Dermot's study a minor classic of the Big House genre.

If you live in the Big House, people will usually believe the worst of you. For example, in the 1830s Sir Robert Gore-Booth decided to evict some tenants because he felt that their plots were too small: well, he would say that, wouldn't he? But not merely did he compensate them for the acquisition of their land, he also personally chartered a ship, the *Pomona* to take them to Canada. It is not an entirely wholesome story – nor is it a wholly terrible one either.

Though the *Pomona* completed its journey safely, a rumour soon circulated that it had been lost with all hands, and the rumour has survived to this day. Tim Pat Coogan and George Morrison's account of the Civil War reports of the *Pomona* that the 'whole shipload of emigrants was drowned within sight of shore'.

Jacqueline van Voris's biography of Constance Markievicz declared that the vessel had a fiendish captain and a false bottom, and the skipper – rather gallantly to my mind – was so determined to finish off these pesky Irish peasants that he perished in the task. The equally silly Diana Norman maintained that the *Pomona* was a coffin ship, which sank with all lives. 'Perhaps not surprisingly,' she opined darkly, 'no evidence for this survives in the family papers.'

Not surprisingly indeed, for the *Pomona* continued to ply back and forth across the Atlantic for years to come – which did not prevent local historian Joe McGowan recently printing a ballad about the sinking, while the broken-hearted young people of Sligo watched their loved ones perish.

Of course, the most famous holder of the Gore-Booth name was Constance Markievicz, whose own account of her plucky conduct on being sentenced to death in 1916 has entered Irish nationalist mythology. Dermot James has retrieved the record of the prosecuting counsel, William Wylie KC, who bizarrely went on to become a High Court judge in the new state. Wylie spoke well of some of the 1916 leaders, admiring their bravery, dignity and demeanour.

But of Markievicz he wrote: 'she crumpled up completely, crying. "I'm only a woman, and you cannot shoot a woman, you must not shoot a woman" … she was literally crawling, I won't say any more, it revolts me.' Of course, this same woman had no trouble shooting poor unarmed Constable O'Brien dead in St Stephen's Green. Yes, she revolts me too – but not for pleading for her life (an eminently sensible policy, and one I would certainly emulate) but for her triumphalist murderousness ('I shot him, I shot him,' she gleefully screamed beside O'Brien's body) and her insufferable vanity.

It wasn't the Gore-Booth status as Protestant gentry that was their undoing, but a combination of Hitler, Churchill and unbelievably bad luck. In the next generation of Gore-Booths, Brian, a sub lieutenant in the British navy, was killed when his destroyer, HMS *Exmouth* was torpedoed in January 1940.

Churchill's military lunacies were so numerous and so abominable that the calamity at Leros three years later cannot by any stretch of the imagination be considered his most infamous — but it's up there, nonetheless. He ordered the British army to invade the Greek island, without air-cover, and the entire task force, including a battalion of Royal Irish Fusiliers, was either killed or captured in a German counter attack. Amongst the dead was Captain Hugh Gore-Booth.

Meanwhile Michael, first-born and heir, had become gravely mentally ill, and was made a ward of court. The court's administration of the Lissadell estate — either through dishonesty or ineptitude: *what*, in this country? — became a national scandal, and inflicted grievous wounds on both the house and the family fortune, from which neither fully recovered. It is an extraordinary, quite riveting story, and one that has found a quite splendid teller in Dermot James.

[17 December 2004]

COUNTRY MATTERS

III.21. Mali & Mayo

It has rained for 109 consecutive days Crossmolina, County Mayo. (News report)
Crossmolina, Crossmolina, you are drowning where you lie
The waters rise before you, they fall down from the sky;
Bearing waves and roaring seas, and bringing weary thoughts to me
Of a sunny dune in Mali, where I would that I could be.
One hundred days of endless rain, one hundred days plus nine
Of unceasing, heartless downpour, a punishment divine
Where the brown boglands echo with the people's plaintive pleas,
Against fresh storms a-blowing from north Atlantic seas.
The people pray in earnest but they also pray in vain,
For their one sure certain portion is another fall of rain.
They plead, they beg, they whimper, prostrate on the sodden sod,
Yet once again are smitten by the rainly wrath of God
For rain in all its guises, rain in its many forms,

Gathers alongside Mayo, in clouds and gales and storms
Gathers there at day break, gathers round the clock,
To cover all Claremorris, and moist pilgrims bowed at Knock.
While wide Lough Conn has risen up, well above Slieve Carr,
A single spire above the waves marks the town of Castlebar,
And priests that prayed for instant drought alongside Achill Sound,
Were caught by an instant flood there, and instantly were drowned.
Then the downpour began to ease, eased to a steady shower
And in Killala's cathedral vaults, they hailed the bishop's power.
The shower fell to a trickle that might fill a brickie's hod,
And the trickle then turned to another soft day, thank God.
The bishop rose up smiling, saying this was a sign from above,
For the Lord he giveth freely in return for our given love.
The prelate bestowed his blessing upon a grateful nave
And vanished still brightly smiling, upon a tidal-wave.
A tithe of Mayo's showers, a hint of the lashes that fall,
Exceed the rainfall in Mali since the end of the Berlin wall.
And maybe that's the lesson, one that we find most emphatic,
To search the common-ground, twixt the bone-dry and aquatic.
If Mali's dunes and Mayo's bogs could in common cause unite,
Might not date-palms flourish the length of Killalla Bight?
Might not the virgin visit her shrine at Timbuctoo
While Tauregs follow the camel trail, from Conn to farflung Clew?
If Mayo spread one day of its rain on Mali for a year,
The two could feed all Africa, from Good Hope to Agadir.
And if Senegal and Donegal agreed a common plan,
They could produce a common food, most agreeable to man.
If Bord na Móna churned the peat the length of the desert land
While bedouin screeched for trade along the Mulrany Strand
We might all be safe home again before the rains resume,
Before ancient truths return, and even older truths exhume.
For it's a strangely human yearning, by kith or kin or breed,
To guard one's mother's offspring, to mind one's father's seed.
The Mayo man detests the rain, the Mali man the sun,
Thus Maliman and Mayoman, must not the other shun.
Crossmolina, Crossmolina, you are where this all began,
Beside Burkina Faso, not far from Ardrehan,
Let's mix and match sand with peat, Capri with County Carlow,
And Cross is now in a place called Mayi, and Timbuctoo in Malo.

[19 December 2000]

III.22. The Meet

The first true sign of spring is the last hunt of the season, the last meet, the last stirrup cup, the last frantic baying of the hounds, the last maelstrom of horses' heels on a cobbled yard, the last flash of hunting pink on a Kildare field. The hunt is not about hunting: it is a celebration of the vagaries of groups of animals and their masters, pitted against the wiles of nature, in which the latter usually wins.

Hunts are so very satisfying because they involve the union of the first two animals which mankind tamed, domesticated and formed personal unions with. In horses and dogs we created dysfunctional versions of the wild animal; wolves that did not kill sheep but which nipped their ankles, which did not eat the dead bird but returned with it intact; horses which did not try to kill the carnivore astride their back but which obeyed it, which accepted the bit in the mouth, the harness and the gruelling plough.

Dogs and horses have been merely bred to possess qualities that resemble human virtues. We perpetuated and refined the DNA of the wolf-descendent whose face registered human qualities, which retained the puppy qualities of licking, of dependency, of affection: but the wolf which remained a wolf was left to the wild or killed. And we simply ate the proto-horse that would not be broken.

The hunting pack is probably the closest to the wolf that the domesticated dog is allowed to revert to. Wolfhound, borzoi, beagle: wolves would recognise them and hail them as kin. But they are not wolves. They heed the whip and hear the horn and know the voice of their master. And most of all, they love the chase; and as hounds are cousins to the wolf, so 'chase' is an etymological cousin to 'catch' and 'capture'. For there is a quarry, and the quarry is a fox, the most artful animal of all. And all else being equal, the fox will get away.

So the Kildares gathered at The Thatch pub in Ballymore Eustace the other day for the last hunt of the season, with the field master Charlie O'Reilly resplendent in the blood-red jacket that goes by the name of its tailor Mr Pink. The precious quintessence of country life assembles at a hunt meet; animals and humans milling in sociable circles, a general air of careless affability, as one tries to put names on faces one hasn't seen in a year.

This is perhaps the only occasion when there is merit to hot punch as it warms the blood and makes the brain just a little giddy. The wine, the cloves, the cinnamon, the diced fruit, the clean air: yes, barely past eleven, but with still a nip in the air, I think I might venture to have a second glass of that, thank you. Plates of sizzling sausages circulate as the excited baying of the hounds that have scented the horses announce their imminent arrival; then they pour into the yard, a grey and cream stream, babbling, sniffing and enquiring, their blood up, the nostrils aquiver. Around them, wheeling in expectation, the polished buttocks of the horses shine like soldiers' toecaps.

A trump from the horn, and horses, hounds and humans all pour away, leaving behind them a ghost town of abandoned horseboxes and lorries, to draw the first covert, in the parkland near Barrettstown Castle. The foxhounds in all their giddy stupidity gallop into a break just as a smirking fox emerges, to double back behind them, before leaning against a tree and lighting a slightly amused cigarette.

The horn again, and the hounds erupt from the drawn cover in an auburn tide, a concerted score of anuses beneath raised tails scampering after the scent of the now vanished fox, the whippers-in cantering in their wake, the riders in an obedient, bobbing stream behind them, all to disappear over the brow of a hill.

The neighbouring promontories provide the perfect place to follow the hunt, as in the distance Wicklow's snowclad peaks shine like sailing icebergs. The yelp of the hounds echoes across the fields, the hunting horn shrieks, the huntsmen's scarlet jackets serving as markers of their progress across the dun countryside, like barium in blood. But then the vast countryside soon swallows the hunt, and even the declamatory pinks vanish. The sounds of the hunt depart, and all one can hear is the bleating of lambs and of their fretful mothers

Human affairs move in tides. We measure our seasons in animal rites. The hounds are put in kennels as spring arrives, and there they yearn for the shortening days and the falling leaves and the departing swallows, twitching in their sleep as they once again scent the spore of that wily old dogfox from Elverstown covert. The horses are stabled, and impatiently paw their straw to return to the field.

Evenings draw on, the cowslips and the primrose burst into colour along our hedgerows and the first of our avian visitors from Africa tentatively begin inspecting suitable sites for nesting. Six months must pass before we can again sip the stirrup cup, listen to the companionable noise of hoof on stone, and the babble of enquiring hounds. However, at a certain time of life, six months pass like six weeks once did: and between now and the next meet of the Kildares lie the flickering of an eyelid known as spring and summer, mere gossamer in the path of a tractor. A sobering thing, time, for when all is said and done, its utter evanescence is all that lies between us and the grave.

[6 March 2006]

III.23. Ragwort and the Corncrake

A Martian coming to these shores could be forgiven for thinking that our national flower and our primary cash crop is ragwort. And if our Martian had heard of that great, diseased and bloated monster called the Common Agricultural Policy, she would assume that our farmers are being paid headage or bloomage or cribbage (or whatever the EU term for bribery is) is for the industrial-scale production of ragwort.

Of course, nobody is paid for growing ragwort, and though it is perfectly lethal, it is everywhere. When it is standing, animals will not touch it; but when cut, their antennae are unable to detect the plant's warning signals, and they eat it. It is deadly poison, killing livestock both when fresh and long afterwards, if inadvertently baled with fodder.

Moreover, it spreads as vigorously as scabies in a brothel. An allotment of ragwort one August can cause acres of it downwind the following summer. And there are no easy ways of dealing with the infected fields. You can plough the plant into the ground, and hope that it doesn't come back the next year; or you dig out the plants by hand, and remove them from the pasture and burn or compost them.

Ragwort is so lethal that it has been illegal to allow it on your property for a very long time indeed. Failure to abate ragwort was one of those few agrarian crimes for which the RIC used regularly prosecute, in between those other periods of tumult which occasionally interrupted the otherwise blissful harmony of Irish rural life. Their successors in An Garda Síochána were equally vigilant in hunting down the growers of this plant, not least because there was a strong neighbourhood taboo against its tolerance. The lazy farmer of one year was causing a lot of sore backs for everyone round him a year later.

Somewhere in the intervening decades, the enforcement of this law slipped into abeyance; and a few years ago, when responsibility for prosecuting ragwort-growers passed from An Garda Síochána to the Department of Agriculture, enforcement just about ceased. Now ragwort is everywhere, poisoning thousands of acres, most especially land that is now lying fallow in that latest EU exercise in fiscal infamy called 'set-aside'. The net effect of this is that farmers are being bribed to create oases of unmanaged land, little unchecked paradises of docks, thistles, brambles and ragwort, which in time will contaminate the pastures around them.

Farmers are not alone in their neglect of their land. Perhaps the greatest culprits are county councils, which own and are therefore responsible for roadside verges, along which ragwort this year is now prospering as never before. Vast yellow armies of invaders now line our roadways, their malevolent yellow heads bobbing in the breeze. Soon, uncropped, their flowers will turn to seeds, and their thistledown will be borne on a breeze in a vortex of unchecked and unpunished contamination. And no one has to pay the price, other than the innocent landowners downwind over the summer months of next year. Lovely, isn't it?

So here we have, once again, a vicious, state-subsidised triangle, sponsoring the contamination of the Irish landscape. EU-supported farmers are being paid to allow their land become ragwort factories, while the government department that is meant to be enforcing the law over these reprobates apparently does nothing whatever about them. Meanwhile, local authorities themselves are also cultivating this poison.

But this year has been the worst that anyone remember, as agricultural delinquency mounts and government passivity becomes positively Bolivian: walk into the Ragwort Suppression Branch of the Department of Agriculture, and you will probably find a couple of RSB enforcement officers snoozing under their sombreros. The consequence is that I, and my farming neighbours, have once again to remove ragwort sent to us in seed form by strangers, perhaps miles away.

And so it was the the other day I was stamping around my humble landholding on a ragwort hunt, spade in hand, the ragwort-hounds – Parsnip, Mumps and Wurrum, mongrels to a man – being generally idiotic around me. A cluster of ragwort attracted my attention on the raised edge of the ménage, where the grass is never cut. I had successfully extracted a dozen of the offending intruders by the roots when I caught sight of about ten blue-green eggs lying in a little flat oval in the middle of the long grass. Beside them sat a large unmoving speckled bird the size of a pheasant – but it was no pheasant.

Frantically ushering the dogs away and back to the stable-yard, I went rummaging for my birdbooks. Could the bird be what I suspected? To Eric Dempsey and Michael O'Clery's invaluable *Complete Guide to Ireland's Birds*. 'Dumpy with short bill'. Yes! Confirmation from other bird books. 'Eight to twelve eggs'. Yes! 'Brown and barred'. Yes! It was a corncrake, a veritable corncrake, here on my field in Kildare!

So, I softly retraced my steps towards the nest until the head of the roosting hen was just in sight, and then, very carefully, and from a safe distance, I shot it. Corncrakes roast beautifully, you know, and are delicious with cranberries; moreover, next day, I breakfasted quite imperially on the eggs.

What? It's not April 1st? All right. I left the hen alone, of course, and by the purest of good fortune, as evening descended a few days later and I was returning from putting a neighbour's horses to bed, I spotted the hen leading her waddling, baffled brood down the road, and away to their new lives. Surely, one of the greatest sights of my life. Heaven guard thee crakes!

And the moral of the story? No ragwort-picking, no corncrake-sighting.

[2 August 2005]

III.24. *The Terrible Month of May*

That was it. That was May, the month that almost always lets us down. Perhaps one May in ten lives up to something like its reputation. But for the most part, May is a grave disappointment. That is its nature, as it is in man's nature to be incorrigibly optimistic about a month that is more inclined to dismay than to please. *The Oxford Dictionary of Quotations* lists 21 references to May, but only seven to the next most cited month, December, and six to March; apparently no one has uttered a quotable word about January.

May is named after Maia, the Greek goddess, but for Christians, it has traditionally been the month of Mary, though it actually begins with the feast day of St Joseph, the carpenter, and of course, her husband: May day is not a socialist invention but an ecclesiastical one. And the entire month of May was once spent in preparation for the feast that is today's, that of Our Lady, Queen of All Saints, Mediatress of All Graces, as the Catholic Church once termed her.

In that distant time when the Catholic Church recognised the power of beauty, it taught its children beautiful language; 'Alleluia, alleluia. Show me thy face, let thy voice sound in my ears; sweet is thy voice, fair thy face,' they would say in the mass for Mary's day. 'Alleluia. From thy lips is dripping the honeycomb, honey and milk are beneath thy tongue, and thy raiment is fragrant with the odour of frankincense.'

As the tide of Catholicism has receded, it has left behind it vast sandbanks of agnosticism on which rests residual rituals of meaningless first communions, a ghastly mumbo-jumbo of fake tans, ruinously lavish dresses and salon-concocted curls. And along with almost any sense of what communion is about, those receding waters of faith have taken with them the incredibly powerful reverence that was once felt for the virgin Mary at this time of year. Barely a child in Ireland now could conceive of what today once was, a day of flower-bedecked parades through every town and village, with large statues being borne on the shoulders of pious young men, and choirs singing the many anthems in Mary's honour.

There are no parades any more, nor any pious young men either, and most of the choirs are gone silent, to be sure; but equally there are no orphanages and laundries which are temples of abuse. For the world turns and values change, but in its essence May does not. May is the month of regeneration, which explains why May is also the month of murder, when the feeding competition amongst animals moves into a killing frenzy. It is the month when magpies and cats stalk the hedgerows massacring helpless fledglings by the thousand. It is the season when animal-parents' feeding duties are almost incessant through the long hours of daylight, so making themselves vulnerable to the compelling needs of other parents, other broods. May is truly the month of Creation's final law, of nature, red in tooth and claw.

Through the long dark nights of winter, we dream of May and its long days and its returning flocks of birds, home at last from beyond the Congo. Fixed somewhere in our collective memory is a notion of a mythic May of dancing maidens and lusty youths, and spring bursting through the warming soil. But May seldom is as we remember it, and certainly never as our collective memory recalls it. Few enough poets depict it accurately. Shakespeare does of course – 'Rough winds do shake the darling buds of May' – and so does the forgotten American poet James Russell Lowell: 'May is a pious fraud of the almanac.'

And he's right. May is a pious old fraud. May is a time of east winds, of sudden, fatal frosts, and even this year, stout gales from the Atlantic. It is the season which kills Aesop's hasty swallow, when one hangs up the heavy coat in the wardrobe one day, and takes it out a couple of days later. It is the season when the grass begins to grow, finally, but you cannot cut it because it is too wet. Most of all, it is the season that is more representative of life than any other month of the year: for its essence is disappointment. It will almost never live up to expectations, and at its end, we invariably say: 'Is that it?'

Three years ago one rare May evening when it was warm enough to sit out, we were enjoying the setting sun, listening to the songs of a pair of blackbirds, a hen and a cock, perched on a tree beside the terrace. The hen began to fly to another branch and had gone about a foot when she was taken on the wing and instantly killed with a talon through the spinal column by a sparrow-hawk, also a hen, which fluttered into a neighbouring bush

After a while of solitude, the cock began to sing for his mate, but of course, she was gone, her destiny to live on in the lives of baby-sparrow hawks. Still he called, evening after evening after evening. And for the rest of the spring, and for the one afterwards, the cock bird stayed on the bare branch calling for his mate in long, melancholy melodies. He has done so again this year, his forlorn song ringing through the twilight air, as he patiently and vainly awaits her return. May is truly a terrible month, and yes, that was it.

[ND]

III.25. Where are the Water Rats?

Where dips the rocky headland
Of Sleuth Wood in the lake,
There lies a leafy island,
Where flapping herons wake
The drowsy water rats.

W.B. Yeats might as well written of ostriches or alligators as water rats in his elegy to Glen-Car, for they are just as absent from there, or anywhere else in Ireland, as the aquatic rodent he invokes in 'The Stolen Child.' Simply, there are no water rats (or water voles: their proper name) in this country. Yeats was merely exhibiting an ignorance of the animals of Ireland, which is remarkably commonplace, and which in part is compounded by the language we speak.

This was, of course, created by a people with a different culture and entirely different history. English is a language rich in Shakespeare, the Book of Common Prayer, and the Royal Navy: every time we use expressions like by and large, in a trice, go by the board, a wide berth, we are commemorating an English rather than an Irish sea going experience.

Similarly English speaks of weasel, kite, nuthatch, vole, mole, adder, nightingale and water rat, none of which exists here. Even many of the birds and animals that do live here have been given Irish names of very recent and often rather self-conscious devising. This reflects a curious attitude within Irish culture towards the land and its inhabitants, which inclines at times towards an almost studied disdain. So many country people can neither name the native birds or beasts of their landscape, nor eat the edible ones. Why?

Apart from the gentry and the middle classes, few Irish people, especially in the country, will eat the rabbit, pheasant, deer, grouse, snipe, woodcock, hare and duck that infest our land, lakes and estuaries. There are virtually no dishes based on commonplace fish such as freshwater crayfish, pike and eel, which most Irish people would regard with horror. A German angler on the Shannon, however, would rejoice to find a pike, rather than a salmon, on his hook.

And how is it that country skills are so very rare in Ireland? There is next to no tradition of ferreting or poaching game anywhere. Nor is there a widespread engagement with our waters. Communities along the Shannon, Barrow, Nore or any other river tend to have been built with their back to the riverside, and there is little or no custom of exploiting the waters as a food source. Why? Gillying, a profession of utmost refinement and guile amongst the Gaels of Scotland, is almost unknown amongst their Irish cousins. Why?

The ravages of landlordism? Possibly – but the Scots had landlords too, and few people in Europe endured the weight of landed nobilities as unremittingly heavy as those of Spain or France, yet these countries have rich and powerful peasant food cultures based on the native produce of the land. There is no equivalent in Ireland. Farmhouse cooking culture here, such as it is, aside from handsome traditions of bakery, is based on limited kinds of tended livestock – sheep, beef, pork, but not goat. Why?

Even culinarily challenged England has regional specialities – Cornish pasties, Bakewell tarts, Melton Mowbray pork pies, Cumberland sausages – and numerous local cheeses. There are virtually no local foods – a Tipperary sausage or a Kilkenny mutton pie, say – apart from that regrettable phenomenon, drisheen. And for all the reverence traditionally accorded the cow, there is no tradition whatever of making farmhouse cheeses here comparable to Stilton, Wensleydale or Cheshire, to say nothing of the caseous cornucopia of France. Why?

There is an appetite for land, to be sure, to be measured in acres on which to graze cattle or sheep, and to be owned at almost any cost, but land itself is neither cherished for what it contains nor what it naturally yields. Nor is it even just a matter of the wild animals and birds that live on it. How many country people pick blackberries, sloes, mushrooms, crab apples, elderflower and elderberries when their season arrives? Very few. In Spain, France and Italy, local markets are full of local produce, but not in Ireland. It's almost as if those who live on the land here are culturally and emotionally disengaged from its essence as a living thing. Why?

This might explain the enthusiasm with which the urban bungalow, containing features wholly inappropriate for both the Irish countryside and weather, has been embraced with such fervour. It is an architectural denial of the reality that surrounds it, a statement of ambition over a mute acceptance of actuality. If you see a restored stone cottage anywhere in Ireland, it is invariably a sign of a complete outsider. Why?

This denial of rural reality might also explain our appalling treelessness; for trees must be planted and minded; and if the absence of a tradition of tree husbandry, of coppicing, pollarding, pruning and ivy-removal co-exists with a tradition of tree-felling, the Micawberesque logic of life will ensure the outcome which we enjoy today – the most treeless landscape in Europe. Even the trees that remain are densely infested with ivy – and nor is this a vice confined to farmers. The surest sign that a woodland is managed by Coillte is the dense green foliage rioting through its broadleaf trees in midwinter. Why?

There is history that explains all of this, but what is it? Was it the Famine? Or the Penal Laws that psychologically distanced the greater part of the people from the land they worked? Or something else? Just one more question. Why?

[30 January 2001]

III.26. The Gadfly

There are many reasons to doubt the existence of a kind and bounteous God – Jacques Chirac, Lurgan, George Galloway, Martin Ferris, athlete's foot, synchronised swimming – but all of these are themselves open to debate. Jacques Chirac is kind to his slippers. Lurgan has exits. George Galloway is not Jacques Chirac. Martin Ferris is an arsehole, and we all need one of them. Athlete's foot might not be pretty to us, but it is to its doting parents. Synchronised swimming sometimes goes wrong, and the performers drown.

The argument over the existence of a benign and generous God is thus unresolved. So what's left? What decides whether or not God is a genial old chap in the clouds, indulgently tut-tut-tutting at our many misdemeanours, or a gnashing, snarling old fiend, showering us with bolts of lightning, afflicting our cattle with the murrain, and littering our bottoms with unlanceable boils?

This time of year provides the clinching argument. It goes by the usual name of 'horsefly', the gadfly in older English and the cleg in dialect. Now the 'horsefly' sounds quite amiable. So too does 'gadfly' because of the coincidence of sounds. The usual meaning of 'gad' is of light-hearted pleasure seeking. However, it is an unrelated word that is the root of the word gadfly, which comes from *gaddr* the Old Norse for spear.

The spear-fly just about sums up the horsefly, known to science as *haemotopota*. My Greek is just about non-existent, but I know *haemo-* all right. Blood. And I may be wrong here, but that *topo-* bit looks ominously like 'place'. In other words, the fly that goes for the place where the blood is, which is fine as it goes. Flies have to eat too, and what to us is a precious blood vessel to them is the works-cafeteria. Moreover, most of us can spare the odd armful of blood or two for our lesser, six-legged friends.

But the real problem about the cleg is what the little lassie feasts upon between her banquets of blood, which is faeces. It's all the equivalent of a cleggy pub crawl. First you stop off at a nice heap of stinking, rotten fox-crap, which you inhale as much of as you can. Then you saunter off to the nearest expanse of exposed human body, and amble into the licensed premises marked 'vein', using the heat-seeking vision of the cleggish brain. You go to the bar, you insert your proboscis, and you insect half an alimentary canal of mammalian excrement into the soft tissue around the vein. This will stop the blood clotting, and now it's time to let rip, and drink your fill, and to wassail away like Pistol, Falstaff and Mistress Quickly as the chimes of midnight ring about their ears.

The brilliant key to the continued survival of the horsefly is that at a certain point, its activities will trigger a response, a small tic, from its host, the equivalent of the barman's 'Have youse no homes to go to?' At which point, the horsefly will promptly depart. Without the tic, so intrepid boys told me in my youth, the fly will continue inhaling haemoglobin until she explodes: they proudly boasted that they had allowed gadflies to do just that on their arms. One minute she's sucking away like an American teenager at a milkshake, next she goes pop! cascading the contents of her tummy all over her gallant host's arm.

Do girls do this? No. Is this because the cleg who browses from stool to vein is solely female? I do not know what the male of the species does – goes to air shows, probably, the poor fool – but he doesn't sup at the pool of poo and then banquet upon human blood, thereby spreading vile infections. And though I know the female of the human species is in other regards a sturdy brute, I can hardly believe that it is sisterliness alone that prevents a girl steadfastly watching a gadfly on her arm gorge itself until it blows up in a shower of blood.

Thus, provided the horsefly is spared a boy's little plucky cunning, she will then depart for its next hostelry, which could be cow dung, dog droppings or wherever Paula Radcliffe had recently been running. And then back to a human vein; and so on and so forth, as this delightful little feeding cycle wends its merry way, with each human guest being injected with a little syringe of bacterial filth which over the next days will become infected septic and swollen.

So wherefore the cleg? Whence the gadfly? Why has God in His wisdom given it such a pernicious food cycle, and moreover, made us part of it? It all seems so gratuitous. Look at other insects. Bees only sting to protect themselves. Wasps the same. Ditto ants. Mosquitoes – like the others, all female – do not choose to spread malaria, but merely want a soupçon of your blood. For they too are the hapless victims of the malaria parasite, and *that* is only doing what any species does, namely, reproduce. It doesn't want its host to die, either you or the mosquito, any more than you want the plane you're flying in to crash.

With the cleg or gadfly, it's different. It is designed solely to inject excrement into human flesh. So, St Thomas Aquinas what do you have to say about a God that designed such a beast? Speak up, St Thomas: we cannot hear you. Ah, struck dumb, are you? I thought as much.

[13 July 2005]

IV. The North

IV.1. Harald, This Is Not Scandinavia

Did anyone explain to those nice, handsome Danes when they took an interest in National Irish Bank what a peculiar country this is? In Denmark, they put bank-robbers into jail: in this country, we put them into government and call it a 'settlement'. We don't even insist on ministers in government leaving their bank-robbing organisations, though we'd prefer them not to participate personally in bank robberies. Government ministers shooting policemen doing their duty can be just a little embarrassing. But government ministers' friends? Oh, that's okay.

Poor baffled Danes. They probably didn't realize that different rules apply to crime in this country. The Australians, who are trying to sell the National Irish Bank, finally did, and were probably holding their breath, hoping to complete a sale before they got clobbered by the armed wing of a government party. Too late, and now Sinn Féin-IRA are counting the loot, chuckling away merrily at what a great thing this peace process is.

And it is a great thing – isn't it? Yes, of course, it has brought us peace, though there were other ways of doing that. But the deal that was done was a masterpiece of amoral fudge and equivocal appeasement, in which the two governments assented to a series of lies, and consented to the existence of two sets of rules – one for Sinn Féin-IRA, and another and entirely different set for the rest of us.

You can't harness a crocodile to a gazelle and expect them to pull a stagecoach – but that's what the peace process did. Moreover, it didn't demand that the crocodile change its carnivorous habits, merely to pretend that it had, and to continue to practise what came naturally in secret. But then the crocodile learnt that there were many unacceptable deeds that it could visibly perpetrate, and it would have to pay no price whatever.

We all know the laundry list of offences that are in studied refutation of the rules of the peace process, the Mitchell Principles, the Belfast Agreement. God knows, I've gone through that damned list often enough here. It makes absolutely no difference. Meanwhile, the peace process has contaminated entire communities in the North – and contamination is the only word you can use to describe West Belfast's response to the funeral of poor Jean McConville a year ago – metaphorically, it turned its back on the most shameful single murder in the entire Troubles.

A moral universe has been created that is wholly antithetical to the ethical system which enables ordinary societies to function, lawfully and decently. The Big Lie has become a way of life. Everyone knows that Sinn Féin-IRA is a single extended organisation, though everyone then pretends that it is not. Everyone pretends that the IRA is not active, though everyone knows it is extremely active, even if in a strictly à la carte fashion.

A society predicated on such flagrant untruths is not a society in practice, because you cannot contain falsehood: it spreads from its source, and permits all manner of untruth to become doctrinaire 'truth'. The peace process is based on a series of Orwellian lies that mean that no contract has value, no word of honour has any meaning, no undertaking is binding. In this diseased and wretched universe, men who kill are honoured; those who do not are abased. And out of this mess of potage, lasting so-called democratic institutions were meant to be constructed.

The political landscape of Northern Ireland was meanwhile littered with the bodies of those sacrificed to keep Sinn Féin-IRA happy. The Alliance Party is a cadaver. The SDLP's death rattle echoes over the drumlins. The Ulster Unionist Party will probably will go meet its maker in the UK general election later this year. Meanwhile, Sinn Féin-IRA are triumphant across both the North and in working-class districts of Dublin. Grinning TDs consort with garda-killers, as toasts are raised to celebrate the biggest cash robbery in Irish and UK history. The poison seeps through society; lawlessness is celebrated, and the lawless are feted.

The IRA will not go away. It was never going to go away, for it knows that organisationally it predates Fianna Fáil and Fine Gael. Moreover, it traces its spiritual roots through to 1798, and onwards to antiquity. That sense of past has given it a unique sense of time, which it measures not as the rest of us do, in weeks and years, but in epochs and in lifetimes. The struggle continues in different ways in different epochs; but it does not cease to be a struggle, and it does not cease to continue. All it requires to give itself authenticity are guns; and it cannot buy all it wants.

But the money is in Northern Ireland banknotes. Really? And that is a problem? For just watch as bank managers across the North over the coming weeks receive visitors with two observations. One, they know where the managers' children go to school, and two, they'd like to exchange these here local banknotes for British ones. This day next week will do nicely. Why, National Irish banks might even have the pleasure of laundering their own money.

Listen, Harald, this is not Scandinavia. Nor is it even a Sicily without the weather, for it is against the law there for politicians to consort with participants in organised crime. In Ireland – aided and abetted by an abject and unprincipled British government – it is the law that elected politicians *must* consort with gangsters, extortionists and killers.

It is called the peace process. Happy Christmas, Harald.

[24 December 2004]

IV.2. *Drawing an End to the Troubles*

You have to be either deeply cynical or deeply stupid not to care about Sinn Féin-IRA On The Runs project. For the Shinners are busy successfully redrafting history, with the aid of two largely compliant governments in Dublin and London, and two political establishments which are either fast asleep (Westminster) or are being drawn by their nationalist nose into the Sinn Féin trap (Oireachtas).

Sinn Féin-IRA demand that presidential pardons be offered to IRA men in the Republic, and that the British grant what amounts to an unquestioning amnesty to unconvicted paramilitary offenders. Yet they also demand that no mercy be offered to members of the British security forces who had allegedly colluded in terrorist activities. Familiar territory: for this is the Black and Tan project revisited. Thus an entirely mythical historical landscape is created in which the only visibly guilty people at the end of the Troubles will be members of the security forces, thereby retroactively legitimising the atrocities of the IRA.

After years of appeasement, the Shinners now routinely expect their disgusting set of values to be accepted by the two governments. So they're now genuinely astonished and indignant that the British government intends to grant to its employees the same pardon which it is offering its enemies.

But why wouldn't they be surprised? Are they not regularly invited to tea and scones at Downing Street and Chequers? Has that brute Martin Ferris not been ushered into the drawing room of Number 10, while the Prime Minister giddily tap-danced in attendance? So how could thugs like Ferris have the least idea how the rest of us feel about him, his vile organisations, and their filthy deeds? Because you can be sure that Blair, playing cutesy mother with the teapot, never told him. And of course, how could he? For Blair is cut from the same moral material as his guests. None of them know right from wrong any more than a tadpole knows a fine-tooth comb from an All-Ireland Final.

Gerry Adams once again spake in Shinnese on the issue last week, when he denied that republicans had double standards in seeking to close cases for republican paramilitaries, but to keep them open if they involved members of crown forces. 'The fact is that hundreds of people have been killed by the British crown forces, and there is an attempt to cover up this issue, and I think people understand that.'

Only in the burlesque world of Shinnery could such preposterous falsehoods exist. Go, as one should daily do, to David McKittrick's *Lost Lives*, to get a measure of how risibly evil the Adams' world view is. Republicans were responsible for 58.3 per cent of all deaths in the Troubles. The regular British army was responsible for 6.5 per cent, and Special Forces were responsible for 1.7 per cent. The RUC was responsible for 1.4 per cent. The UDR (as UDR) killed 8 people, just .2 per cent. Yes, point two per cent. The regiment's dead numbered some 200 – surely, the highest disproportion in any conflict anywhere. The Royal Irish Regiment contribution to the trouble's dead? 0 per cent.

The British army was responsible for 158 civilian deaths, i.e., 4.27 per cent of the total. The IRA killed 644 civilians – 17.4 per cent of the total. The IRA also killed 163 republicans. In other words, republican fratricides accounted for more deaths than the total number of civilians killed by British soldiers. Moreover, many killings by soldiers were in return-fire incidents, which had been initiated by terrorists, and young soldiers had to make instant and often impossible decisions about whom to shoot and whom not. Such killings of the innocent cannot usually and decently be called murder. Moreover, the pressure of terrorist warfare explain 13 'blue-on-blue' security force killings of their colleagues.

Nationalist Ireland has been tiresomely but predictably huffing and puffing about the 'scandal' of letting security force colluders go free. And in Tony Blair's abject and craven attitude towards Shinnerdom, he might even give ground here, with British soldiers thus finding themselves in the dock, while republican and loyalist terrorists are effectively pardoned for far worse crimes. If that is so, then Blair may now withdraw his troops from Iraq, before they mutiny there, or more probably, stay in barracks, reading porn.

For, as a group, the British army suffered massively in the Troubles, with 688 dead. And how many terrorists were convicted of involvement in murdering soldiers? 400? 100? No. Just 81. Which meant that the deaths of 597 soldiers went without any punishment whatever. Moreover, most of those convicted were in fact bit-part players, while the really serious killers the snipers, the bomb-makers, the land-mine detonators, the point-blank assassins – why, they have mostly never been punished for their crimes.

The simplest way of drawing an end to the most purposeless, stupid and unproductive terrorist campaign of the twentieth century in Europe is to say its crimes will not now be judicially revisited. The dead are dead, the guilty are guilty, but there can be no question of creating a legally binding hierarchy of victimhood, of rightness and wrongness. We may all have many our different opinions on this, but to incorporate such a hierarchy into formal and lasting political agreement is merely to recreate the mythology of Black and Tan evil, IRA saintly, and thus generate the DNA of further Troubles.

Not that Blair cares for such decent concerns. The most amoral British Prime Minister since Lloyd George, no infamy is too infamous for him, no indecency too indecent. Beneath the rule of this unprincipled reptile, almost anything is possible.

[8 December 2005]

IV.3. Conflict Resolution

'The moment the very name of Ireland is mentioned, the English seem to bid adieu to common feeling, common prudence, and common sense, to act with the barbarity of tyrants and the fatuity of idiots,' the nineteenth-century essayist Sydney Smith once famously said. He would amend his sentiments today as follows: 'The moment that the name of the IRA is mentioned, the world seems to bid adieu to common standards, common history and to common sense, and to act with the fatuity of infants and the gullibility of fools.'

Henry McDonald in last Sunday's *Observer* revealed that Gerry Adams shared a platform at a conference on 'religion, conflict and reconciliation' in New York with Holocaust survivor Elie Wiesel. But Gerry Adams is the leader of the only organisation in Europe that holds an annual knees-up or goosestep to honour a Nazi collaborator, Sean Russell, at the latter's statue in Dublin. No one else does this. No one. This would be tolerated in no other country. Such demonstrations would be banned by governments or broken up by counter-demonstrators.

But not here. The Sean Russell Nazi-lovers were apparently at their capers again the other day, once again honouring their hero, and of course there was no counter-demonstration, because either people mostly do not care that we have a bunch of unrepentant Nazi-loving goons in our midst, or because they are scared. A bit of both, I'd guess.

Consider the supine passivity towards the IRA by the much of the Irish people, a section of whom actually elected Mary Lou McDonald to the European Parliament even though she had been present at a we-revere-Sean-Russell rally.

I wonder: does she regale the MEPs with her own version of the Nazi anthem 'Horst Wessel', now retitled 'Sean Russell'? So, perhaps it's hardly surprising that there's no counter-demonstration, not any attempt by Dublin Corporation to remove this abominable statue to an abominable man.

But what on earth was Elie Weisel doing sharing a platform with Gerry Adams? It was he who coined the term, 'to remain silent and indifferent is the greatest sin of all ...'. Was he not doing both in the company of a man whose organisation yearly honours a Nazi collaborator? Was he not sharing a platform with a man whose father, as a member of the IRA, actually lit bonfires on the Black Mountain to guide Nazi bombers to destroy Belfast in 1941? Was he not sharing a platform with a man who repudiates or disavows neither of these deeds?

Maybe Elie Wiesel is a little old to know such things – but surely he gets advice from someone or other. Could the Israeli government or the Simon Weisenthal Centre not inform him of the political pedigree of people with whom he cavorts?

Still, we have to congratulate that grisly confection, the Clinton couple, with their utterly perfect timing for their conference on 'religion, reconciliation and reconciliation', as Orange thugs tore apart the capital city of the province they profess to love. 'Conflict Resolution' has been the political art form in vogue around the world for the past fifteen years or so, during which we have had Rwanda, Dofar, Bosnia, Chechneya, the West Bank and Iraq, and the cult of suicide bomber. So much for conflict resolution.

The truth is that genuine conflicts are not resolved. They are won or they die down of their own accord. Human agencies are incapable of peacefully interfering where genuine conflict exists and creating enduring institutions that permanently bring opposite sides together. The very act of 'resolution' institutionalises the conflict. Extremes are bribed to be in government: therefore, why not be an extreme? Thus Sinn Féin-IRA was put into government, and continued to behave as it always did, smashing kneecaps, robbing banks, plotting murders, and so forth, just as Orangemen continued to behave as they have always done, marching wherever they weren't wanted.

You cannot put a cat and a dog in a bag and expect them to make apple pie. The hoary old example of conflict resolution is South Africa, where the conflict was not resolved, but won, by the majority black community. The white man stays on in South Africa with the permission of the majority: but that permission could be revoked at any time, as it has been in that other model of conflict resolution, Zimbabwe.

In the North, the tribal difference has been deepened and prolonged by the unprincipled Belfast Agreement. This particular IRA campaign is over, but the war declared in the Proclamation of 1916 is not. Yet for years we have been regularly treated to inane RTÉ and newspaper reports declaring that major IRA decommissioning is imminent, followed by months of non-decommissioning, followed by fresh headlines declaring that major IRA decommissioning is imminent, followed by et cetera, et cetera.

So of course the IRA knows that the rules that apply to others do not apply to it. Everywhere else, Nazi-sympathisers and their celebrants are excoriated, but not if they're IRA, in which case they might find themselves publicly cosying up to some Holocaust survivors. Everywhere else, people who cross the globe to train narco-terrorists in Colombia are utterly reviled in their home countries, but not if they're IRA.

Everywhere else, fascist terrorists who murder ambassadors, or blow up old people and children in a boat, or take civilians off a bus and massacre them, are objects of contempt. But in our wretched country we have degraded democracy in order to put such vile people with their filthy practices into government. This is rip-off Ireland all right, but in principles, not prices: the original Hobbesian nightmare.

[21 September 2005]

IV.4. The GFA (Good Friday Agreement)

There is nothing in the Good Friday Agreement which declares that convicted terrorists should shut up for good, and complain about nothing for the rest of their lives; but nor is there anything in the Agreement which commands the convenient amnesia that former paramilitary leaders desperately yearn for. Amnesia has been one of the great enabling factors in the cycle of Troubles over the years. Amnesia liberates from consequence, conferring innocence on the guilty, and banishing the slaughtered dead to a permanent exile from popular memory. So it is not spiteful or revanchist to remember. It is morally necessary. It is the guard against a fresh infestation of violence.

So it is not in the least in a spirit of vindictiveness that I refer to the letter from Danny Morrison, former Sinn Féin publicity chief and a convicted terrorist, published last Monday, complaining about the appalling travails he recently had had to endure trying to get breakfast on the Enterprise Express to Dublin, the poor lamb. I must say: I admire his nerve. I really do. Perhaps, next a letter soon from Paul Kefa Mukonyi complaining about the rough treatment he received on a British Airways flight to Nairobi?

Ten years ago, Danny Morrison was found guilty of being an accomplice in the kidnap and interrogation of a police informer, Sandy Lynch, who had been held and interrogated by the IRA for two days in 124 Carrigart Avenue, Belfast. The court was told about the fate of a previous such captive at that address, Joseph Fenton, a father of four, whose treatment, in every detail except the final outcome, was identical to that of Sandy Lynch.

Joseph Fenton was bound and blindfolded, just as Sandy Lynch was. He was deprived of food, just as Sandy Lynch was, and indeed, as poor Danny Morrison was the other day on the train from Belfast (though only for a while, you'll rejoice to hear: he finally got a fry in a soda farl). Both were forced to make tape-recorded confessions of guilt. Both were compelled to record pleas for mercy. Both were told that judgment on their future would be made by men not then present in 124 Carrigart Avenue. The confessions recorded, the tapes were taken away for judgment.

In the case of Sandy Lynch, some time later, Danny Morrison arrived at the house and was arrested in a police raid. The trial judge ruled that Morrison knew that Sandy Lynch was being held captive and was a supporter of IRA terrorism. Sandy Lynch told the court he was convinced that he was about to be murdered. Others would agree. He was, however, freed before any further harm befell him.

No such liberation awaited Joseph Fenton. Whoever arrived at that house with news of Joseph Fenton's fate was able to ensure sentence was carried out, without interference from the RUC. His body was found with gunshot wounds to the head in Bunbeg Park, Lenadoon. Sinn Féin played a copy of his taped 'confession', including the futile plea for mercy, to his father Patrick. Perhaps we may believe the assertion that it was Joseph Fenton who had earlier fingered a married couple, Catherine and Gerard Mahon, as RUC informers, in order to deflect suspicion away from himself; perhaps we may also believe the allegation that Fenton did this on the instructions of his RUC handlers.

I don't know the truth about these assertions. But I do know Catherine and Gerard Mahon were captured by the IRA and taken to Turf Lodge and interrogated there. Were they deprived of food there, as Sandy Lynch was, as Joseph Fenton had been, and as poor Danny Morrison was to be, on the Dublin train before Christmas? I don't know that either. But I do know, regardless of who brought the news of their fate in whatever house they were being held, that the end that awaited the Mahons was the same as that which was to await Joseph Fenton. Both were shot dead.

Six years later, Gerard's brother Colm was shot dead by a man he had barred from a pub he managed. It was an apolitical act of mindless thuggery. The killer, Crip McWilliams, joined the INLA while in jail. Three years ago, he shot dead LVF leader Billy Wright in the Maze. McWilliams is now free, under the terms of the Good Friday Agreement, but the daughter of Colm Mahon, is not: 'Since his death, I have felt alone and empty,' she told a rally four years ago. 'One of the most important people in my life was gone. One wish I have is that no more people suffer the way my family and other families have suffered.'

There is suffering and there is suffering. There are myriads of relatives of the dead, who must try to make sense of the emotional calamity of bereavement and the suffering inflicted by those who have enjoyed early release from the Maze; and there is the suffering of poor Danny Morrison, unable to get his breakfast just when he wants it on the train to Dublin.

Now Danny, I don't know what you've got on your conscience and what you have not. All I'm sure of is that I'm glad it's your conscience and not mine. So do us this small favour, please: endure the slings and arrows of life's little misfortunes in silence. In other words, Danny my boy, you're alive, and thousands are not. So shut up.

[4 January 2001]

IV.5. *The Rubric of Republicanism*

Reading the rubric of republicanism is never easy. In that culture, words are plastic things to be shaped as needed. What makes this process all the more sinister, all the more powerful, is that the speakers embrace the new meaning of the word the moment they have framed it. This is Nescafé-speak: instant belief.

Sinn Féin-IRA call the present Executive, formed from the most rigged election in Irish history, democracy. They genuinely believe that is what it is: democracy, and since even the Nescafé-speak version of democracy is better than the armed struggle, I will continue to sip at the pallid, bitter brew of the Good Friday Agreement, though killers are free, and unelected terrorist chieftains are government consultants. The people of Ireland consented to this deal. So be it.

So be it not, apparently. Ruairí Ó Brádaigh recently said that the Good Friday Agreement was made 'under duress, like the Treaty of 1921 and as such is not binding any more than was the political surrender of 80 years ago'.

No, don't ask me what he means by duress, only take my word for it: he means it. He has dedicated his entire life to The Cause: what riches might he have enjoyed if he had put his brain, his single-mindedness, his courage, to the business of making money? How much unswerving devotion to a belief does it take that a man might spend half a century plotting and conspiring about a single politico-military object?

He belongs to the unregenerate old school of republicanism, which traces apostolic authenticity from the 1916 Rising through to the one true election in Irish history, 1918. He speaks for the tradition of Republican Sinn Féin: Catholic, virulent, unrelenting, a ferocious, pagan world teeming with Fenian martyrs and righteous killers. It is a religion, full of the ambiguities that all religions employ, and which republicanism invariably has. Has not the implausible twin face of Sinn Féin-IRA, one face armed and lawless, the other unarmed and law-abiding, often both represented by the same individuals, curious resemblances to the equally implausible notion of the divine trinity?

The Real IRA is a more contemporary version of an old tradition: the Douay rather than the King James version. Its birth lies in more recent roots, yet invoking the same ancient divinities of the Continuity IRA, but in more modern, more accessible, but less colourful language. The Real IRA probably doesn't give a fiddler's about the 1918 election. What it wants is what the Continuity wants: Brits out, by force of arms, preferably. It has a stomach of tempered steel. Despite Omagh, despite the still staggering monstrousness of what happened there, it is sticking to its guns (Croat, as it happens: careful lads, Yugoslav mags are not inter-changeable with AK mags). Its war continues.

We could have wrapped up the Real IRA after Omagh. Imaginative and unrelenting policing such as that which followed the murder of Veronica Guerin, could have closed the operational base of the Real IRA in Louth. That did not happen. Tragically, the political will to do so was absent.

Agreements will not make these people go away. They have seen ETA sur-viving a similar such agreement, seen how it is possible to conduct a ferocious war without any popular support. Indeed, terrorist purists find something reas-suring in their sense of isolated, intransigent virtue. We cannot stop them feeling this murderous moral superiority; all we can do to ensure they feel it in the cold of a prison cell.

We have taken a reactive policy to the Real IRA. We wait for them to move before we respond. This will not work. Nor will the promise of a deep kiss from the next First Lady if they start behaving themselves. They are busy recruiting. Both Continuity and Real IRAs were touring pubs in the Liberties last weekend, as brazenly as the Salvation Army clinking boxes.

This is ridiculous. These people were given the chance to come in to the light. They chose dark. Their decision. Let them stay there. Settlements, agree-ments, nor even a hecatomb of human misery can stay they hand or sway their beliefs. They are on the brink of war again, and this time we cannot wait for them to decide when and where the war should be fought; and certainly they cannot be allowed to wander the streets of a democracy, raising money to overthrow that democracy by force of arms.

In this perilous time, we should ask: who is South Armagh loyal to? Is it constructively ambiguous in its pledges, assuring both Real and Provisional IRAs of its devotion to the leadership, biding its time before deciding which dialect of Nescafé-language it will speak? What British commander in his right mind would surrender the militarily vital watchtowers while the hedgerows there soon might seethe with furtive movement, as young wives in England dread the chaplain's knock on the door?

These terrorists neither respect us nor believe us; and they certainly don't fear us. Frankly, I don't give a damn about the first. But here in this state, they should be made to believe that unless they declare an unambiguously permanent ceasefire, they will come to understand what an amnesty-free future in prison means. They should start to fear us democrats very seriously indeed.

As a matter of interest, if Martin McGuinness were Minister for Justice in Dublin, what do you think he would do about the rejectionist IRAs? I think, for once, he'd agree with me. Someone should ask him.

[21 December 2000]

IV.6. The Troubles, 1919–1921

'During the Anglo-Irish War, the British press had teemed with reports of unconscionable extremities – of brutal assaults, degrading tortures and an endless train of assassinations perpetrated by Republican forces ...' writes Richard Bourke in his recent book *Peace in Ireland*. 'Up until then, the Royal Irish Constabulary had been acting in open defiance of their civilian duties, while Britain's Auxiliary Forces had terrorised the population.'

So here we go again: and I'd really believed that all the wider scholarship of the past decade or so would have firmly registered in that curious creation, the Irish academic mind, that during the period of 1919 to 1921 the IRA really did commit atrocities, even war crimes, and the RIC was not a force composed entirely of murderous blackguards.

This is not a review of Richard Bourke's book, which has been widely praised, but a response to his summary of the Troubles of 1919 to 1921. Though he admits to 'guerrilla outrages', he seems to believe that IRA atrocities existed primarily in the pages of the British press. So no mention of the hundreds of ex-servicemen murdered; no mention of the many secret murders and burials; no mention of the campaign of terror against Cork Protestants.

Meanwhile, according to the Bourke thesis, the RIC had decided to defy their policing obligations to the Irish people. What a bunch of scoundrels: somebody should have taught them a good lesson or two.

Actually, somebody did. Over 500 RIC officers were killed between 1919 and 1921 by the IRA: we don't know the accurate figure because some were murdered and secretly buried. Half of the men killed were shot at home or while walking with their wives or sweethearts. The RIC had a strength of 9490 in 1919; in the following three years, aided by a twin campaign of terror and boycott, nearly 7500 men – about 80 per cent – resigned. Proper policing ceased throughout much of Ireland.

You cannot blame the victims, the RIC, for this, but the culprits, the IRA. Right across the country, police huts and barracks were abandoned, as the RIC retreated, abandoning their civilian duties, to be sure, but in general not defying them. They had no choice.

A moral disparity in the perception of the deeds of the time is one of prevailing characteristics of subsequent nationalist historiography. Michael Collins' ruthless use of pre-emptive murder attracts respect and admiration, but any possibility of the crown replying in kind is viewed as low and dastardly.

Thus, one of the standard 'justifications' of the Bloody Sunday massacre was that the so-called 'Cairo gang', was closing in on Collins. Now it is true that one man had been killed in operations by this group of intelligence officers – the blameless John Lynch, probably in mistake for Liam Lynch.

But murder was not at the time within their *modus operandi*. Consider, after all, the fate of three of Collins' senior intelligence – Liam Tobin, Frank Thornton and Tom Cullen, who were taken into police custody in October 1920. British intelligence unquestionably knew who they were, questioned them at length but didn't torture them, and in time released them. What would Collins have done to their British equivalents? It's not a hypothetical question; he provided the answer, on the morning of 21 November 1921.

Michael Collins introduced cold-blooded murder as a political weapon into Irish life. He proved that you could disrupt and intimidate society by such methods, but you couldn't create political institutions with them. Arbitration, negotiation, give and take: these are the currency of politics, which republicans abandoned for the bullet, and to which they had in time to return. And the lives meanwhile lost in the sordid struggle that followed were lost in vain; vast treasuries squandered about no good purpose; and the grief and the sorrow of thousands unaccompanied by any remotely proportionate reward.

Collins was an utter failure; a homicidal, dysfunctional buffoon who corrupted an entire generation of young men, yet achieved nothing for his epic exercises in blood-letting. Yet he has been sanctified and mythologized. Yearly Fine Gael, the party of law and order, mutter mumbo-jumbo about rededicating themselves to the values of Michael Collins. Which values? The values of shooting men in bed with their wives? The values of murdering unarmed men on buses? The values of giving guns to teenage boys and indoctrinating them in the ways of Cain?

All this could matter little if we weren't seeing a comparably grisly sancti-
fication being bestowed on the current leadership of Sinn Féin-IRA. But unlike
with Collins, the libel laws prevent the press from disclosing what we know about
these men: though most journalists are aware of the name of the now eminent
man who was responsible for Jean McConville's murder. Meanwhile, the moral
contamination of the peace process has elevated men we know to be merciless
killers into national folk heroes.

And so liberated from the ordinary rules of civilisation do the Shinners
feel that *An Phoblacht* recently published a photograph of four Sinn Féin TDs
– Sean Crowe, Aengus Ó Snodaigh, Martin Ferris and Caoimhín Ó Caoláin
– grinning alongside Martin Walsh, the killer of Detective Garda Jerry McCabe,
in Castlerea Jail.

When you tell lies about your history; when you blame the victims of terrorists for the fate that befell them; and when you exalt their killers; then sooner
or later you will wake up, and it will be too late. You will find elected politicians
cheerily consorting with the murderers of a good and honourable police officer.
That, now, is the abomination to which the peace process has reduced us.

[16 September 2002]

IV.7. The McCartney Sisters

Man, a bear in most relations – worm and savage otherwise –
Man propounds negotiations, Man accepts the compromise.
Very rarely will he squarely push the logic of a fact
To its ultimate conclusion in unmitigated act.

Thus Kipling in 'The Female of the Species', a poet our Shinner friends have no
time for, but not for his opinions on women. It was men who propounded the
peace process negotiations, men who accepted the compromise. It was men who
declined to push the logic of a fact to its ultimate conclusion in unmitigated act.

And it was men who coldly butchered Robert McCartney to death in Belfast,
because they thought they could: and it was women, the McCartney sisters, who
have pushed the logic of that fact to its ultimate conclusion in unmitigated act. For
women have greater moral courage than men: men hunt in packs and follow the
morality of the hierarch. Contrary to mythology, women do not form lynch mobs.
That is a male prerogative and a male instrument imposing male laws in male ways.

Men are physically braver than women, to be sure: women are poor racing
drivers and fighter pilots, and if you wanted to clear an enemy machine-gun nest

using female warriors, prepare for disappointment. But society does not function largely according to such requirements. It needs are more modest in scale, and more demanding of morality than mere mortal man can supply. Morality might be enforced by men, but it emanates from women. Even in outwardly male societies, where women go masked, the family ethic is established in the home by the mother.

It is the unwavering female desire to protect kin, even by association, which caused Jill Morell to campaign for John McCarthy during the long years of his captivity in Beirut, though the British Foreign office told her to go away and to stop being such a silly woman; the poor chap's dead. He wasn't; and nor was his co-tenant of a single radiator, Brian Keenan, whose name was kept alive in Ireland by the tireless campaigning of his sisters.

Physical courage is useless when faced with the mountain of getting up each day, and making the same phone calls, the same futile trips to the same government offices to meet the same bored officials, with their excuses and their scarcely concealed irritation, just as you did the day before, and the week before and the month before, just as you will the next day, and the next week, and the next month, for all the years to come.

No. What you need for that is moral courage, moral certainty, moral stamina, and moral focus.

> She is wedded to convictions – in default of greater ties;
> Her contentions are her children, Heaven help him who denies! –
> He will meet no suave discussion, but the instant white-hot wild
> Wakened female of the species warring as for spouse and child.

And in the case of the McCartneys' brother. Nearly thirty years ago, another band of women tried to bring the conflict in the North to an end, after the three Maguire children were killed by an IRA getaway car. They were bulled, jeered and harassed off the streets by the young men of Sinn Féin-IRA, assisted by a few females. But the sexes classically divided over the question of peace and war – and the men, with their physical bravery and their reverence for violence, catastrophically, won. We know with what results.

For Northern Ireland is a truly macho society – so much so that Brid Rogers and Iris Robinson aside, no woman has had any impact on political life since Bernadette McAliskey left the scene. Thus when peace came, it was through a classically male agreement, bereft of any morality, and steeped in an ethical compromise which enabled the Shinners to proceed just as they wanted. Forget Mo Mowlam: that cursing, vulgar creature was a she-male, imitating men without having the endocrinal wherewithal to do it successfully.

If Margaret Thatcher had been in Downing Street and Mary Harney had been in the Taoiseach's office, the steady drumbeat of murder, arms importations and ceasefire violations of the past decade would have been met with a stern, unbending response. The Shinners would have known that beneath those female breasts beat female hearts implacably opposed to the moral compromise that is the slippery slope to sewer rods, gouged-out eyes, cut throats, and an entire pub intimidated into silence.

That silence reached across the month of February, while Ireland busily pretended it had other preoccupations. No doubt the Northern Ireland Office hoped the murder would simply go away, as so many inconvenient IRA murders conveniently have. The Shinners must have thought that yet again they had won: but they reckoned without the dauntless moral courage of Paula, Catherine, Gemma, Claire and Donna, Robert's sisters.

Have you the least idea how much resolve those women had to possess to organise an anti-IRA rally in the Short Strand, under the very noses of the men who beat and slashed their brother to death? I have absolutely no idea whether the savage slaying of this unfortunate man will be a turning point in our affairs: but I do know that their remorseless pursuit of justice is a reminder that no deal can work unless it contains a moral heart. For ethics is the glue of all societies. It is learned in the female institution of the home, not in the male institution of the school. We had a peace deal without women, and therefore without ethics: and now we know with what abysmal results.

[3 March 2005]

IV.8. Suicide Bombers, 7/7 and 1990

The convenient fiction of recent times has been that the London suicide bombings of 7/7 were the first in the UK, and never you worry, chaps; the stiff upper lip is back, and we're not going to back down before such terrorism! Well, actually, chaps, the British have already experienced suicide bombings, and back down they bloody well did.

For back in 1990 the IRA dabbled in suicide bombing, though not quite on the London model, which at least has the merit that that those intending to kill also intend to die: the IRA's variation on the theme was the involuntary suicide bomber. In October 1990, terrorists made poor Patsy Gillespie drive a lorry-bomb into a British army vehicle checkpoint outside Derry city, where it was detonated – presumably by remote control – killing five soldiers.

The afternoon before the attack, Martin McGuinness and his brother had arrived at the checkpoint, and started shouting and slamming the car-doors. The guard was stood-to, which might – had they been interested in such things – enabled the two men to count the number of soldiers on duty. Needless to say, the attack some hours later was wholly coincidental and utterly unrelated to the events of the afternoon. That same evening the IRA volunteered another involuntary suicide bomber to enjoy the pleasures of dying for Ireland, when James McEvoy was forced to drive his lorry-bomb to a VCP outside Newry, where it exploded. A young Irish Catholic soldier of the Royal Irish Regiment, Cyril Smith, sacrificed his life saving his comrades.

The Islamic suicide bomber chooses to die, with 74 virgins waiting to tend to his every need. However, Patsy and James had rather more prosaic concerns: they were told their families would be butchered unless they obeyed IRA orders. Nothing – apart from a patch of beard – was found of Patsy's body. James, miraculously, survived with extensive injuries, but only briefly: a broken man, he died of 'natural causes' a few months later.

So. Let us consider. How did the governments of Ireland and Britain treat the organisation that brought the UK its first suicide bombers? Did they sonorously intone about never surrendering to terrorism? Did they hound it to extinction? Did they agree that it must be repressed, whatever the cost, and no matter the means?

No they did not. Instead, they made the Unionist population of Northern Ireland share power with the representatives of the organisation responsible for these suicide bombings. Thus the man who had so coincidentally been at the VCP in Derry, eight years later became the Minister for Education, responsible for teaching the schoolchildren of the province – amongst other things – to count. Moreover, the British government unconditionally freed all IRA prisoners and provided the suicide bomber organisation's representatives offices in the Palace of Westminster. Why, it even gave the IRA money, though the latter ran – and runs – the largest criminal conspiracy in Ireland.

Did the authors of the UK's first suicide bombings do anything in exchange? Did they declare that their terrorist war was over, did they cease to recruit and train and organise terrorist operations against the British, or disarm and disband? Absolutely not. Indeed, they systematically broke their word whenever it suited them. Did nationalist Ireland accordingly shun these killers? No: quite the reverse. There are no more welcome guests in the Department of the Taoiseach than the groomed and grinning reptiles of the IRA. And now, ten years on, and we're still hearing government-sponsored bilge about the imminence of IRA decommissioning.

Appeasement is a seamless robe: thus we heard the Taoiseach the other week querulously remind any would-be suicide bombers that Ireland is non-aligned. Of course – why not? – for non-alignment is the absolute guarantee that you will not be bombed! Bali in Indonesia was not aligned. Tanzania was not aligned. Kenya was not aligned. And that saved them from Al Qaeda terrorist attacks, didn't it? And look at the happy example of Spain, and how it benefited from its gallant de-alignment after the Madrid bombings!

Hold on. Now that I come to think about it, were not hundreds of blameless Indonesians blown apart in Bali? Were not scores of hapless Africans explosively despatched to kingdom come in Nairobi and Dodoma? And Spain's reward for capitulating to Al Qa'eda? Why, it is now in a permanent state of terrorist alert.

And so on these islands we have now finally arrived at the time of steel, and the dawn of a long existential struggle, when we might have to fight tenaciously for Western European values of democracy, law, sovereignty and, most of all, tolerance of whom we disapprove, but only those who tolerate our disapproval. Or shall we allow the brainless high priests of campus-multiculturalism, with all their blithering mumbo-jumbo, to delude us into tolerating the imams of jihad and mullahs of bigotry? Survival of our culture means that there can be no room for ambiguity, no penumbra between the light of law and the dark of terrorism.

But how can we expect such vital realism from our pathologically Laodicean political class, which did not condemn Trevor Sargent's address at a rally backing the terrorist insurgency against Iraq's democratic government? In other countries such a disgraceful deed would mark the man as a complete knave or an irredeemable buffoon, and either way, utterly unelectable: but here in Appeasement Central, he's actually a party leader. So in this intellectually and morally enfeebled culture, with those responsible for protecting our Constitution boastfully consorting with its sworn enemies, what meaningful action against terrorism can we seriously expect?

[19 July 2005]

IV.9. Internment

It is quite amazing how reverence for the Easter Rising enables intelligent, well-informed men to marshal the facts, to analyse them carefully, and then come to the directly opposite conclusion than the evidence indicates. Take Barry Andrews TD – who clearly knows something of our history – who accused Joe Lynch, a writer to this newspaper, of belittling Fianna Fáil when he said that the party had 'crushed traditional republicanism by harassment, draconian laws, imprisonment and executions'. Belittle? Barry should have proudly accepted Joe Lynch's words. Not to be draconian in the face of armed fascism at a time of war is to be terminally frivolous.

Barry recalled the consequences of de Valera's clemency towards armed republicanism. Two IRA men, who had been released by the government in a gesture at reconciliation, promptly murdered two gardaí, no doubt as an eccentric way of saying thank you. Barry did not name any of the men. The two gardaí who were cut down with Thompson sub-machine gunfire at point-blank range were Detective Hyland and Sergeant McKeown. Their killers were Tommy Harte and Patrick McGrath, later shot by firing squad, who were only at liberty because of the good offices of de Valera; two of his good officers paid the price.

This might suggest that Barry Andrews was leading us round to the concept that political violence in Ireland is counter productive, and that nothing whatever is gained by further glorification of an unmandated insurrection of ninety years ago, especially since it caused such calamitous loss of life. But no: he goes in the opposite direction. He justifies the revival of celebrations to mark the 1916 Rising.

So why does he consider the murder of two armed gardaí in 1939 unacceptable, and the murder of two unarmed DMP in 1916, Constables Lahiff and O'Brien, acceptable? What part of the killing of these latter men is morally justified? The Easter Rising was not a mythic event. It was a real event in which hundreds of people died. No vote was taken at any level that it should happen, outside a tiny coterie of the Irish Republican Brotherhood. How can democrats draw inspiration from such means, and such appalling consequences?

The lesson from Irish history is that any appeasement of armed republicanism merely whets its appetite. The British allowed most of their captives after 1916 to go free, unconditionally (a rather different method of dealing with armed insurgents than would have been practised by the insurgents' gallant allies, one feels). Did this clemency soften republican aspirations? The very reverse. One of those released was Michael Collins. The price the British paid for this folly was rather similar to that de Valera's government was to pay 20 years' later.

Ed Molony's *Secret History of the IRA* is easily the best account of the IRA's role in the most recent Troubles. One of the points which he raises – but sadly does not pursue – is that the primary reason for the revival of the IRA's fortunes after 1975 was not the oft-cited release of Gerry Adams from jail, but the unconditional ending of internment. Before that, the IRA in Ardoyne was down to a couple of men. With internment ended, the IRA ranks rapidly refilled.

So what was the point of ending internment? To be sure, this satisfied the demands of two constituencies, those of nationalist Ireland, north and south, and the liberal-left human rights lobby. But neither faction then urged nationalists to support the RUC, by recruitment and information, as a *quid pro quo*. In other words, this was the kind of appeasement that the British had tried in 1919, as did de Valera (briefly) in 1939. The result was the same: a steep increase in bloodshed.

Yet by 1975, there were no 'innocent' internees, loyalist or republican. All internees drilled and obeyed paramilitary orders. So who could possibly gain from their release? Only the movements to which they belonged, but certainly not the causes of peace, harmony, civility, freedom and democracy.

The introduction of internment in August 1971 – brutal, one-sided, stupid – was a catastrophe. However, by 1975, internment had crippled the IRA over much of the North. But the British then opened the floodgates of the Maze and out poured hundreds of well-trained terrorists, back into the ranks of the IRA. Twenty years later – TWENTY YEARS – the same amount of time between the British unconditionally and idiotically releasing their IRA prisoners and de Valera doing the same – the IRA went on ceasefire.

Now, this cannot be described as a successful management of a terrorist insurgency. Moreover, the luxury of hindsight reveals that the interweaving green and pink strands of Irish nationalism and the civil liberties lobby protected the rights of IRA terrorists, and wilfully, obscenely, and murderously ignored those of their hundreds of victims. Many of the worst atrocities to come – most notably the La Mon massacre in which 12 Protestants were incinerated by IRA bombs – were perpetrated by former internees.

All of those prisoners pouring out of the Maze in the mid 1970s to report back for duty in the ranks of the IRA would have regarded the Easter Rising as the moral authorisation for what they were about to do over the coming two decades of misery and bloodshed. Only the selectively amnesiac would now seek to sanitise and acclaim that moral authorisation, for the Easter Rising was quite the worst and most undemocratic event in Irish history in the twentieth century, and the very inspiration for so much heartbreak and suffering, then and ever since.

[4 November 2005]

IV.10. Disbanding the Northern Irish Regiment

Almost beyond parody, with the IRA intact, its proceeds from the Northern Bank still in its coffers, its intelligence files enriched by the Castlereagh raid, its arms dumps bulging, and with the destruction of RUC Special Branch complete, the British government now obliges it by disbanding the Royal Irish Regiment.

Yet contrary to virtually every single breathless analysis on the airwaves, even more abysmally moronic than usual, the IRA has offered neither to disband nor disarm. For disposing of *some* weaponry is not disarming. You cannot be part virgin, and you cannot be part armed.

So here it is. The IRA is not going away, and neither is its careful use of language. For example, whenever the IRA wants to say 'all', it says 'all', as in 'All IRA units': whenever it doesn't want to say 'all', well, it doesn't, as in the rest of that sentence: 'have been ordered to dump arms'. So, some arms will be dumped, but not all. And contrary to the implication that 'dump' implies waste material about to be disposed of, this is how the OED defines the noun 'dump' in the military context: 'The site of a store of provisions, ammunition, equipment, etc, *deposited for later use*' (my italics).

Now, of course, some of these dumps will be disposed of under the beady eye of a Canadian ex-general (who has been enjoying the retirement from hell) and a couple of obliging, tail-wagging ecumenical peace-process dog collars, but others will not. Why? Because the Provisional IRA owes its existence to the nationalist calamities of 1969 in Belfast, and the graffiti covering the walls of nationalist ghettoes subsequently declared: IRA = I Ran Away. The Provisionals are no more going to disarm totally than become Beefeaters in the Tower of London.

These particular Troubles are over, to be sure, but they could have been ended a decade earlier if the security forces of this Republic had assisted in the closure of the IRA's operational base in South Armagh. Instead, we pursued security policies of a diseased and cowardly querulousness. Thus for 30 years Slab Murphy's farm complex straddling the border was a major terrorist and smuggling base, well known to soldiers and police, from where he openly mocked the rule of law and scorned all notion of civilisation.

In 1986 Murphy even had the unspeakable gall to sue for compensation for damage allegedly done to his house by an IRA bomb that killed two British soldiers. (My, I bet that explosion came as a big surprise to him.) Nearby and not long afterwards, a soldier and two policemen were killed in a landmine blast. One of the RUC men was Bill Laurence, a young Catholic and former GAA man from County Down who had chosen the path of law and civilisation above the call of the tribe. He bequeathed all his effects to Mother Teresa.

Some weeks later, five IRA attackers were seen fleeing into Slab Murphy's cross-Border complex. Guided by an army helicopter, some British soldiers entered the property from its Northern side. They saw two civilians, and a Scots Guardsman, Private Robinson, moved towards them, inadvertently crossing into the Republic. The two men grabbed him and held him, as gardaí arrived. Far from arresting the terrorist-suspects, they arrested Private Robinson and hauled him off to that bastion of IRA intelligence, Dundalk Garda station where he was held for six hours. The occupants of the Murphy farm were neither questioned nor arrested.

What an utter triumph for pedantic jurisdictionism at its most diseased! Lives were daily being lost in a brutal terrorist war, yet gardaí were meanwhile on their knees with tape-measures, trying to determine which was north and which was south of the Border running through the most evil terrorist-complex in Europe. So what possible chance was there of ever defeating the IRA in South Armagh, if by moving a single foot, IRA men were immediately protected by the Republic's law, and by moving that same foot, Northern security forces would be arrested and detained by An Garda Síochána?

The melancholy truth is that from its centre, this state lacked the political will to strangle armed republican terrorism in its heartland; instead, it chose a policy of abject appeasement, now known as 'the peace process'.

Eight years ago last Sunday week, James Morgan a 16-year-old Catholic boy set out to hitchhike from Newcastle to Castlewellan, County Down. He was picked up by loyalist terrorists, who, discovering his religion, savaged him with a hammer. They then took James to a ghastly sink-hole, traditionally used to dispose of dead farm animals. Having finally beaten this boy to death there, they set fire to his corpse, before immersing it amid the rotten cadavers.

One of James Morgan's killers, Norman Coopey, was sentenced to life imprisonment for murder in 1999. The following year, he was released under the utterly squalid terms of the Belfast Agreement.

A society is not made by an accord that can allow such filth back into society: nor can peace be constructed from a culture in which killers are acclaimed, as they are today in West and North Belfast, while the kin of victims – such as those of poor, brave forgotten Bill Laurence or Jim Morgan – silently and invisibly grieve. So who can say what long-term damage has been done to Ireland's moral health through the failure of this state to enforce its law, and most of all, its order, over republican terrorism? We have been steadily injecting poison into our veins: and in time it will reach our very heart.

[3 August 2005]

IV. 11. Pardons for Executed Irish

No doubt Senators Brian Hayes, Fine Gael, and Paschal Mooney mean well when they asked the Northern Secretary Peter Hain for pardons for the executed Irish of the Great War. But pardons change nothing – moreover, Irish-alone pardons would contribute to that tiresome sense of historical victimhood that now is surely due for retirement in The Sunset Home for Outmoded Attitudes.

Irish soldiers might well have been executed in disproportionately large numbers. I don't know. I do know that the allies and their enemies were fighting total war. It was one of the most utterly barbaric episodes in human history, and to go back into history and administer the grace of political absolution to 26 Irish soldiers amid the millions of dead is faintly grotesque.

In recent times, we have come to grasp a far firmer picture of the catastrophe of this time, thanks to the work of Irish amateur historians. One of these is James W. Taylor, who produced an outstanding history of the 1st Battalion, Royal Irish Rifles, and has followed it up with the equally splendid history of the 2nd Battalion of the same regiment.

An index reference in the most recent book takes us one of the most out-rageous court-martials of the entire war, that of 21-year-old Private Patrick Downey of the Leinster Regiment. He had failed to follow an order to fall in on parade, and then refused to put on his cap when his officer told him to. Poor Downey was court-martialled, and the presiding officer, his own commanding officer, decided that the volunteer soldier should be shot because morale in the unit was poor. The officer in question was Captain Robert Otway Mansergh, of Rock Lodge, Ballyhooley, County Cork, kinsman of Brian Hayes and Paschal Mooney's colleague in the Seanad, Senator Martin Mansergh. Maybe they should have a word with him.

What was done to Patrick Downey was, by any standards, murder. It was a time of murder. Last weekend, the Sinn Féin IRA celebratory blood-fest moved its sordid caravan to Kilmichael to celebrate the massacre of 17 Auxiliary police officers there in 1920. Reasonable people who have read Peter Harte's account of the Kilmichael ambush cannot doubt that many if not most of the Auxiliaries killed at Macroom were shot after they surrendered. No one can be in any doubt about the fate of Cadet Guthrie, who escaped the ambush and had nearly reached sanctuary in Macroom where he was picked up by the IRA, interrogated for two long days, and then shot before being secretly buried in Annahala bog. And nor can anyone be in any doubt about Cadet H. Forde, who survived massive head injuries, and spent the rest of his life as a drooling, epileptic quadraplegic.

Nor indeed can there be any doubt about the fate of two police officers of the Macroom detachment – both ex-soldiers: Thomas Walsh of Dublin and Lionel Mitchell from Somerset – who had earlier been taken off the Macroom train by the IRA, interrogated (whatever horror is thereby implied), murdered and secretly buried. Their bodies have never been recovered.

Now is anyone going to propose retrospective benedictions upon these nineteen dead victims and one vegetative victim of the IRA, murdered 85 years ago last weekend? Is anyone going to insist that the Irish government say that they were unjustly killed or unjustly turned into cabbages with fits, but dear God, one hopes, with no sense of self? And is anyone going to say anything about the 77 anti-Treaty IRA men executed by the Free State government in the course of the Civil War? The government can hardly be expected to pardon them, because the dead were, so to speak, its own men.

No sense can be made of any of this – for sense is impossible when people propose irreconcilable projects as being complementary ones. You cannot 'pardon' some executed war dead and not others. Nor can you rummage around in history and re-order it to suit your contemporary requirements. For if retroactive rearrangements of history were possible, those of us who wear the poppy would certainly reach back in time and undo the Somme, Ypres and Gallipoli. We detest the reason for the poppy. But republicans, both the kneecapping variety and Martin Mansergh's lot, are proud of the Easter Rising. They don't commemorate it. They celebrate it. Not for them the rearrangement of history that would mean no Rising. Hell, they *love* the bloody thing.

No doubt the Shinners were quietly celebrating the massacre at Kilmichael last Sunday, and no doubt soon they will be having annual celebrations at Narrow Water. But as they have drawn a prudent veil over the butchery of Protestants not far from Kilmichael eighteen months after the massacre of the Auxies, I imagine another veil is being woven to conceal the 14 Protestants fried alive in a napalm attack at La Mon in 1978, and the 14 dead at Enniskillen, and nine dead at Frizzell's fish shop and the … no, no, not again, not another list of IRA atrocities.

But somehow or other, such lists seem to be necessary, because if people like me don't supply them, who will? For I am with the good senators in one regard: the proposed capitulation to Sinn Féin-IRA by the British government on the issue of on-the-runs is quite shameful. Moreover, it is actually part of a wider republican programme to rewrite history, and thereby exclude its own vast litany of war crimes. That is why the senators are wrong to seek a pardon for our boys executed by firing squad. Leave history there as it lies, in all its sordid horror.

[31 November 2005]

IV.12. Education in the North

Perhaps the greatest and perhaps even defining feature of Irish political culture is its central *laissez-fairism*: leaving well alone. This was bred into the DNA of the Free State which had inherited so many existing institutions – such as schools and hospitals – from the British days, and since most were run by the Catholic Church, there was neither the political courage nor the appetite to subvert existing authority.

This deference thereby curtailed the normally powerful interfering instincts of those who govern. This is quite unlike the obsessive, centralised control-freakery that two world wars and the creation of a ruinous welfare state have helped create within British political culture. Busybodyism is its now defining feature, personified by the wretched duopoly resident in Downing Street, who believe that there is nowhere that the state should not be interfering, no conversation it should not be eavesdropping on, no thought it should not be shaping. This is the diseased mentality that recently saw an Irish student actually being charged with a hate crime because he asked a mounted policeman if his horse was gay.

Mix that busybodyist culture with the poisonous and arbitrary authoritarianism of Sinn Féin–IRA, and what you get is the ghastly hybrid, the demented griffon that is education policy in Northern Ireland. Throughout thirty years of Troubles, the grammar schools of the North were the bright shining stars that helped navigate ten of thousands of pupils safely away from the sirens of violence to the shores of civility, education and self-advancement. And now the demented griffon wants to kill those schools.

The griffon was sired in Martin McGuinness's last minutes in office, as the Executive was brought down by his Sinn Féin–IRA colleagues in the Provisionals' intelligence department. It was not agreed policy by the Executive. It was not even discussed. And paradoxically, it was the very terrorist instincts of the Provisionals that gave him the chance to destroy the greatest educational institutions on this land, for his departing fiat could not then be overturned by an Executive that his chums had, in essence, destroyed.

The final signature of a departing terrorist-warlord should have no more power over a constitutional politician than a Brazilian butterfly's wing-beat upon the path of a migrating Arctic ice floe – but that is to ignore the busybodyist instincts of British politics, as represented by the Northern Secretary Peter Hain. He has taken time from preening his distinguished greying temples before the mirror, not to throw the McGuinness fiat into the waste bin as he should have done, but to implement it as policy.

Pure, unadulterated ideological madness: busybodyism at its most demented, and worse, at its most irresponsible. Schools are like ancient salad bowls that convey a unique memory of garlic into every generation of lettuce that is tossed in them. It is just about impossible to make a new school as good. Old schools have survived through Darwinian principles; by retaining the best habits and traditions, tested over time, they will know in their corporate bones what is good for their students individually and corporately. Yet for all their strengths, you can destroy them in a moment, as scores of superb English grammar schools were by that lunatic Shirley Williams 30 years ago.

No one supports the permanent separation of pupils at 11, nor the creation of second-tier education for the less academically gifted. The task for any education minister is not to destroy what works, but to fix what doesn't. And the grammar schools of Northern Ireland work better perhaps than any comparable educational system in Europe, for no students anywhere have had to contend with such trying circumstances.

Working-class accents are almost unknown in universities in the Republic. They are commonplace in Queen's University Belfast and the University of Ulster. Indeed, Northern Ireland's grammar schools are responsible for creating probably the most upwardly mobile working class in the entire EU. This is the system the Hain-McGuinness griffon wishes to destroy, and put in its place a post-code selecting process to match pupil with new comprehensive schools.

This is precisely the hypocritical system which that contemptible caste, the Islington socialists, favour: they cluster in a single area where only the rich and privileged can afford to live, and of course, their local comprehensive school contains only the children of the upper classes. Meanwhile, in the London equivalent of Ballymurphy or Ardoyne, intelligent, ambitious working-class pupils are held back by the aggressive indigenous cultures of boastful failure and gang violence that are endemic in British sink-schools. The same will inevitably happen in Northern Ireland, except that the gangs will go by the names UVF, IRA and UDA.

With a Bangor in each of his bailiwicks, no doubt the Northern/Welsh Secretary gets a little confused: I daresay he often studies his in-tray and wonders sighingly if he will ever master the intricacies of Sinn Cymru or Plaid Fein. Possibly he expects to hear male voice choirs in the Coalisland and Llurgan Valleys. All very confusing.

Prudent pro-consuls on the edges of the Roman empire did not attempt to govern, but merely administered, interfering as little as possible in the traditions of the natives. Peter Hain is now guarding the marches of the last remnant of the British Empire, a poisoned chalice made more deadly by the depraved appeasement of terrorists and their incorporation, with their murderous and unrepentant ethos intact, into the body politic. But the destruction of those educational bulwarks that have stood against total tribal war down the decades will be perhaps the most enduring evil that the peace process has yet wrought.

[19 January 2006]

V. Wheels

V.1. Driving Test

It would be logical – would it not? – to assume that when the 100,000 people in the Republic waiting to sit their driving tests are finally tested, there will accordingly be 100,000 new and unaccompanied drivers on the road. Ah; would that it were that simple. Drivers with provisional licences can already get into a car on their seventeenth birthday and drive away, though they possess the automotive skills of a dog, have the eyesight of a mole, and the intelligence of a car-jack. Merely the possession of a provisional licence, for which no test whatsoever is required, enables anyone to sit behind the wheel of a ton or two of moving metal and vanish into the wild blue yonder or the casualty wing of St Vincent's Hospital.

'It is highly irresponsible of the deputy to suggest that, because a person holds a provisional licence, there is a danger to people travelling on the road,' puffed Bobby Molloy indignantly the other day to Brian Hayes TD, who had had the outrageous temerity to suggest that having so many unqualified drivers on the road was having a detrimental effect on road safety. Well spoken Minister! Stand by the right of the untested, the untrained, the unskilled, the unqualified to be free to drive however they want on our roads. To suggest that driving requires specially learned techniques that are difficult to master is clearly absurd.

We should all take a leaf from the book of the driver of a pickup truck who was recently (and by our standards wholly wickedly) arrested by police in the Argentinian city of Trelew. He was completely blind. However, he had the visual skills of his 13-year-old daughter in the passenger seat to assist him. 'The blind man was driving fairly well, although he made some pretty abrupt manoeuvres, which attracted the attention of a patrol car,' a police spokesman said.

I see. And this is what passes for freedom in Argentina, is it? A chap can't go out driving with his daughter without the heavy hand of the fuzz descending on the shoulder? Caramba! Thank God we order these things better in Ireland, and have done ever since that golden day 20 years ago when Sylvester Barrett, Bobby Molloy's illustrious predecessor, blazed a path for liberty by declaring that anyone who had had two provisional licences could claim a full licence without doing a test. That is to say, people who had repeatedly sat tests, and who had scared generations of testers into gibbering witlessness by their utter and incontrovertible proof that they were incapable of driving, were, without more ado, now entitled to drive unaccompanied.

So Prudence Entwhistle, that venerable granny from Kingstown who had first yearned to drive when watching the Gordon Bennett rally in 1903, and had been sitting tests since the time gels got the vote, failing every year since, suddenly realised her hour had come. She could leave behind her that unfortunate collision involving a crocodile of girls from Holy Child Killiney (but how pretty the massed wreaths had looked!). And the unlucky occasion when she'd chosen reverse instead of first and had backed into the day-trip of the pensioners from the Kingstown and District Presbyterian Sewing Club, crushing five – now mere history! And as for the time when the driving instructor had vaulted out of the car, even though they were bowling along at 70 m.p.h. northward on the southbound lane of the Naas dual carriageway? Lord, how she laughed. Prudence's heirs are everywhere to this day, and they have, thank God, their defender in Bobby Molloy. The freedom-loving spirit of Sylvester Barrett and Prudence Entwhistle still informs so much of our attitude to roads and driving. We still erect road signs that employ two measurement systems, metric for distance and imperial for speed, but sell cars whose meters measure distance in imperial only. About half of our drivers think the outside lane is for having a good natter in, with maybe the possibility of a right turn in about 20 miles, oops, 38 kilometres, meanwhile continuing the conversation with the hand gestures of a Neopolitan knitter.

Fully 10 per cent of drivers either think that signalling on roundabouts is a frivolous waste of energy, or even worse, they indicate in the wrong direction (the most common error being to indicate left simply because one inevitably turns left on entering the roundabout, and then leaving the indicator on during the jolly circumnavigation that follows).

A vast body of laws seem never to be enforced at all. How many JCBs have roadplates on? If they are not registered to be on the road, they cannot then in law be insured. When has any JCB making its stately passage down the centre of the road, without road tax or insurance, ever been stopped and its driver prosecuted? When has the cheery dumper truck that zips platelessly all over the President's highway ever been flagged to the side of the road and its operator been given a touch of the Argentinian treatment?

Never. It doesn't happen. We live in Barrettland, its principles of freedom stoutly defended to this day by Bobby Molloy. By Jove, sir, it makes you proud. And sometimes dead.

[30 April 1999]

V.2. They Drive Porches, Don't They?

Prudence Entwhistle sat in the sun-room at her home in Kingstown, gazing at the sunlight on the glittering waters of Dublin Bay – or rather, she would have done if somebody hadn't built a block of flats in the way when she, Primrose and their brother Cuthbert had been off shrimping in Bognor Regis. Now a tower of windows gazed down upon her little Regency home.

No matter. She had seen the waters of Dublin Bay on ten thousand evenings, and in more tranquil and leisured times than these! She cast her mind back to when they would all cram excitedly into Bertie Protheroe's Daimler and Algie Blenkinsop's Alvis and would absolutely zoom off to the Featherstonehaughs in Greystones or Jed and Clemmie Hackett's place in Queen's County.

Poor Jed. Bought it on the retreat from Mons. His brother Nigel was gassed at Ypres. Algie copped it on the Somme. Even Clemmie went west – sunk in the *Leinster* just out there ... Prudence's eyes opened to search the glittering seas for a last glimpse of the *Leinster* vanishing beneath the waves, its propellers churning futilely in the air. But of course neither she nor the sea were there, only the tower block of flats, with those strange low cars without roofs parked outside in the car park. They were named after part of a house. Verandah, was it?

'Sherry, Pru?' quavered an elderly voice beside her.

'Bless my soul, how you startled me!' cried Prudence to her sister Primrose. 'I do wish you wouldn't do that. I was looking at that beastly building there, and those horrid, horrid cars, what do you call them -window-sills is it? – and thinking of those happy days when we could see the sea. Yes, I'd love a sherry. Where's Cuthbert?'

'In the WC,' said Primrose, mouthing so that no one could hear. 'Trouble again with the waterworks.'

'There's no need to mime, dear, there's only the three of us, and my water-works are no longer the force they once were, alas.' Waterworks. Her mind suddenly raced back to a day long ago, when she and Algie Blenkinsop had slipped into the bushes during a soiree in in the viceregal lodge and he had kissed her and had run his hand up her leg and she hadn't stopped him and then he had …

'Are you having a sherry dear?' asked Primrose. 'We have some of the Dry Fly here, I think, or perhaps a touch of that rather nice Findlater's own sherry, perfectly good to my mind.'

'I think I'll have the Findlater's, if you please,' as the memory came back to her of one of the Findlater boys taking her by the hand behind the rocks near Seapoint. He had raised his finger to his lips. Shhh, he mimed. He didn't need to. She knew what she wanted. Such a warm day too. How could she have been so confident that they would not be disturbed? And they weren't, either. The Findlaters. One lost in Gallipoli, the other on the Somme. Handsome boys, rogues the pair of them. She smiled as the memory of two young men lodged in her memory like a hot-water bottle in a cool bed.

There was the sound of distant flushing, followed by an agitated shuffle as Cuthbert approached. 'Have we any Angostura, Prim, dear?' asked Prudence. 'Cuthbert's allowed back on the sauce tonight, and he has been such a good boy. He really does deserve his pink gin this evening.' What was the name of the car? Balcony?

The door burst open, in as much as any door being propelled by a centenarian is ever capable of such explosive movement. Cuthbert was clutching the evening newspaper, the one that they were obliged to take now that the *Evening Mail* had mysteriously vanished, and brandishing it joyfully.

'The trams,' he cried. 'They're back! Glory be!'

'The trams, dear? I don't think so. That Mr Andrews got rid of them ages ago.' Hearths?

'No, it says so here in the newspaper. They're going to reintroduce the trams! I always knew it! I knew once the plain ordinary decent Irish people got their senses back, they'd see the error of their ways. Served with 'em in the trenches. Salt of the earth. Just need a touch of firm leadership and they'll follow you to the ends of the earth, rifles in their hands.'

'Pink gin, Cuthbert?' said Primrose, adding: 'Luas, isn't it?'

'No, not the Lewis, that was the machine-gun. I meant Lee-Enfield. Pink gin would be topping. Don't you see? This is just the beginning. Trams one day, viceregal lodge the next, the King on the stamp next, back into the Empire the following day, you mark my words. Chin chin,' he said, raising his drink.

'I rather think those days are past,' said Primrose sadly.

'Never,' declared Cuthbert. 'We'll see the Grand Fleet sail into that harbour one day now, and not a day too soon.'

Prudence stayed silent. They could bring back the trams, and they could rename this place Kingstown, but it would make no difference. Not merely was their Ireland dead and buried long ago, but so too now was the one that had replaced it. An entirely novel Ireland was even now uncontrollably taking shape on this island, one she knew nothing whatever about, except that it zoomed around in strange cars.

'Porches,' she said suddenly. 'They drive porches.'

[5 August 2000]

V.3. The Garda Press Office

It seems I've been writing about the needless death toll on our roads since Mercedes first met Benz. In that time, the numbers killed have remorselessly risen, and we seem utterly unwilling to stop it. At the most obvious level, in our policing and in our courts, we are failing. We are failing the dead, those about to die and all their families as they plummet into the worst days of their lives. Eddie Shaw, chairman of the National Safety Council, recently told an Oireachtas committee of the wholly unnecessary death toll: 144 killed and 1200 injured.

God knows how he got those statistics. A rather simpler statistic was provided by Assistant Garda Commissioner Edward Rock: that there were 9050 drink-driving arrests up to September 30 this year. A nice round figure, as it happens, because that means there were a fraction over 1000 arrests a month, or 250 a week. Which comes to 9.6 per county per week. Or, if you like, 1.4 arrests per day per county. Or better still, one arrest for drunk-driving every seventeen hours, per county.

When I wrote on the absence of visible policing on the N81 last January, Superintendent Kevin Donoghoe of the Garda Press Office in a letter to this paper offered what the poor fellow apparently ploddishly imagined was a rebuttal. He said, 'The roadway in question stretches a total of 55 kilometres and is policed, both covertly and overtly, by a number of Garda districts and units 24 hours a day. For the year 2004, the total number of Garda checkpoints on this roadway was 462.'

In other words, 1.26 roadblocks per day over fully 55 kilometres – that included them all, visible and invisible. And I'd be surprised if each one lasted much over an hour. Let's be generous: allow an hour and a half per roadblock. In other words, out of the nearly 11,100 hours of 2004, the N81 had roadblocks deployed for around just 693 of them; thus the N81 had no roadblocks on it for 93 per cent of the time.

Superintendent Donoghoe also triumphantly declared, as if it were some astounding vindication, that there had been some 35 drink-driving arrests on the N81 in 2004 – or, if you like, just one for every thirteen roadblocks. Put another way, a drunk-driver was found on the entire 55-kilometre length of the N81 once every ten and a half days. My. What sober folk live in Wicklow.

Now these dismal figures are not the headline-making revelations of a brilliant investigative journalist, but the boastful declarations of the superintendent of the Garda Press Office. Yet instead of attacking me, as he did in a highly personal and dismally self-defeating letter, a more talented press officer than Superintendent Donoghue – and that is not hard to imagine – would have provided the real explanation for the lack of policing on the N81, namely, a lack of police. As I discovered when I needed An Garda Síochána earlier on this year, there simply weren't any officers available. Not even the most efficient individuals can be in five places at the one time, which is what is now expected of rural gardaí.

Let's look at the figures in a rather simplistic but nonetheless impressionistic way. There are 12,000 gardaí in Ireland. Excluding overtime, each works around 310 days a year. But it takes three gardaí working eight-hour shifts to provide a full 24-hour coverage per day. So in this abstract, there are only 4000 gardaí available for duty at any time, and taking into account annual leave, that works out at 3,400. But we have a population of over four million: which means there is a garda officer on duty for every 1200 of us: and every time a crash attracts the attentions of, say, 10 gardaí, 12,000 of us are left without any garda-cover at all.

In other words, we are so short of gardaí that you would have to be a desperately stupid or an astoundingly unlucky drunk-driver anywhere in Ireland to be caught by the guards. Thus large tracts of the country are now, even by the boastful declaration emanating from the Garda press office, effectively without policing. The result is that all over the country, drivers are getting tanked up and then weaving their home in the early hours, knowing they need little fear of roadblocks. And incredibly, many people apparently have to die before policy is changed. It needed a catastrophic series of fatal crashes in Donegal before a unit of the Garda Traffic Unit was finally established on the Inishowen Peninsula last month

But of course, as we know, people are sometimes caught drink-driving, as Vincent McCormick was last December, but only after he had killed two people – father of two, Martin Connor, and mother of three, Theresa Smith. The killer was so drunk that he had already unknowingly hit one other car, forcing it off the road.

McCormick briefly appeared before Roscommon Circuit Court last week, to receive a €1000 fine and a ten-year ban on driving, before walking free. No jail sentence, suspended or otherwise. This faithfully reflects the politically correct and bankrupt morality of our wretched state. To put this derisory punishment into perspective, a year ago two pub owners, Ronan Lawless and Kieran Levanzin were fined a total of €6400, with another €3000 in costs, merely for smoking on their own premises, and allowing others to do likewise. Drunkenly slaughter two innocent people: a €1000 fine. Light up a fag, effectively, the best part of a €5000 fine. Sick, sick, sick.

[2 November 2005]

V.4. The Red Cow Roundabout

The Red Cow Roundabout says all that we need to know about how Ireland is managed.

It takes incompetence and stupidity on a quite Olympian scale to blend traffic coming from the south, the east into and out of Dublin, and most traffic from the North to Munster, into the one circular system. Elsewhere, the standard rule is that the complete separation of vehicles moving in different directions is vital for efficient traffic management.

At the Red Cow, however, we put all such traffic into the one blender, so that even traffic going in opposite directions, and which should never touch, now manage to contribute to the jams obstructing one another.

Moreover, we mixed two different traffic-management systems. We combine the personal initiative-based roundabout with the command-based traffic light: like putting turf into a petrol engine.

We didn't do this on the Soloheadbeg–Fethard cow-track, which would have been bad enough: no, we did this on the busiest traffic exchange in the entire country, where traffic orbiting the capital, and entering from and going to the south, the north and the west, conjoin: nearly one million vehicles a week meeting at a football pitch.

It wasn't a totally unique experiment in structural cretinism: we did exactly the same for traffic going to Belfast, which has to compete for space on the same roundabout with traffic going to Dublin Airport. But the Red Cow Roundabout is the *piece de resistance* of state imbecility. The M50 has probably cost £1 billion: the Red Cow is the ha'p'orth of missing tar.

Most of us assumed that the Luas system was going to spare its travellers the Byzantine horrors of the RCR: that they would be immune to the traffic jams into which thousands of people have disappeared in recent years, never to be seen again. Wrong.

For now we know that the Luas trams are in fact going to enter the Red Cow Roundabout space-competition: and far from Luas reducing the delays at this vast folly, it will increase them.

The Luas will have to negotiate three lights each way at the roundabout, at three level crossings. Six in all, in and out, 70 seconds a time. And car drivers will park on and obstruct the tracks at the level crossings, because they're usually desperate to be free of this mad-cow roundabout.

We know this, just as we know that Irish lorry drivers are specially trained to enter those yellow boxes at rush hour when all exits from it are blocked, and stay there, picking their noses, just as gardaí are trained to turn their backs when they see this happen.

So to sneak any advantage, some Red Cow drivers will creep onto the tracks, and the trams might have to wait till the track is clear, possibly not once, but even thrice. Moreover, since the lights will be green for Luas for 70 seconds every two and a half minutes, road traffic on the most congested roundabout in the state will lose nearly half the time currently allocated to it. Listen to 'AA Roadwatch' and weep.

It gets better. Traffic from Dublin entering the M50 to go northwards – as hundreds of lorries from the industrial estates do – will face four traffic lights in about 200 circular yards. The icing on the roundabout cake is this: some 5000 extra lorries per day will soon enter the Red Cow system to reach the docks when Dublin City Tunnel opens, while the roundabout closes every two minutes or so to let a train through.

The Red Cow Roundabout is the Most Favoured Place of breakdown in Ireland, and it's also where people behave like Nazis. Never give space; never give way; jump the lights; sound the horn; yield not an inch. It's where the Celtic Tiger caught rabies.

And into this overcrowded cauldron of aggression and stupidity and frustration, the most congested roundabout in Ireland – and at vast capital cost – the state is introducing a light railway system. A jolly good idea. And since we're at it, put Busaras on the Red Cow Roundabout. And the new terminal for Dublin Airport. And the Bertie Bowl, and perhaps Houston Station as well.

The Luas project exemplifies everything about state projects. We bought trams years before they could be of use, since when they've been rusting in storage at – where else? – the Red Cow Roundabout: and meanwhile not earning a penny while we were paying for them.

The Americans got a man on the moon in the time we've spent on Luas, and it still isn't close to running.

And then you read the explanation – 'the decision on Luas was taken a long time ago, when maybe traffic levels were less'. Jesus Christ Almighty; that was supposed to be the bloody point of Luas – that it was intended to cope with future demand.

Now this would be bad enough if it were an exception: but it's not. It's the norm. Those who undertake any major state enterprise in this country seem to think that planning is something you need permission for and foresight is a saga on television.

Wherever we find government or political involvement anywhere in this country, at best we find incompetence and stupidity of Red Cow proportions: at worst we find corruption and criminality. The state's response to all this? Well, it's to transfer money confiscated from the citizens going gibberingly berserk at the Red Cow Roundabout into the pockets of lawyers, and then to carry on as before.

Wake me up someone. This nightmare's gone on long enough.

[5 June 2003]

V.5. LUAS on Stilts

Madam, – Your columnist has kindly vacated his normal space to allow me to dispose of the preposterous notion from the Minister – a Mister Brennan, I believe – that I should be raised on stilts when I finally reach the Red Cow Roundabout. Madam, I am a tram.

Nuns do not walk the high wire. Popes – unless they were once bishops of Galway – do not go to lap-dancing clubs. And trams do not go on stilts.

That is in our nature. We cannot help it. That we are – idiotically – being treated as non-trams, and being made to rush out from the centre of Dublin to the distant Red Cow Roundabout like some vulgar rapid transit system, doesn't diminish our essential tramness. I know whereof I speak, for I come from a along line of trams. And trams are trams, Madam – not buses, not trains, not undergrounds, not charabancs.

To be sure, we are not 'exclusive' in any snobbish sense about our identity. For example, our feelings about trains are cousinly. We would not actually engage in what you might call love-making, but we have been known to flirt, if you take my meaning. But as for buses, oh we loathe them. Always have. Promiscuous little hussies that go anywhere at any time. I have seen buses up country lanes, Madam, touting for business, their doors wide open for all to see within. Shocking but true. I trust I have not offended your delicate sensibilities.

Buses and trams are long since sworn enemies, and the history of transport is littered with accounts of the bloody battles between track and tyre. There was the famous Bradford & Bingley bus–tram war; the Inchicore & Clondalkin conflict, of tragic memory; the appalling massacre of Tramco, in which an entire section of McTramalds was butchered and damned by the treacherous Campbuses. And each November we gather to remember and honour those who have lost their grooves in the cause of tramdom.

The last post is sounded; electric arms are lowered; tracks weep; and the senior tram present intones: 'They shall not grow mould as we that are left grow mould …' In other words, Madam, we have our history and our sense of pride. And now we hear that Minister Brennan wishes us to clamber up stilts, and allow all and sundry see our underneaths. Madam, not even my husband has seen my underneath, and I have allowed my doctor to make his inspections there only through sheets, and in the presence of a lady tram of the Reformed Faith, with her electrical arm upraised lest he try to take liberties. The modern tram might wear the raiments of the twenty-first century, but in our hearts, we remain true to our Victorian origins. Unlike that good-time trollop the bus, all bench-seat and no suspension.

Yet we hear this Minister is so deluded with lust that we wishes to raise not one of us, but all of us – and many of us are unmarried ladies, our bogeys still untouched by oilcan – up in the air, so that he may gaze Where No Gentleman Should Ever Set His Eyes. One has to ask: what other indignities of an intimate variety has he in mind for us? I can assure him now, he is getting nowhere near my grooved underparts at the strangely named Red Cow Roundabout.

This intersection is the primary interchange between Limerick and Cork, Dublin, Dublin Airport, the north-eastern and the north-western seaboards and the Dun Laoghaire ferry port. When I first heard this, I assumed that the Red Cow Roundabout was a vastly complex traffic system, like Spaghetti Junction outside Birmingham.

However, because the agency responsible for 'masterminding' – and what pleasure that term gives me – the Red Cow Roundabout scheme bought me ages before I would possibly be used, I have had the time to give much thought to the subject of the Red Cow Garage. Why I was bought and paid for fully two years before I was earning any money? And why has Ireland made its prime national route less like Spaghetti Junction and more like macaroni cheese out of a tin?

Madam, it seems that this country has finally managed to create a twenty-first-century version of the West Clare Railway – and this at the height of your boom. It is of course your right to squander your riches as you may. But if you think your Minister is using this ineptitude as an excuse to get his grubby fingers on my armature brush, or to try stroking my step-down transformer while I am trying to rise above the Cork–Dublin, Belfast–Munster, Dun Laoghaire–Dublin Airport and Donegal–Wexford traffic, he has another think coming.

The stilts will protect me against such outrages, you may say. Madam, I know men. Once one has seen my underneath, there'll be no stopping him, the little pervert. He'll have ministerial ladders against the stilts, and in no time at all he'll be waving me down, wearing one of those big raincoats that his type go in for. And the moment I stop, he'll clamber aboard, his raincoat wide open, a big rapacious grin on his face as he … no, no, I cannot go on.

Madam, I appeal to you. Stop this obscenity now. Far from taking us out to the Red Cow Roundabout, the Minister should be turning most of us around in the centre of Dublin. The reason he isn't is because he has an unhealthy interest in my bottom.

Yours, et cetera, Luas Lane.

[24 September 2003]

V.6. Bridge Building with the NRA

Alas! – I have been unable to follow the exotic tale of Tom and his sister Ellen Roche and their legal dispute over their humble little family home in Blackrock, which went for €47 million last month. No doubt some of you have been worrying with me about who will foot their legal bill. Worry not: for rest assured, we will.

The Roche family sit on top of the Cement-Roadstone empire, which is a pleasant enough peak from which to view the world – but not nearly as pleasant as from the West-Link toll bridge, surely one of the most bizarre state-protected monopolies in all of Europe. The only way across the Liffey Valley outside Dublin's city centre is via the West-Link, along the state-owned M50. But instead of the state owning the entire length of the M50, it franchised out the final length connecting the bridge to the Roche family.

Building bridges is not difficult for most societies. The Nile – a somewhat mightier water-course than the Liffey – was first bridged in 2650 BC. The Romans built the 87-mile long aquaduct of Carthage from the springs of Zaghouan nearly 1900 years ago. The Lake Pontchartain causeway is 24 miles long. Closer to home, the Humberside suspension bridge is nearly a mile long.

So, though the Liffey Valley is a moderate hurley-puck over its width, this state decided it was simply unable to manage such a heroic feat and contracted the construction, the maintenance and the resulting tolls to the ill-named National Toll Roads, even as it built the motorways linking it to the rest of the world. This is utter nonsense. Without the state building the M50 to the bridge, the latter is useless: yet the state surrendered control of a stretch of the orbital system around the capital to a private company, not just once, but twice, when NTR were allowed to build a second bridge across the Liffey.

The tollbooths are an artificial and privatised bottleneck that cause immense disruption to traffic around Dublin, but for the Roche family they are an assurance of a vast Niagara of gold, no matter the outcome. The economist David McWilliams writing in *The Sunday Business Post* last weekend reports that it might cost the state €300 million to buy the Roche slab of concrete over the Liffey.

In other words, the state effectively owned a monopoly, which it surrendered to a company, which it is now buying back at huge expense. Does anyone understand this? Can anyone explain how such nonsense occurs? Is anyone in public office answerable for such a preposterous waste of government resources?

The answer to these questions is: no. When TDs tried to get to the bottom of how the National Roads Authority works, they failed. They found the NRA – No Reason Anywhere – unhelpful and arrogant. The NRA lives in a world of its own, one in which it is apparently answerable to no one, creating policies that are conjured out the very thin air of NRA cerebral activity, and which are utterly unrelated to reality.

Mankind discovered about 70 years ago that median crash barriers on motorways were essential to prevent horrific head-on crashes. Every country has learnt from that primary experience. Except us. Our NRA state agency decided to build motorways on which vehicles can freely cross over the central reservation – with the entirely predictable result of collisions with oncoming streams, and hideous results that are predictable to all but the geniuses in the NRA.

There's no point in asking the NRA state agency why, because you won't get an answer. I asked years ago why the signpost on the new access point on the orbital M50 merely pointed 'north' and 'south' without explaining to motorists what destinations lay north and south, and haven't got an answer yet. The enigmatic sign remains in place.

The motorway system linking Munster with Leinster and Ulster has been built without restaurants, petrol stations or public toilets. Those that exist pre-date the implementation of NRA's plans. Thus – and I have written about this before, many, many times – when travelling on the N7 northwards, the petrol station just before Kill in Kildare is the last you will encounter before you reach the Border nearly one hundred miles away.

The NRA's policy was outlined in reply to an indignant letter to Bord Fáilte from an English visitor, which has been passed on to me. That reply said it was actual policy not to provide any facilities on the new road network because it would require the NRA to enter into agreements with third-party developers – though this precisely what it has done with National Road Tolls. Lay-bys were being built where motorists could rest, but very deliberately, without toilet facilities.

Well what about private enterprise operations near the motorways? How could strangers know about them? The NRA letter was delightfully frank about this. Its letter continued: 'It is NOT [my capitals] the policy of the National Roads Authority to provide for signage for individual premises providing services or facilities.'

Now how can this blithering cretinism be construed as 'policy'? Why are not heads rolling by the dozen around that colossal monument to brainless NRA ineptitude, the Red Cow Roundabout? And how long before this arrogant NRA imbecilism is brought to an end?

[23 December 2004]

V.7. Dublin Corporation and Traffic

Dublin Corporation is pleased to announce its new traffic management scheme. Drivers from the northside heading to the southside should enter the free-flow axis heading from Castleknock to Navan.

There they will be able to join the exciting new park'n'ride scheme: for a mere €20 they can leave their cars for the entire day, and the bus journey into Dublin is completely free of charge. Passengers will change buses at Ashbourne and Coolock before alighting at Phibsborough, from where they will have to walk the rest of the way. (A bit of exercise will do you no harm. Look at the belly on you.)

Traffic emanating from Killiney and Dalkey will be directed on to the M50, and thence to the Red Cow Roundabout, where a Luas should be along in a few weeks. CIÉ is expecting some tents to arrive from its North Korean manufacturer any day now, which should make it easier for travellers at the encampment. U2, on their way to Dublin airport, were among those obliged to join the Red Cow Roundabout Reservation. On his second day there, Bono tried to address the residents of the Roundabout on Third World hunger. He was promptly killed and eaten by some strange-looking nuns. He was, one said, flossing her teeth wistfully, possessed of a strange, minty flavour, rather like ... what was it? Seaside rock? Polos? No. Humbug.

Even more dramatic developments are expected for traffic in the city centre. Vehicles around St Stephen's Green will now move in an anti-clockwise direction, except for those intended to exit on to Leeson Street, which will move in a clockwise direction – but only during office hours, in months with an 'r'. Otherwise they will move in an anti-clockwise direction, which of course will make it impossible for them to turn into Leeson Street at all. City engineers are working on a solution to the problem, and have given themselves the pressing deadline of 2008 to sort it out. In the meantime, motorists wishing to exit St Stephen's Green at Leeson Street are advised to stay at home until this small teething problem has been solved.

There are comparable problems for motorists wishing to exit the Green at Cuffe Street, Dawson Street, Merrion Row, Harcourt Street and Earlsfort Terrace. All such vehicles should travel clockwise, except on Leap Years and during Rogation Days, plus Advent. But we still haven't worked out a safe way of exiting the Green. So, for the time being, until safe exit strategies have been worked out, cars on the Green will stay on the Green.

Meanwhile, traffic coming down Harcourt Street will be obliged to turn left onto Cuffe Street, but will not be allowed to enter St Stephen's Green. Nor is any provision being made for it to find a way on to the Green once it has been directed away from it. (Screw you anyway. What were you doing on Harcourt Street in the first place?) In fact, the only way of getting on to St Stephen's Green is via Leeson Street, and the only way to get to Leeson Street is via the Holyhead ferry and Dun Laoghaire.

So very simple: start your journey in Wales.

What is really exciting about our new traffic system is its integration. The jam of cars on the Green will integrate perfectly with the jam of Luas: if synchronised correctly, this will cause a jam at the Merrion Gates, hence preventing the DART from moving in either direction. This should cause huge build-ups of passengers at DART stations across the city, and of course, cars in traffic jams will of necessity be illegally parked, unmoving in the centre of the road, and will be clamped, generating absolutely zillions in revenue.

Which brings us to another leg in the joined-up traffic system – the Arrow trains from Kildare, breaking down without explanation at Maynooth, Sallins, Celbridge, Hazel Hatch and occasionally Carlow – that is, when there's an 'r' in the month, or it's a feria day. Which doesn't explain why the Kildare–Dublin commuter once broke down in Belmullet. Our chaps are still working on that. We'll let you know.

The central point is that just before the Arrow train arrives at Heuston Station, the connecting buses for the city centre depart, leaving the passengers to scamper on foot down the quays. Ah yes, the quays. Haven't mentioned them yet. Vital.

Absolutely vital. So here goes ...

The quays will remain one-way: that is, traffic will move in the same direction on both quays, away from the city centre. Vehicles wishing to head towards O'Connell Bridge from upriver are urged to take the alternative route to Slane, which will be clearly indicated by 'diversion' signs. These will be Irish diversion signs, which will simply cease to exist once they have drawn the drivers across a Meath bog into a particularly virulent housing estate, which is full of cul-de-sacs containing burnt-out cars, but has no more diversion signs, street names, or exits.

There, they will find themselves surrounded by staring crowds of gnarled, unwashed folk with large eyebrows and small foreheads, who all resemble the love child born from the sex scene in *Deliverance*. But stay! Are they not strangely familiar? Indeed they are – some of their sisters became nuns, and are at this very moment busy flossing away on the Red Cow Roundabout. There's also a park'n'ride scheme in this estate, but it involves no buses.

There now. With these simple, easy-to-follow measures, we in Dublin Corporation are confident that – finally – we've cracked the problem of Dublin traffic.

[8 July 2004]

V.8. Planes, Trains ... and the Dublin Bus Corporation

Maybe it happened in Eden. Possibly after. Whenever it was, the difference between the sexes is nowhere more strongly marked than in the business of packing.

Being a perfectly typical male, when I pack a suitcase, I normally manage to include several bottlers of wine, a beer or two, some Sellotape and a packet of crisps. This is fine for the first week or two, after which the absence of any clean socks, underwear or toothbrush and paste tend to oppress strangers. When horses shy and hotel receptionists swoon at your approach, it's time either you went on a suitcase-packing course, or surrendered the entire business to your wife, if she's willing, or divorce her, if she's not.

Thus it was I arrived at Dublin Airport with a perfectly packed suitcase, en route to a lecture in England. I presented myself at the Ryanair desk and proffered my passport to the girl in blue. The photograph is a little bit old and very flattering, so I'm used to airport eyes flicking back and forth to compare the pictorial Adonis with the car crash that is reality.

This time, it was different. The Ryanair eyes slowly went backwards and forwards several times before their owner said: 'And you really mean to tell me that you're Rachel Nolan?' Rachel had asked me to make just one contribution to my departure: to pick up my passport. I had gone to the filing cabinet, picked up both our passports, looked at them both very carefully, and then with equal care, had placed my passport back in the filing cabinet, and then put hers in my pocket. A psychiatrist can perhaps explain such conduct. I cannot.

Listen. Merely because you're a journalist doesn't mean you can bypass the Berlin Wall of Ryanair Blue. I could not identify myself with any photographic evidence, and therefore was not allowed on the flight to Bournemouth, the last of the day.

There are a number of words to describe my predicament, but the most apt is that ancient Greek term, 'phukt'. Yes, I was well and truly phukt.

I was now a snarling madman. For I had arrived by hackney from Kildare. She-who-packs was now she-who-shops, as in Christmas, as in, with her mother. There are some things – Requiem Masses, marital consummations, and mothers and daughters hitting the credit card at Yuletide – which one does not in all decency interrupt. Moreover, I could hardly ask to her to claw her way down the dark and unspeakable horror of the M50 in the late afternoon, as static as a British car-assembly line circa 1981.

So this madman did something he hadn't done in many years: he caught a bus into Dublin city centre. Not a coach, but an ordinary bus, one that stopped at stops. It was incredible. It cost only €5, left from just outside the terminal doors, and was not merely air-conditioned but heated. Why, it felt more like a Stockholm bus than a Dublin bus. I asked the driver which was the best stop for Jervis Street, and he told he would let me know. And sure enough, over the public address system, he kept assuring the passenger for Jervis Street that now was not the stop to alight at. Finally, the instruction came to abandon ship, which I duly did.

I had a bit of time to spare, so I chose to walk to Connolly Station and get a seat ahead of the mob. The balance so far? I'd lost the cost of the flight. I'd had to buy another ticket for a flight to England the next day. I was missing a small party being held for me at the other side. On the other hand, I'd been in a Dublin bus that was amazingly clean and efficient, and the driver was attentively courteous in an old-fashioned way. And here I was on Luas, which I criticised recently for the time it takes to cover the journey to Tallaght; but maybe I should rethink that criticism, because this tram left on time – to the second – and it really was exceedingly pleasant. A group of postal workers began to sing carols – though needless to say, not well. Still, their shambling forays into the lower registers of 'Silent Night' added a festive note to the journey.

Then we stopped. More passengers came aboard, and in their midst was a wheelchair. The occupant was a young woman, and she propelled that wheelchair by hand. Not merely did she have no legs, but she appeared to have no lower abdomen either. As far as I could judge, her torso ended somewhere in the region of her navel. She was about 22, and she was alone.

Minutes before, I had been cursing my luck over my missed flight.

She clutched a packet of cigarettes to her chest. With a priggish sanctimony, we as a society have decreed that if this young woman wants to have a smoke while in a pub, she must go outside. But that's as far as our Pharisaic morality goes, for we have also decreed that she must propel herself around by hand. In any other country in Europe, the State would have supplied her with an electric wheelchair.

We came to her stop and, alone, she wheeled herself off, leaving a score of sobered minds behind her. I flew to England the next day, and then – naturally – missed my flight home. I didn't care.

Oh, who are you, my girl? What catastrophe befell you that the grace of God spared the rest of us? And this Christmas, of all times, what more should we be doing for you?

[15 December 2004]

V.9. Irish Rail on Track

Last month an Offaly man who was hit by a train and lost a leg while lying drunkenly across a railway line was awarded substantial damages at the High Court. Mr

Justice Donovan – clearly a clever fellow – assessed gross damages at €740,539 (don't you just love the €39?) but, because he held the 'victim', Derek Raleigh, 85 per cent negligent, Hopalong will receive just 15 per cent of that – €111,081.

Is that what they teach you in law school? How to divvy up responsibility when a man gets paralytically drunk and lies down on a railway track? By Jove, it sounds a rare old art form indeed, as difficult to master as chicken-sexing. So Derek Raleigh gets €111,081 for getting legless: happy Christmas indeed.

One August night in 1995 Derek Raleigh and his girlfriend went to a stretch of the Clara–Tullamore railway on which most people regularly socialise – really, really stupid people, that is. They had to mount a 4ft 6in wall and clamber down a steep bank to join in the drunken revelries. His companions later left, but he and his girlfriend fell asleep on the tracks. Then, toot-toot! A toot too late.

Judge O'Donovan declared shrewdly: 'I cannot think of anything more irresponsible than that a grown man would sit on a railway line in the middle of the night with a feed of alcoholic drink on him.' He concluded that Derek Raleigh, who had been often enough chased off the line before, was 'largely' the author of his own misfortune.

Here: what's with this 'largely'? Nobody made him drink, or climb over a wall, or climb down a steep embankment, or gather with his friends on the track, or drink six or eight cans of lager, and/or lie down and go to sleep on the tracks.

Yet all this not withstanding, the judge ruled that he must also reflect the rail company's responsibility for failing to take appropriate steps to prevent trespass, which it must have know was taking place, by an apportionment of fault, albeit small. (Lawyers tend to regard a sum like €111,081 'small'.) The company had implicitly facilitated or tolerated access to the railway over the wall by its failure to take appropriate steps to prevent access to the railway, but he was not persuaded that the train driver was in any way to blame.

Not 'persuaded' that the train driver was to blame? Well, bully for the poor old train driver; but had anyone attempted to persuade the judge that the driver was to blame for some drunken cretin lying down on a railway line in the middle of the night? And has the driver thought about suing the inebriate imbecile for the nightmares people in his profession quite often have after then run someone over? (Think about it, Mr Driver.)

Which leaves the question: how on earth can Iarnród Éireann now make its railway lines free from the Derek Raleighs of the land? After all, it had chased him off the track many times before. Some moonless night, he might hop back on the track and hazard his remaining leg. And of course, he can't properly be chased away any more, for that would be discrimination against the disabled. Moreover, once he has lost that surviving leg, he has two arms still to go. He might then even chance his arm (so to speak) with some of his other protuberantly profitable parts to lay on the line, collaring 15 per cent every time.

But it's not just Derek and his corporeally reductive habits that our national railway has to worry about. Iarnród Éireann has hundreds of miles of track for nocturnal revellers to caper on. How is it meant to seal it all off to prevent these incursions occurring? With barbed wire and watchtowers along the entire length? The could prove rather expensive to the government, the ultimate owner. In 2002 the national railway company was given a€155 million subsidy by the State – €3 for every ticket bought, plus another €20 million for track safety.

This was, of course, before Derek made his own little inroad on the Iarnród piggyback. Twenty million won't build you much of a wall alongside our railway network: ask the Israelis, who know all about building walls to keep people out.

But then, what about all the people who fall off the wall when trying to join the on-track festivities? Since wicked old Iarnród Éireann will probably have made no attempt to erect safety nets to catch tumbling revellers or to supply them with parachutes, it could be 15 per cent liable for damages there as well.

Do you know, I'm not sure Iarnród Éireann is up to this task. After all, it's not Swiss railways, which last had a train late in 1944, after its engine was hit by Allied bomb as it left the station. The footplatemen towed it the rest of the way. It was still five minutes late and the driver was fed live to the herd of wild cuckoo-clocks in Zurich Zoo.

Irish Rail timetables, however, are based on the calendar, not hours and min-utes – the trains standing at platform two is the Sligo express, departing around January, sort of. Iarnród Éireann can't even manage to erect signs outside Sallins railway station saying 'station'. So how can it possibly protect hundreds of miles of track all around Ireland? Ah well. At least Derek Raleigh has answered one question. Now I know what the French call it *chemin de fir*.

[14 January 2004]

V.10. Travelling with the Tattooed Classes

What a glimpse into the face of the new Ireland one gets when one travels by Dublin bus. I made such a journey recently, on the upper deck of the 65, from the city centre to Blessington, with large numbers of the tattooed classes as travelling companions, certainly as far as Tallaght.

Now life has taught me to treat people with tattoos with the deference I nor-mally reserve for Garda officers with Uzis who have just been stung by wasps. So when a Tattoo lights up in a no-smoking zone, in general, I inwardly counsel timidity, which in my lexicon also goes by the name of prudence. An Australian tourist sitting near me on the 65 was clearly unacquainted with that lexicon, for when a young she-tattoo beside him lit up, he asked her, very politely, would she mind putting her cigarette out, because she was showing no respect for other passengers.

'She the f**k up,' declared the hospitable paragon loudly, 'and f**k off back where you came from, you f**kin' bleedin' foreigner.'

Well, *really*. One can just about endure other people's illegal tobacco smoke, and perhaps even maintain a certain heroic aloofness while doing so; but there is something in the old system that rises in ungovernable revolt when visitors to this country are thus addressed, especially if they are called a 'fuqqin forddennor'.

However, I am at a disadvantage when talking Tattoo, for not even my fondest admirer would concede that I am a master of Ireland's numerous argots and accents; and Tattoo is quite beyond me. Turning to the young and fragrant creature, I simply said: 'Our young visitor here is perfectly correct. It is against the law to smoke on a bus. Might I suggest you put the cigarette out?'

My memory is sometimes an able instrument, and there are certain things which it can recall that should be beyond its power of retention but which strangely are not. But alas, it cannot do credit to the ensuing stream of abuse and contumely, which would have drawn a nunly pallor to the cheek of a sergeant major. In essence, and converting her terminology to more Latinate and more circumspect language, this petal of Irish womanhood simply informed me to mind my coital business, that I was a copulating pendulum, and if I didn't button my copulating lip, she would coitally well defenestrate me, using a boot about my conjugating private parts to achieve that objective.

Well, something along those lines, anyway.

And then she embarked upon a different tactic. 'Who the phuc do you tink yew are anyways, wid your shoes, and your suit, and your phuqqin' *Sunday Independent*? A phuqqin' solicitor?' The creature was clearly unacquainted with any broadsheet other than that august organ emanating from Middle Abbey Street, so she assumed that the copy of this newspaper that I was reading was the *Sunday Independent*. But that did not hurt quite so much as the presumption that I belonged to the lawyering classes; here, now, was a crushing blow, and one that left me speechless.

At which point my antipodean friend chose – I think on balance inadvisedly – to speak up again. 'Look,' he said, in a voice plangent with sweet reason, 'would you please put that cigarette out?' To which St Theresa of the Roses replied (loosely translated): 'Hearken well, oh gentlemen of foreign extraction, and stay silent, else I shall rearrange your copulating reproductive organs with my coital feet – do you catch my conjugal drift?' And so saying, the She-Tattoo sat back in her seat, her face triumphant as she received the congratulations of strangers around her. And with the principles that she had so bravely defended now vindicated, her neighbours then promptly lit up.

I confess that my reserves of valour, limited at the best of times, by this time had been squandered in the futile assault on her single cigarette, and I was no more capable of storming the veritable fortress of cigarette smokers now around me than I was of converting Alabama to Islam.

There was such a time when a foreign tourist such as the (now silent, scarlet cheeked) Australian would have been defended by most natives in such circumstances. That time, it now seems, is past. No doubt there has always been a tradition of not obeying the law; but there was an equal tradition of courtesy and hospitality that would have caused a large group of Irish people to have defended an outsider against such vile abuse. Instead, the She-Tattoo was hailed as a hero – or perhaps heroin would have been a better word – and our visitor was left to muse upon what an enchanting country Ireland has become.

Travelling by bus into the city doesn't even save time: this trip of 20 miles took two hours (a journey made all the more fascinating by a journey through most of Tallaght's back streets). How often does Dublin Bus management actually travel on the upper deck of its vehicles to see how truly abominable it is up there? How many people have been prosecuted for illegal smoking and for threatening passengers who complain? And how really stupid must you be to travel by Dublin Bus when you have a car?

Here is a promise. Mark it well, Dublin Bus management, and weep: regardless of how long I have to sit in my car in a Dublin traffic jam, I will never travel on one of your sanguinary copulating omnibuses, ever again.

[28 October 2001]

VI. Destination Ireland

VI.1. The Declaration against Racism

'We the undersigned wish to protest at the torrent of abuse that has been stoked up against asylum seekers. The most vulnerable people fleeing persecution, oppression and war are being blamed for the ills of Irish society ... Instead of attacking refugees, we should condemn politicians who led an opulent and corrupt lifestyle while they told the rest of us to "tighten our belts"... We particularly condemn attempts to associate refugees with medical illness. People from divergent countries with different experiences should not be dehumanised in this way ... We believe that asylum seekers deserve our compassion and help.'

Thus runs the Declaration against Racism which has been signed by 10,000 ordinary people who are opposed to racism, plus, of course, the usual suspects – the literary types, the left, and, naturally, our kool right-on showbiz dudes. All very predictable. Thirty years ago, comparable petitional pieties were being uttered by their English equivalents as the tide of Commonwealth immigration rose cross-channel.

Now I'm not opposed to anti-racism. Quite the reverse. Racism is a foulness in the human spirit which must never be allowed to triumph. But it is, alas, a widespread foulness, and because it is so easily aroused, we must be careful how we address it: for we will never ever defeat racism with falsehoods or prating humbug.

Of what group is the Declaration Against Racism speaking? Solely and exclusively 'asylum seekers' or 'refugees'. But we all know these terms are largely false; they are simply congenial and convenient euphemisms for illegal immigrants. Few of our recent guests are genuinely seeking 'asylum', that is, immunity from seizure, or are refugees who have been forced to flee their homelands. Far from condemning such illegal immigrants, I applaud their enterprise in getting here. Since we have crippling labour shortages, my instinct is to give them work visas, and to start the process of naturalisation immediately, regardless of race or country or origin.

Yet that in itself is a piety, because I live in the middle of the countryside, and it's unlikely that large numbers of Africans are going to be my neighbours. But they will be – indeed, already are – neighbours to large numbers of Dubliners. Now there has never in the history of the world been an occasion when two ethnic groups have begun to mix for the first time without misunderstandings, mutual dislike, cultural disdain. If large numbers of Afro-Caribbean people manage to settle in areas of Dublin which have been poor, working class, white, Irish and Catholic for centuries, and do so entirely without friction, it would be an utterly unprecedented miracle.

Such friction normally expresses itself predictably – they're taking our jobs, they're taking our women, they're on the dole, et cetera. Amid all the spurious mythology of such prattle, the last thing the inner city natives need are sermons from castles in Dalkey about their duty towards 'asylum seekers', which, as we all know full well, is what the vast majority of our immigrants are not. Moreover, why are we enjoined to condemn corrupt politicians who led an 'opulent and corrupt lifestyle while they told the rest of us to tighten our belts'? The corruptness of our politicians is irrelevant, a sanctimonious red herring to throw into this simmering pot of public holier-than-thouness.

By the by: are the members of U2 perfectly at ease condemning the opulence and corruption of politicians? When they've finished telling us that they are, maybe they would tell us how much tax they pay a year. No doubt they're utterly law-abiding, but multimillionaires with clever accountants should be slow to deliver sermons from the Mount to anyone.

But stay! Who else is giving us sermons on public duties but two men who were named in the Northern Assembly as members of the IRA army Council. What? Am I to receive anti-racist homilies from the leaders of an organisation that has not repented by the merest molecule of a truly atrocious sectarian war which took thousands of lives? Am I to listen to condemnations of racism from men whose comrades blew up Protestants pubs, machine-gunned Protestant workmen, butchered two impoverished Pakistanis for the crime of serving tea to British soldiers, murdered British businessmen for the crime of being British, and for whom the very word 'Brit' is the foulest term of racial abuse? By gum, this is rich stuff indeed.

The petition condemns 'attempts to associate refugees with medical illness'. What? Is the state not to give AIDS tests to immigrants? With glutinous PC circumlocution, the petition declares that 'People from divergent countries with different experiences should not be dehumanised in this way'. But are we not told often enough, perhaps even by some of those who signed this petition, that we are not doing enough about AIDS in Africa? Are we now to establish parity of neglect and wait for full-blown AIDS to develop here before acting? And then how would U2, in their sermons from the turrets and embattlements in Dalkey, describe the state's failure to treat infected people properly when they first arrived? As dehumanising, perhaps?

A black Englishman now resident in Dublin told me recently that he had never personally encountered any racism of any kind; but he thought all the talk about racism and how-horrible-we-Irish-all-are might exaggerate whatever racism there actually is. I don't know, either way. But I do know we will never tackle this problem properly so long as we prefer to posture with weasel pieties than to speak the plain truth plainly.

[29 July 2001]

VI.2. Exploring Masculinities

A certain reader was kind enough to send me a copy of *Exploring Masculinities* some time ago; and as with most such things that are sent my way, I did nothing with it until I fell over it, just the other day. It's a big book, and the really surprising thing is that I hadn't fallen over it before. Indeed, as an obstacle of any kind I could recommend it heartily; and you would not need too many to make a decent-sized wall from it.

That's just about where its usefulness begins and ends. There is at least the consolation that though this farrago of multicultural, politically correct drivel is being served out in our schools, we know from history that ideological educationalists invariably fail to create the attitudes amongst their pupils that they want. If it provides no other lesson, at least Yugoslavia is good for that.

By happy chance, my vast purple tome fell open at what is called the labelling theory. This is multiculturalism at its most ideological and its most cretionously self-contradictory. 'When someone is named, for example, as a nigger or a queer,' it witters witlessly, 'what is happening is that they are being labelled.'

So what does *EM* then do in its a campaign against labelling? Why, it simply labels. Under the term, Objective, we are told by *EM* that students may explore the key question: 'What do I admire about Black Culture and Black people's lives?'

What is this thing, Black Culture, please? Does it equally encompass an Australian Aborigine, an East African doctor, a pygmy in the Congo rainforests, a Tory MP from the shires, and a nuclear scientist at Harvard?

There's no such thing as 'Black Culture' any more there is such a thing as 'White Culture'. The colour of your skin no more offers you entry to a culture than it enables you to speak a particular language. However, such racist mumbo-jumbo would be perfectly understood by the ideologists of *Die Sturmer* and the *Broderbond*; how interesting to see the ideological multiculturalists embracing the same epidermal frivolity.

Unsurprisingly, multiculturalists have added a new spin to the word black. It doesn't just mean people with some African blood in them, but it now means not just anyone who is not white, but also anyone supposedly without power. In some funny, fuzzy way, black transmutes into whatever you want it to mean.

So, in the list of people from which fellow students are asked to compile a guest list for a theoretical dinner party, the following are included as 'black' guests: Tiger Woods, Kahlil Gibran, Julius Nyerere, Arundhati Roy, Mahatma Ghandi, Chaim Herzog, Rigoberta Mechnu, and Ken Saro-Wiwa. Famous people not on the list may be chosen, provided they are not white: and for this purpose, white also means white Christian. Presumably, a practising Jew may be invited; his Catholic brother may not.

Tiger Woods is said to be an African-American. His mother is Vietnamese, which is not very African. So why does the African part predominate? Or would the authors of South Africa's pass-laws, and the Nazi definitions of Jewishness give us a few helpful tips here?

Khalil Gibran was a Lebanese poet, and was as African and black as Adolf Hitler. Julius Nyerere – 'the wise old man of Africa', is how *EM* terms him – nearly bankrupted his country with his absurd socialism and his forcible tribal translocations. Any European responsible for comparable follies in Africa would be rightly vilified by educationalists. To hold up such a man as a sort of hero because he is 'black' is inverse racism at its most condescending.

Arundhati Roy is a high-born Indian who has invented a poverty-stricken past for herself. She's about as black as Jean-Marie Le Pen. But listen, *EM*-people; if you want to know whether Hindus are black or not, why don't you pop into a gathering of Bombay Brahmins and tell them they share the same culture as the people of Rwanda?

The Irish Jew Chaim Herzog who went to become President of Israel is also on the list of blacks and sort-of-blacks: welcome to negritude, Chaim. The same surprising discovery might be made by Rigoberta Menchu, an ethnic Mayan from Guatemala.

At least Ken Saro-Wiwa was African. His execution 'resulted from his campaign for the protection of the rights of the Ogoni people and against the environmental exploitation of the lands of the Ogoni people by a major oil producing company,' declares *EM*.

Actually, Ken Saro-Wiwa was executed for his role in the murder of four of his Ogoni opponents who were hacked to pieces and burnt to death by a mob, some of whose members even ate their victims' body parts. Despite this colourful little episode, BP petitioned the Nigerian government for clemency for him.

And still on this subject of Saro-Wiwa: were his executioners representatives of 'Black Culture'? Were Idi Amin and Emperor Bokassa? And are Halle Berry or Colin Powell be called African-American, when her mother is pure white, and he is considerably paler than I am during a good summer (meaning, not right now).

The dismal experiences of imperialism, Nazism and apartheid have shown that it is useless to categorise people politically, culturally or artistically by race or tribe. That way leads, at worst, to evil – and usually – unworkable laws, at best to fatuous rules and absurd categorisations, which intelligent students will see right through. They'll certainly see through the risible rules of the *EM* programme. That's the truth about ideologies that ideologists never learn: intellectually, they inevitably disprove themselves.

[11 June 2002]

VI.3. Tolerance Has its Limits

The standard liberal way of discussing immigration in Britain was usually to mis-represent the arguments of those who counselled caution and control, and then triumphantly to denounce the disingenuous caricature of their own devising as bigoted or racist. I am therefore intensely grateful to Ronaldo Munck of Dublin City University for providing me with a little jewel of intellectually grubby mis-representation of a column I wrote a couple of months ago. He replied in this newspaper as follows.

'Kevin Myers writes that: "The present good relations and general harmony, are typical of the early days of immigration' but he sees this as only a 'honey-moon period''. Diversity policies lead to fundamentalism: "Jews are attacked in the streets of Antwerp by Islamic militants expressing their own form of diver-sity." Ahead of us lies the spectre of Rotterdam that "will shortly be the first European city with a racially and culturally non-indigenous majority". Diver-sity for him leads to murder and national identity surrender. This is reactionary nonsense, but it also reflects the confusion in Ireland today over migration and multiculturalism.'

Well, thank you Ronaldo for that intellectual guano, culminating in that classic piece of undergraduate name-calling, the r-word. God, I remember doing that in UCD: categorising an entire argument as 'reactionary', and dismissing it as nonsense; and then exiting with a supercilious smirk on my odiously smug little face. To judge from your powers of logic and ratiocination, you are probably in first year, Ronaldo: but with time and patience, there might be hope for you yet.

As a matter of interest – though clearly not to you, Ronaldo – I simply didn't say that diversity leads to murder and national identity surrender. I didn't say it because I don't believe it. Nor did I say that diversity policies lead to fundamentalism; indeed, I didn't use the word fundamentalism once in the entire column. Not once. It looks like DCU have got an uphill struggle with you on their hands, young Ronaldo.

But after welcoming immigrants, as I continue to do, what I said last May – and I say even more emphatically now, with two score and ten dead bodies in London – that we were in the honeymoon period for immigration in Ireland, and that we had better face reality, because immigrants are here to stay.

So, we might get some marriage guidance counselling in, nice and early: and the first thing the counsellors – let's make them Dutch – will probably tell you is that you do not emphasise diversity. You do not put up signs in many languages in schools, thereby giving parity of esteem to foreign cultures, foreign norms. Instead, you emphasise and celebrate commonality, within a native culture of tolerance. But let's make it clear: our tolerance has limits …

Well, we learned what those limits were on July 7th. Indeed, we could have learnt them long ago, but here in Ireland, with the lessons of virtually every other country in Europe to benefit from, we have chosen triumphantly to embrace the witless mumbo-jumbo of unprincipled, doctrinaire multiculturalism. We are apparently not content for the Dutch and the French and the Spanish and the British to have their own home-grown Islamic jihadists; we've got to have some too. So we'll state-fund some madrassahs, and then studiously ignore what is being taught in them, and who knows, if we're really lucky, in ten or fifteen years' time, we'll have our own home-made martyrs blowing up the Luas and the Dart.

The column that triggered the Munckological essay in witless piety was itself in response to the new multicultural state guidelines for our primary schools. These even include formal proposals for multilingual signs in schools. In explanation, Mary Hanafin said that Auschwitz must never happen again. Well, of course, if we don't have signs for toilet in Arabic and Kurdish, the gas chambers are just round the corner. Remember, we were also told that if we didn't all accept the EU Constitution, the next step would be Auschwitz. The same is probably true if Dingle is allowed to remain Dingle.

Aside from the sheer immorality and intellectual sloppiness of deploying the death camps to stifle discussion on anything, who is the more likely to have an interest in reviving an Auschwitz? Europe's hand-wringing multiculturalists, or Jew-hating Islamo-fascists? Or put it another way. Would the train bombers of London not have resorted to an Auschwitz if they could, with the rather idiosyncratic Islamic refinement, that this time the guards get into the gas chambers as well?

And in Britain they're asking some pretty agonised questions today. How did they allow immigration policies that have resulted in one third of 1.6 million British Muslims – that is, half a million – thinking that the society they live in is immoral and should be brought to an end? Or that a similar number would not report potential terrorist activity to the police? Or that one-quarter of them sympathise with the motives of the London bombers?

Answer. In large part through an ignoble and doctrinaire multiculturalism, as represented most classically by our spotty young undergraduate friend, Ronaldo Munck, 1st year, Surrender Studies, DCU. So, the next question is – provided we are interested in learning from other people's experiences, and there's absolutely no evidence that we are – how can we prevent the same phenomenon sooner or later occurring here? By compulsory educational assimilation of all immigrants, as has been so successfully achieved in the US? Or by having helpful little signs in Arabic in our schools: suicide-bombing classes this way?

[27 July 2005]

VI.4. ... and the Burka

I am being made dizzy with this all this mumbo-jumbo of 'multiculturalism', a term that is unfailingly invoked in every pious homily about immigration. However, I note that Martin Ruhs, of the University of Oxford Centre on Migration, Policy and Society, and of the Policy Intitute at TCD, does not seem to use it all. Good man Martin. He raised the point recently that sustainable immigration policies cannot be achieved without a comprehensive and structured debate – 'something that has eluded many other countries with much longer histories of migrant workers than Ireland'.

As my careful and considered contribution to a comprehensive and structured debate, I politely suggest that the entire concept of multiculturalism should go and shag itself. I simply don't believe that all other cultures are as good as the Western European and North American democratic models. I regard the fundamentalist Islamic cultures that oppress women as utterly loathsome, as I do the variants which have appeared throughout the Middle East. In some parts of that benighted region, the pharaonic circumcision of girls is a 'cultural norm', as is the practice of honour killings of women.

So, if you defend multiculturalism as parity of esteem for all cultures, and please, make yourself at home in Ireland of the Welcomes, well, you're in essence saying that you respect cultures which mutilate little girls and justify the murder of rape victims because they are unclean (a common practice in Jordan and Pakistan).

India has given us a startling insight into the complexities of 'multiculturalism' (protected in the longest and most incomprehensible constitution in the world, one which makes the now-dead European Constitution seem like the Gettysburg Address). A Muslim woman named Imrana was raped by her father-in-law in a village in Northern India. Because she is now alleged to be 'unclean', the powerful Islamicist Darul-Uloom seminary has ordered her to leave her husband, that is, her rapist's son.

Under ordinary Indian law, she would be entitled to alimony from her husband; but strict Islamicists, such as those at Darul-Uloom, insist that alimony is contrary to Islam. And in India, family law depends on your religion: if you are a Muslim woman, Indian law obliges you to abide by the interpretations of powerful Islamic clerics. So although you are an Indian citizen, you are nonetheless deprived of the protections of Indian secular law: just another joyous item in that colourful mosaic known as multiculturalism.

Twin legal codes for Muslims and non-Muslims exist in Malaysia too. Is that what we want? Do we want people moving to Ireland, and within the unprincipled licentiousness of multiculturalism, establishing different marital and family norms for themselves? Don't say it won't happen: it already has in Britain, where half a century after mass immigration began, there is a growing Islamic demand for Shariah law to be recognised as having the same judicial validity as British law. And demographic change can come with astonishing swiftness. In the Leicester of my childhood, there were five Catholic churches, a score of Church of England churches, and perhaps as many non-conformist chapels. In the Leicester of today, there are 160 mosques.

When I see a woman shrouded in full burka in the centre of Dublin, my heart does not race with pride and joy at the evidence of multiculturalism we are importing. For in such cases, we are not importing any such thing, but an aggressive and monocultural intolerance, one that is a studied and disdainful refutation of our ways. For the burka is both an extravagant declaration of its wearer's modesty, and an insulting and explicit declaration of the immodesty of women who do not wear it.

So, let me put one libertarian foot in the multicultural door here. It should be made illegal to go masked in public in Ireland, in any context other than a carnival parade or street theatre. If Islamicist women and their wretched menfolk do not like such restrictions, then they can go and live in glorious places like Saudi Arabia, where such horrors are the norm.

And I do regard the burka as a true horror: for masks are one of the most disturbing artefacts any culture knows. Their purpose is always sinister: that is why even clowns, with their feature-concealing comedic make-up, cause us unease. We know deep down that there is something wrong about a concealed or artificial face. For our primary form of communication, antedating and anterior to speech, is the look on the human face. Babies respond to faces, not voices. Moreover, voices tell lies more easily than do faces.

When we eradicate the face from our communications with one another, we are dehumanising those communications; we are listening to a cloaked speaking machine, who sees us, but we do not see her. And we are made profoundly uncomfortable by that. It is no coincidence that the primary social tool of secret police everywhere, from the Ton Ton Macoutes of Haiti to Mugabwe's goons in Zimbabwe, is a pair of sunglasses.

Yes, and no doubt, some people will say the burka is part of their religion. Very well, go and practice your religion where its public display doesn't offend the norms of the indigenous people. Scandinavian nudists do not promenade on Saudi Arabia's extensive beaches, waiting forlornly for the tide finally to come in. They have taboos in Saudi, which they expect us to adhere to. In Ireland too, we have very strong taboos against the concealment of the human face. If you want to walk our streets, respect our taboos. *Si fueris Romae, Roman vivito more.* Or just stay away.

[16 September 2005]

VI.5. *How the British & the French Deal with Immigrants*

The year in Ireland is not 2005. It is about 1965 in terms of the French and British experience of immigration. Forty years on, let's see how things are going in both places. July, and suicide mass murderers in London. More recently, in Birmingham, riots between Asians and Afro-Caribbeans, which were not designated 'racial' by the police because no whites were involved. This is no doubt good news to the family of the black IT specialist Isiah Sam-Young, who was murdered by Asians. So maybe they killed him because they didn't like his shirt or his taste in music. Whatever it was, it apparently wasn't his race. What a relief.

The French tend to wait for a longer time before they act, and then they explode, their revolution being their enduring template. Which does at least show that, in one regard anyway, the descendents of immigrants to France behave exactly like the aboriginal natives. So in what has been a virtual racial insurrection, hundreds of towns and cities have been hit by riots, with tens of thousands of cars destroyed, leaving big smiles only on the faces of Messrs Citroen and Renault.

The French way of dealing with immigrants was to deny there could be any difference in attitude or culture between the children of incomers and those of the native French. The glories of French culture would embrace all with *liberté, egalité et fraternité*, but of course, like all ideological claptrap, such simple solutions didn't work. However, the belief that La France in all its gloire, unlike perfidious Albion, was capable of seamless integration of immigrants prevented the French chattering classes from chattering about what desperately needed to be chattered about.

Meanwhile, across La Manche, perfidious Albion similarly refused to discuss immigration – not out of hubris, like the French, but from a desire not to appear beastly, all because of a single disastrous speech by Enoch Powell. Which doesn't say much for the intellectual courage or imagination of the thinking classes in Britain. Thus Britain stayed silent as the immigrants poured in: and now, immigrant communities are many millions strong.

With France's deep traditions of anti-Catholicism, the state's political culture separating Church and State was invoked to outlaw ostentatious displays of Islamic difference in schools. I suspect this is one key, if largely unspoken, reason why Renault and Citroen will soon be working double shifts, and why French insurance companies are even now scanning their small print, searching for exemptions from payouts which involve religious riots. Insurance companies always scan the bottom line, after all, and they spell Mahomet's title one way only: profit.

The British, on the other hand, decided to embrace 'diversity' by abolishing anything that appeared to be too non-immigrant. Guided walks of the Lake District were hastily scrapped when it turned out that the participants were all white, and perhaps even worse, middle class. The Christmas holiday in Birmingham was renamed the 'Winterval', so as not to offend immigrants, it apparently being assumed that native Christians had no feelings to be offended. Derby City council earlier this year decided not to re-erect the once much-loved statue of a boar damaged by a German bomb in 1941, lest it offend the rather more recently arrived Muslims. One workplace elsewhere in England outlawed public displays of pictures of pigs, even cartoon pigs, for the same reason.

This nonsense came to a splendid high point a couple of years ago in High Wycombe, where the librarian refused to allow a Christmas play be performed by the local school in the town library because it would be offensive to the multicultural nature of the building. Only later did it transpire that the librarian had not long before allowed a Hindu festival to be celebrated there.

The latest British chapter in multiculturalism was the decision of Suffolk county council to ban a subsidy for local Christmas lights on the grounds that it would not match 'its core values of equality and diversity'. Which merely shows that these words are meaningless mumbo-jumbo for what diversity or equality are possible if you have already abandoned local ways for others to be diverse from and equal to?

George Bernard Shaw was once propositioned by a beautiful woman who said: 'Imagine our child, with your brains and my looks.' He replied, 'But madam: what if it has your brains and my looks?' And multiculturalism can work just like that. Mixing British with Bangladeshi doesn't necessarily mean you get an Islamic Tom Stoppard, but a skinhead thug called Ahmed. Irish crossed with Moroccan might give you Riverbellydance: or equally, it can produce Sean, the suicide bomber.

We have piously modelled our response to immigration on British lines, loudly proclaiming the virtues of anti-racist programmes, as if society can be constructed around either virtue or programmes (as in, say, our amazingly successful anti-drugs programmes, ho ho ho). Moreover, we share a fatal reluctance to be realistic with more than the failed models of France and Britain. For the European Union itself is a very masterpiece of denial, with its urbane and witless embrace of unprincipled secularism.

Thus the one common feature of Europe, out of which all European cultures grew – Christianity – was excluded from the now-dead, though enduringly preposterous constitution: space travel, however, was included. Such drooling, deracinated idiocy does not befit a continental power, which is what the Brussels Eurocracy still dreams of. But a continental power is something Europe will never be – unless, in about a century's time, it becomes an Islamic one – as well it might.

[10 November 2005]

VI.6. In Defence of an Earlier Column

Illuminated by the burning fires of Birmingham, London and France, I wrote a column about immigration last week. It had no racist content because I am not a racist. To judge someone by their race is the mark of a fool or a bigot. However, I did not say so at the time, because one shouldn't have to profess virtue endlessly in order to discuss matters of national importance.

Michael D. Higgins TD issued a statement in reply to that column. It was headlined: 'Myers scrapes the barrel again: this time on race during anti-racism workplace week.'

It continued: 'The Irish Times through Kevin Myers has, once again, reached the sewer level of journalism. And once again, no doubt, The Irish Times at editorial level will stay silent.

'The contents of his column today go beyond his usually crafted cowardice, staying one step on the safe side of prosecution for incitement to hatred or racism.'

Now this is an actionable allegation. It reeks of malice. It accuses me of habitual professional cowardice, when my job calls for the very opposite. Worst of all, it clearly implies that I am a racist who is going as far as I possibly can to incite racism and hatred, without falling foul of the law.

Needless to say, Higgins was quite unable to produce any examples of racism or racist implications from my column, because there were none. The rest of his statement consisted of a meandering pile of intellectual inconsequence and sanctimonious drivel such as those who have ever had the misfortune of being publicly addressed by him will be well acquainted with.

He quoted this section from my column. 'George Bernard Shaw was once propositioned by a beautiful woman who said: "Imagine our child with your brains and my looks". He replied, "Madam, but what if it had your brains and my looks?"'

And multiculturalism can work just like that. Mixing British with Bangladeshi doesn't necessarily mean you get an Islamic Tom Stoppard, but a skinhead thug call Ahmed. 'Irish crossed with Moroccan might give you Riverbellydance: or equally, it can produce Seán, the suicide bomber.'

Higgins then asked: 'Does *The Irish Times* stand over this kind of writing? Many have been asking for some time what principle of balance requires such gratuitously insulting and hurtful language. Certainly the anodyne and dry editorial on 'Fighting Racism' could hardly be considered provocative.'

Now this paragraph would disgrace the pen of a third-rate undergraduate. It contains no cohering logic; its three sentences are utterly unconnected, as if they have been plucked at random from what passes as thought in that preening, self-regarding organ, the Higgins mind.

Yet from its largely witless melange, one is able to identify a key element: the language of feeling. This has invariably been the weapon of choice for the defenders of the politically correct. If they see something they disagree with, why, they are promptly, hurt, offended, insulted. Their sensibilities alone are the touchstone of whether or not something is acceptable.

But what is gratuitously insulting or hurtful about telling the truth? And the truth is that the cultural fusions in Britain have produced violent youths of Asian background who behave like English skinheads. No? Then ask the family of Isiah Sam-Young, the Afro-Caribbean man knifed to death by Asians for the crime of being black. And though we have not so far seen a suicide bomber called Sean, we have certainly seen one called Richard.

Yet the Higgins statement, for all its defamatory viciousness, raises a vital question. Why would henceforth anyone go to the bother of discussing race and immigration in this country in a serious way? Almost nothing is to be gained by it, as poor Mark Dooley of *The Sunday Independent* found out when he was invited on to *The Late Late Show*, where he was ambushed by Fintan O'Toole and Shalini Sinha, and roundly and triumphantly denounced for his racism.

Now, as it happens, I was subsequently invited to a discussion on racism and immigration by the Smurfit Business School. I asked, who else was to be on the panel? Why, Fintan O'Toole and Shalini Sinha, of course. Which pretty much sums up how debate is conducted in this country. See a lynching on *The Late Late Show*? Excellent! Let's have another one on campus, on pretty much the same lines! Debate becomes a morality contest in which the winners are the side that can most loudly declare their love of immigration as they denounce sceptics as racists.

Naturally, I declined the invitation – not merely because of the entirely predictable nature of my fellow panellists, but also because there wasn't a fee. The school – I was told – didn't have the funds to pay guest speakers. So is this how the Smurfitt School of Business normally operates? Do its lecturers, working for free, urge their students to go out and bestow their services without charge? Does Michael Smurfit give away boxes?

Official figures show that approaching 10 per cent of our population are foreign-born. But immigrants are for the most part are in their 20s and 30s – so our immigrant profile in that age group will be vastly greater. What is it? Thirty per cent? Forty per cent? And with immigration running to at least 100,000 a year the proportion is bound to grow rapidly. So – are we going to discuss this extraordinary phenomenon? Or are we to watch it in mute piety, silencing anyone who raises questions about the long-term impact of these population changes with shrill Higginsesque shrieks of 'racist'?

[16 November 2005]

VI.7. The Callis Case

It is now four months since Osagie Igbinidion was found not guilty of the reck-less endangerment of the life of 29-day-old baby Callis Osajhae, who died after being circumcised by him.

And as interesting as the outcome of the trial and the observations of the presiding judge, Mr Justice Kevin Haugh, has been the public response to the tragic death and the acquittal of the man who occasioned it, which has been precisely none.

190 | VI. DESTINATION IRELAND

Why is this? One simple reason. The baby who died so tragically and need-lessly was a boy. Had the baby who died been a girl undergoing a comparable operation, a tidal wave of anger would – very properly – have rocked through Irish life. And at the very least there would have been cries to outlaw the female version of the bungled operation which killed little Callis, namely genital circumcision.

This newspaper reported on the case, in part, as follows. 'Addressing the jury before they retired to consider their verdict, Judge Kevin Haugh said it was important for jurors not to bring their "white, Western values" to bear upon their deliberations.'

He described the case as a 'clash of two cultures'. 'This is a relatively recent matter that Ireland will have to deal with now that we have a significant migrant population. You are not asked whether this form of procedure is acceptable in Ireland. If you start thinking along those lines, you are doing Mr Igbinidion a great injustice.' He added that Mr Igbinidion did not have the benefit of being tried by peers who would understand his background and culture.

Excuse me, but why should an Irish jury be told they should not bring the values of their 'white, Western' civilisation to a case? For the values of our civilisation are precisely why we have a jury system. The people of Ireland – not the people of Tibet, Peru or Lapland – and their values are represented through the jury. We have a binary justice system in Ireland. The court provides the legal component of a trial, while the jury provides the social component.

And as for the accused man not having the benefit of being tried by his peers who would understand his background and culture – well, there would have been two ways of ensuring that he might have got that. The first was for him to have stayed in Nigeria, and I rather wish he had. The second was for the jury to be chosen on racial – and specifically Nigerian – grounds.

But no doubt, that is not specific enough; maybe he should be tried only by members of his own tribe, or better still, by his own trade – he was, we are told, a fourth-generation circumciser. Maybe such folk can better sympathise with bunglers who cause children to bleed to death after needless operations.

So after this case, are we to have two laws in Ireland? May you ineptly cir-cumcise an Irish boy-child and cause him to die if you are African because of your 'culture', but not if you are Irish? It would seem so.

Irish law, we may guess on these principles, counts less than the culture from which the accused comes – but only up to a point. For if the dead child had been female, I believe that no jury would have been told not to bring their white, Western values to bear on the case – or if they had been, we may equally be sure that the judge would now be dangling from the nearest lamp post in the bar of public opinion.

Moreover, the issue is not simply one of bungling. Do we protect the integrity of a child's body or not? The penis has a foreskin for protective reasons as sound as the existence of female labia. The violent and permanent exposure of a little boy's glans for religio-tribal reasons is an antiquated barbarism which both permanently changes the sexual sensitivities of the victims and endangers their health. Merely because Jews also do it doesn't make it right, or immune to criticism.

One of the problems about a new multi-ethnic society is that immigrants cannot always recognise the difference between social norms and profound, though non-legal, taboos. Some of our norms – saying hello to strangers or thanking bus drivers – are mere quirks. Others are so central to our way of life as hitherto to be beyond the need of law. One of these is the integrity of our children's bodies, free from mutilation by freelance butchers on house calls.

So, as waves of immigrants arrive, we shall simply have to incorporate at least one taboo in our legal code. We must make all circumcision illegal, unless by doctors for sound medical reasons. No doubt our ideological multicultural feminists will declare it still acceptable to mutilate male genitals, thought not of course female; but girls, girls, what about your equality agenda? If it is lawful to remove a baby boy's foreskin, then why not a girl's labia or even her clitoris? You cannot justify one and not the other.

It will inevitably become an issue here. In Britain, some immigrant Somalis insist on circumcising their daughters, and if not by some local harridan of a witch doctor with her rusty, trusty razor blade, they send them abroad.

And if you blindly accept the fashionable theories of value-free multiculturalism – as most soft-focus Irish lefties do – then what is to prevent immigrants in Ireland celebrating their 'culture' by mutilating their children's genitals? Not our legal system, clearly.

[11 January 2006]

VI.8. The Two Faces of Judicial Clemency

Agenda: the Latin plural gerundive, meaning 'things to be done'. Agendas govern our lives, even when we're unaware of them. Take, for example, the seizure of three golliwogs from a shop window by police in Herefordshire in England last week. They were apprehended on suspicion that their presence in the shop window might cause 'alarm, harassment or distress' under Section 5 of the Public Order Act. After an 'investigation' of some kind, the offending dolls were returned to their owner, with the advice that they should not be displayed 'insensitively'.

You are Irish Times readers. You do not need the obvious pointed out to you. The golliwog might – or might not – have its origins in some outmoded racial caricature. But that it irrelevant. Is it the business of the police to seize children's toys that convey messages their chief constable might possibly disapprove of? And if they do, are the police not following some agenda that no chief constable's mission statement would ever consciously allude to?

Consensual unspoken agendas are particularly powerful amongst journalists. Take three adjoining stories that appeared in this newspaper last week. The first was headlined, 'Woman who took €100 after act of kindness convicted'. The affair concerned a Claudia Dragusin who used her baby to con her way into a young mother's house in Blackrock, where she stole a handbag and ran away. Throughout the story this convicted criminal was referred to as 'Ms Dragusin'. In the final paragraph we were told that she was a Romanian national, was the mother of three, and that she, her husband and her three children receive €344 a week in state benefits.

Next to that story was one about a similar crime, involving an Inga Janacuaskiene, who attempted to steal an elderly woman's handbag on a bus. Her nationality was not mentioned, and the one reference to her name contained no title. I would take it from her name that she is not Irish, but of course, that is mere surmise. Samantha Mumba and Olwyn Fouéré are not Irish names, but their owners are of course Irish.

However, a neighbouring story was altogether more forthcoming about the national origins of the offender. 'Briton dealt drugs in Temple Bar', ran the headline. The opening sentence was equally informative. 'An English electrical engineer will be sentenced by Dublin Criminal Court after being caught in Temple Bar selling drugs,' it declared. After naming him as Dean Matthews, all further references to this convicted drubs dealer referred to him by his surname alone.

So what is going on here? A woman who unscrupulously plays upon the charitable instincts of a young mother and then robs her in her home is referred to by the title 'Ms' throughout a news story, which of course implies respect, and her place of origin is kept to the final paragraph. In another, a similar robber appears to be foreign, but if she is, we are not told. And in the third story, not merely are we told the national identity of the criminal, but it is the main feature of both the headline and the opening paragraph.

Let's switch the terms around. If Dean Matthews had been Nigerian, would that have been in the headline? Would the fact that he was an Ibo have been the opening to the news story that followed? If Claudia Dragusin had been Claude Dragusin, and he had been found guilty of cruelly duping a woman and robbing her, would he have been referred to as 'Mr Dragusin' in the story reporting his conviction?

We know the answer to all these questions. Moreover, we know that the term 'Nigerian' or 'Romanian' are now allowed into headlines only if there is an implicit victimhood in the stories that follow. If there is any question of culpability, then their national identities would not be a main feature of the story. And if this were an all-embracing norm, it would be fine: except it is clearly not, as the example of Dean Matthews suggests.

There is an agenda here, but because it exists in the unconscious, and is unquestionably assumed to be culturally normative, its existence is largely unsuspected. I use the examples presented by this newspaper out of convenience – but much the same culture informs most newspapers and RTÉ. Liberal political correctness infuses our media, with our own particular dialect of it: both the *Irish* and *Sunday Independent* have cravenly now even taken to asterisking the word 'bastard'.

The most fascinating aspect of this faith without a Church is how its guiding dogmas, its terminology and its rules are generally understood without ever being discussed or defined. In terms of journalistic respect, at the bottom of the heap are white, middle-class heterosexual British males. It is possible to say almost anything about them in an Irish headline (though any British newspaper that made such a feature of the national origins of an Irish drugs dealer would be denounced by our quiveringly sensitive tribal guardians on the airwaves for 'racism').

Next in the inverse hierarchy of legitimate targets are their Irish equivalents. At the far end of a subtle and complex spectrum involving gender, orientation, race, class and ethnicity (i.e., Traveller/Romany/gypsy) would be an asylum-seeking, circumcision-fleeing, Nigerian Lesbian Traveller, with children in Laois and Lagos. And whereas the Briton's nationality would implicitly be part of an accusation, the Nigerian's would be invoked in exoneration. But the really beautiful thing is that the people who so religiously follow this quasi-liberal, politically correct agenda would hotly deny that it even exists.

[7 March 2006]

VI.9. *The Equality Authority*

Is there no end to the absurdities, the grotesqueries and the ideological idiocies of the Equality Authority? It has its own thought police, and uniquely and probably unconstitutionally, it has its very own judiciary: theirs is a world in which investigating officer and presiding judge are cut from the same ideological timber of egalitarian mumbo-jumbo. If they were some strange cult living in a bog in Offaly with nude witches, British Sunday newspapers could send their magazine colour-writers to describe their weird habits and even weirder beliefs. But they are not. They sit in the heart of government, with their own inspectorate, their own bureaucracy, their own gibbering agenda, and their own mad laughter at midnight.

The latest insane ruling from this bunch of looneys concerns a Somalian gentleman named Mohamed Haji Hassan, who is now an Irish citizen. He went to Western Union to collect £50 sterling that had been sent to him from Britain. But Western Union told him that the money had been withheld by the United States Treasury, and a copy of his passport would have to be sent to the FBI before the money could be released. This was because Western Union had a policy of suspending transfers to anyone whose name resembled any on a list of terrorism or drugs-dealing suspects.

Mohamed Haji Hussan complained to the Equality Authority, and an inspector considered the case. She ruled that Western Union was entitled to freeze the money transfer under a European Council ruling. But she also ruled that that there was no requirement under the European Council regulation for Western Union to check Mohamed Haji Hassan's name in the US.

She then – get this – ruled that Western Union had *indirectly* discriminated against him on religious grounds, and awarded him €4000 in compensation. Now at what point was he discriminated against on religious grounds? There might or might not have been EC regulations to check his name with the US authorities, but the fact that Western Union did so is unrelated to his religious practices, whatever they are. Moreover, Western Union is a US-registered company. Federal law obliges it to report any financial transactions it is concerned about.

But I have a sick, sinking sensation at the bottom of all this. It is simply that Mohamed is called Mohamed, and that therefore to check his name at all is to discriminate against him. But of course this is a circular argument. The only religious war in the world, defined by its participants as being solely religious, is that being waged by Muslim fanatics against the rest of us, including other Muslims. And of course, many Muslim men, peaceful and terrorist alike, have some version or other of the name Mohammed – Ahmed, Mahomet, Mahmet, Mohamed – within their own name. Does that not mean that to investigate any Muslim because his name is similar to that of a known Islamicist terrorist, is to discriminate against him?

Therefore the only people one can lawfully investigate for their involvement in Islamic terrorism are those who are clearly not Muslim. People called Cohen, Goldberg, Singh, Christopher, Bernadette, Jean-Battiste, Immaculata, are legitimate targets of enquiry: but anyone with a name like Mohammed Atta, the lovely lad who crashed the American Airlines Boeing 767 from Boston into the North Tower of the World Trade Center obviously cannot be investigated.

Using that same principle, it is clearly discriminatory to investigate an Irish person for involvement in the IRA. Enquiries henceforth into Provisional terrorism will be confined to Sikhs, Tories, Ulster Unionists, Congolese pygmies, Eskimos, Finns and Australian Aborigines.

So welcome to the wonderworld of the Equality Authority, whose chief executive and high priest, Niall Crowley, declared of the Hassan case: 'It highlights difficulties experienced by the Muslim community.' No it doesn't. It highlights how our society has been hijacked by agenda-driven ideologues who do not live in the world the rest of us live in, the one in which the real threat of terrorism means that innocent people like Mohamed Haji Hassan have to be investigated so that guilty ones like Mohammed Atta can be stopped before they massacre thousands.

And so what is Western Union to do now with financial transactions involving men whose names resemble those of Islamicists? Is it to be fined €4000 every time it sends a Muslim's name to the FBI for investigation? Or is Ireland's role in the war against terror now to be the safe money-laundering depot for Al-Qaeda, courtesy of the Equality Authority?

Which brings us to the real contradiction at the heart of this case. The government department to which this band of barking brothers answers and which actually finances their lunacies, is the same government department charged with fighting terror: the Department of Justice. Moreover, this same Department is in contact with the FBI and other US intelligence agencies every day, supplying information about the activities of Islamic terrorists in Ireland. Has the Minister for Justice called in Niall Crowley to hear the Equality Authority's new cardinal rule, which apparently is that the only people who may not be investigated for participation in Muslim terrorist groups are Muslims?

I can't say I know Michael McDowell all that well, but he does rather strike me as being a chap with quite a shortish fuse. Which leaves me with just one question. Has the Minister for Justice called in Niall Crowley to explain to him the broader equality industry's new cardinal rule, which apparently is that the only people who may not be investigated for participation in Muslim terrorist groups are Muslims?

[24 March 2006]

VII. The Arts & So On

VII.1. The Opera at Garsington

It is one of the deceits and the conceits in English-speaking countries that opera is primarily a musical art form; but of course we say this, because we are largely unable to follow the text. Opera is thus often reduced to being barely more than a concert, in which the performers show how adept they at multitasking by moving around the stage in funny costumes as they sing. For most of the audience, the relationship between the music and the narrative is often tenuous, or even non-existent.

The usual way round that problem has of course been the opera synopsis, the writers of which have traditionally striven to make as incomprehensible as flat-pack assembly instructions for an electron microscope. Even if you could understand the ludicrous opera plots after they have been reduced to a few words, it doesn't mean you can remember them as the drama unfolds before you, and you try to recall who is Bartolo and who is Basilio. Moreover, even if you can remember the plot, it means of course that here are no surprises, in a narrative which might be full of them. The entire purpose of the drama is thus subverted.

We have accepted this destruction of the operatic form as normal, which is sad, and unnecessary, as a recent production of *The Marriage of Figaro* I attended in Garsington in Oxfordshire testifies. One of the keys to the triumph of Garsington festivals is that every aspect of the opera must be enjoyed, and the drama that is locked in the Italian language is opened by the technological key of surtitles. Thus the recitative in particular, that strange half-melodic formula for carrying the true narrative of the opera, is carried in illuminated text slightly above the players. The entire plot is opened up: the transformation from a strange, dysfunctional concert to true musical drama becomes possible, and real opera is triumphantly born.

The revelation about *The Marriage of Figaro* which the use of surtitles makes clear is that it is a truly hilarious comedy, requiring great comic timing as well as serious acting skills. And in the middle of this opera buffa there are the great jewels of Mozart's arias, so absurdly beautiful, so magnificently and extravagantly rising above their comic setting. It almost like an Alan Ayckbourne play with great music, one, moreover, which allows the singers both to sing and act. One of the cast is Irish – Doreen Curran, playing a male page with a delightfully funny and roguish sexual ambiguity, as befits the quite explicit bawdiness of the genre.

Garsington is sort of outdoors. The audience is covered by an awning, as is most of the stage and the pit. Last week, nature decided to take a hand in the proceedings and lined up a thunderstorm that rather resembled the battle for Berlin, April 1945. It made its appearance during the long interval allowed for dinner (the opera begins at 5.30 pm), and proceeded to unleash a violent Niagara over the stage and the auditorium. Winds gusted madly, and the awnings cracked like whips. The result was sensational.

Now the conductor, Jane Glover, was notionally in cover. But some meteorological freak caused a torrent of rain to advance sideways under the tarpaulin over her head, and to drop vertically the moment it detected her handsome Scottish scalp. In other words, for her the evening was like conducting from within the power shower at home. Around her, waves of rainwater were with nonchalant malice washing over the strings, while their players huddled together like shipwrecked survivors on a rock, grimly sawing, bowing and plucking, and being generally rather gallant.

The stage meanwhile resembled the National Aquatic Centre. The admirably named D'Arcy Bleiker is perhaps the first singer to play Figaro using the breaststroke. Julian Tovey, the Count, however, negotiated the rapids in which he was immersed by means of the Australian crawl. His maid, played by Lucy Crowe, propelled herself to the shallows by a powerful backstroke.

Doreen, as is the way of her transvestite role, was changing costumes repeatedly: it is to the regret of us all that she never resorted to a tasteful swimsuit. Singers did not make entrances so much as plunges, and rather than stand when they delivered their arias, they simply trod water. Breathing, of course, is central to the presentation of good singing, but for this production, instead of inhaling between lines, the players more usually imitated spouting gargoyles.

Moreover, the opera did not proceed in acts but tides. Lesser functionaries swam in and out of the narrative, as thunder exploded overhead and the canvas snarled and boomed. Occasionally, there was the plaintive little cry as a member of the choir was washed out to sea, a tiny hand waving in the surging main, to which we bade a sad and sodden farewell, before redirecting our attention back to the opera.

I don't actually know how it all ended – it's hard to keep track of things when doing the doggy-paddle – though end it did, and happily. Moreover, and against all the odds, Jane Glover clambered like a seal from the ocean that was the orchestra pit, alive and apparently well. She is the first person ever to conduct Mozart in a wet suit and flippers. She briefly paused during the tumultuous applause that greeted her miraculous survival to remove a haddock from about her person, and then took a final bow, before we all eddied to our beds, conveniently downstream, after the most splendid night's opera perhaps any of us have ever known.

[6 July 2005]

VII.2. An Affair to Remember

There is absolutely no point in having your own little column unless on occasion you can use it to manipulate the market, as follows. I recently asked in my local DVD outlet – what can DVD possibly stand for, and how did any brand manager permit it? – for a copy of *An Affair to Remember*. Far from having it, he had never even heard of it.

This is like never having heard of *Hamlet* or Beethoven's *Ninth* or a Bentley Continental or *The Importance of Being Earnest* or the Beatles or Leonardo. For *An Affair to Remember* is film at its most filmic: disbelief is not so much suspended as despatched into earth orbit by the cinematic witchcraft of one of the great masters of the medium, Leo McCarey.

I have never met anyone called McCarey, and I suspect it is a confection-in-exile, rather like McMurphy and McSullivan; it barely matters, for Leo was a film-making genius. He directed some of the best Laurel and Hardy movies, as well as the most brilliant Marx brothers film *Duck Soup*.

But primarily, he was the master plucker of heartstrings, as he proved in that sumptuous display of sentimentality that is *Going My Way* starring Bing Crosby. There is not a more extravagant example of maudlin excess in all of cinema than when the elderly priest, Barry Fitzgerald, is finally reunited with his unbelievably ancient mother, almost in a mummy's shroud, whom Crosby has brought over from Ireland as a surprise. Despite this grand guignol in glucose, the film was a box-office triumph, and was followed by the even more successful *The Bells of St Mary's*.

If you read *Time Out* or *Halliwell's Film Guide*, they will generally sneer at McCarey and his works, because their compilers are cineastes who think that cinema is primarily a cerebral art form. Yet that most intellectual of film-makers,

Jean Renoir, said: 'Leo McCarey is one of the few directors in Hollywood who understands human beings.'

The need for a love story is universal, and Leo McCarey produced an almost perfect filmic jewel within the genre, in *Love Affair* starring Charles Boyer and Irene Dunn. Yet though it was a classic, he remade it 17 years later, this time with Cary Grant and Deborah Kerr.

This is insanity, the equivalent of the original directors remaking the 1988 films *Die Hard*, *The Last Emperor* or *Rainman* today. Yet far from not working, *An Affair to Remember* is one of the great Hollywood movies, and a truly brilliant exercise in audience manipulation.

Cary Grant is cast as a playboy who meets Deborah Kerr on a transatlantic liner, and the usual shipboard romance follows. He was 53 when the film was made, and she was 17 years younger: a not impossible gap, but for the purposes of filmic romance a pretty large one. During a break in the cruise, they go to visit Cary Grant's grandmother, played by Cathleen Nesbitt. But she was only 16 years older than Grant, and would have had a hard time playing his mother, never mind his *grandmother*.

In other words, we are expected to believe that the character that Cary Grant is playing is a generation younger than the actor himself – yet the film manages to meet and match that implausible requirement. Film-maker and film audience agree on a contract to overlook the inconvenient. And why wouldn't you, in order to include the greatest filmstar of all time, even if he never won an Oscar for a film role?

An Affair to Remember – *AA2R* – was shot in Eastmancolor, which is not as garish as Technicolor, but it nonetheless adds a level of chromic unreality to the proceedings – which of course, is actually central to the film. For true film is not realistic. It indulges itself in filmic culture, in tight cutting, sumptuous settings, sharp one-liners and music – the fairly appalling theme song exists only within the film: as a romantic ballad in its own terms, it is valueless, as its modest two weeks in the 1957 British charts (reaching just 29) suggest.

The passionate affair is followed by a trial separation, with an appointment on the top of the Empire State Building on a certain date if both are interested in renewing the relationship. He turns up. She doesn't. And now the heartache begins …

I have seen *AA2R* a dozen times on television. Girls, I have wept every time. Why not? I believe an appeal to sentimentality to be an entirely justified and emotionally rewarding dramatic technique. In the US, where they are less snobbish about sentimentality than Europeans, *AA2R* is a cult classic, and is the leitmotif for *Sleepless in Seattle* (the primary virtue of which is to show how superior both McCarey films were).

'Guys just don't get this movie,' says one of the female characters in *Sleepless* as they watch *AA2R*. Well, this one does. Which might mean that I am a closet homosexual/transsexual/hermaphrodite in need of some surgery and counselling: so be it. I am also in urgent need of a good cry, but *AA2R* is never on television, and I yearn to see it again. And the only way DVD outlets will stock is if there is a demand for it.

Men generally are heartless brutes, so there's no point in asking them to do the necessary. This request is thus addressed to my she-readers only; storm your local DVD outlet now, threatening to set it on fire unless it immediately stocks *An Affair to Remember*. Then reach for the Kleenex ...

[19 October 2005]

VII.3. An Irish Luvvies' Exchange

Speaking at a memorial service to Richard Harris recently, his fellow actor Gabriel Byrne declared, 'We never once talked about filming, or acting or theatre. We talked about Ireland.'

Begod, they must have been interesting conversations. 'Hmm, Richard. A penny for them.'

Richard Harris stared mournfully up from the brown study in which he had been engulfed. 'I was thinking,' he intoned, 'of Ireland.'

'Ireland,' replied Gabriel Byrne, sitting down suddenly. 'Ah now. There's a thought indeed. Ireland.'

'Ireland,' agreed Richard Harris. 'Ireland. Do you know what it is, Gabriel? I do seldom be thinking of anything else these days. And I do be longing for Ireland, and I do be yearning for Ireland and I do be dreaming of Ireland. And when I do fall to thinking and dreaming and yearning, and with Ireland in my heart and in my soul and on my lips, I do hear myself talking strangely. And I do find myself beginning sentences with 'and'. And I do be employing more auxiliary verbs and present participles than does be strictly necessary.'

Gabriel Byrne bit his lip, and stifled a manly sob. 'I do be knowing the feeling. Sorry, I mean, I know the feeling. We've got to stop talking like this.'

'You're right, Gabriel, you're so right, but whenever I think about Ireland, something inside me gives, and I come over all weak and soft, and I see the sun go down over Bloody Foreland, and I hear the laughter of children at Mizzen Head, and on the cobbled stones of the ancient Liberties, I hear the cry of the fishwives a-selling gleaming mackerel, fourpence each, a shilling for four. And from the Plains of Royal Meath, strong men came hurrying through, and Britannia's sons with the long range suns sailed in through the Foggy Dew.'

Gabriel Byrne wept the tears of the exile; they were strong tears, and manly tears, the tears of a man far from his native shore, far from the hearth where once he had heard the cricket's song, while his mother stirred the bogwood fire. 'Do you ever think,' he asked softly, as he gazed reflectively into the distance, 'of your childhood days, the days of innocence, of a goodness unsullied by so-called "success" and by the meaninglessness of that meaningless bauble "acclaim"? Do you Richard? Do you?'

'I think,' said Richard Harris, gazing at that self-same remote if invisible object, 'of little else. Success? Pah! Acclaim? Fiddlesticks! No, Gabriel, all I think of is the Ireland of my youth: the hurlers of a summer's evening a-pucking the sliodhar over a Limerick meadow; the hooker's red sail in Clew Bay; curlews calling across the peaty waters of the Corrib; and I think of that glenside where I met an old woman. A-plucking young nettles, she ne'er heard me coming. I listened a while, to the song she was humming. Glori-oh, glori-oh, to the bould Fenian men.'

'STOP IT! YOU ARE TORTURING ME! TORTURING ME! TORTURING, DO YOU HEAR?'

'Forgive me, Gabriel, it is only the unquenchable love that I feel for my native land which has me talking this way. In Kinsale, the fishermen are mending their nets. In Crookhaven, a laughing boatman is hauling in his kreel of lobster, and in a wayside tavern in Westmeath, a piper is lamenting the lost civilisation of Gaelic Ireland, the ancient keen of our forefathers drifting over Lough Ennel, as flights of lapwing head home towards the setting sun. A bittern calls, a sad desolate note: from the reedbanks comes the croak of the corncrake; and amid the stand of beech beside the old Protestant church, an owl hoots. All is still. Night falls on Ireland.'

'Aye, and I know that night too well. See, the shooting stars streak silently through that eerily clear dark sky. Hear the rustle of the wind through the trees. A willow-o'-the-wisp darts across the bogland, as the labourer wends his weary way homeward to his cottage, where his barefoot children await him, the parlour alive with the sound of laughter and innocent games.'

And now Richard Harris sobs. 'Too much. Too much. You are breaking my heart. But stay! Hark! Do you hear it? The spinning wheel – do you hear it?'

'Yes, yes, I hear it!' Gabriel Byrne cries, rising from his seat. 'I hear it!'

Richard Harris's eyes mist over. He speaks as if in a trance. 'Mellow the moonlight to shine is beginning, close by the window young Eileen is spinning, bent o'er the fire her blind grandmother, sitting, is crooning and moaning and drowsily knitting.'

'Ireland! Ireland!' cried Gabriel Byrne. 'Shall you never leave my thoughts?

Is every waking hour to be spent thinking about you, longing for you? Am I to be plagued with my love of you, down all the years of my life?'

'We could, I suppose, always go and live there,' mused Richard Harris, as a knock came at the door. 'Come in!'

It was merely room service at the Savoy Hotel, in London, where Richard Harris lived the last ten years of his life, arriving with their dinner.

'Live there?' riposted Gabriel Byrne. 'Jesus Christ man. You're bloody joking, surely.'

'I am of course. But my heart never leaves it. Never. Do you hear me? Never. EVER. Waiter, if you please, we ordered the Chateau de Cantin St Emilion Grand Cru '83, not the '85.'

[25 March 2004]

VII.4. Twixtdandf

This column, as part of its annual task of improving this world, is not going to allow that non-consonant which is twixt 'd' and 'f' in any of its columns, again. This is a fairly gallant ambition, but it is worth trying, if only to show that nothing is so vital that this world cannot do without it.

So, from this point, I will call that non-consonantal unit 'twixtdandf'. Now today is it is our duty to say only truths. This twixtdandf is an arrogant strutting thug, it truly is, putting its busybody proboscis around all sorts of locations that it has no right to stray into. It's only right that a columnist should finally confront this odious Twixtdandf, knowing that humans can start and finish a total column without it, and without noticing that it's not around.

And how blissful this world would turn out without this monstrous virus of twixtdandf! Just think of so many words that contain it! Vil★, and ★vil and abomi-nabl★ and wick★d and so on. Do you not find it odd that our robust four-unit words which folk usually complain about and which can usually turn up in print as c★nt or f★ck or w★nk or sh★t do not contain a twixtdandf?

So what's going on? How is it right in your ordinary journalistic world to print c★nt with a twixtdandf, but not with a 'u'? Why is a small coin all right, but not part of a groin? Why is it all right to ask a man or a woman about having forty winks; but if you put in an 'a' for that 'i', why, big rows start, and all sorts of tribulations follow.

So, non-consonants within particular words can significantly modify con-notations and transform a primary import. That's why this columnist is trying for a column from start to finish without a twixtdandf.

And just think. Why this curious fact, that twixtdandfs simply do not find a way into any of our daily taboo words but do find a way into many thousands of sanitary words in books, journals and talk? This is not funny: in fact, it's distinctly odd, and you must ask, why this is so?

Is it that our chum, twixtdandf, brings chastity to a word? Most truly 'bad' or impolitic words subsist without it; but many good words contain it in almost miraculous amounts. Think of that family of words for 'kind' or 'good', coming from Latin, and which start with 'b', with an twixtdandf following, with an 'n', and with a twixtdandf following again – I think you know which words I'm thinking about. Isn't that amazing? So, I must ask: is this small calligraphic unit a custodian of a particular kind of humanitarianism?

Firstly, you must admit that curious oddity of twixtdandfs, that it is so ubiquitous, and still, so without impact upon any words containing it. Look, say, at a word such as 'many': it sounds as if it has a twixtdandf following that initial 'm', but this is not so. So why is an 'a' doing that visual duty which is rightly twixtdandf's? Why is that twixtdandfs can land without a sound in many thousands of words, but at that point that it is truly vital, as in 'many', or 'any', it abandons its duty, obliging poor 'a' to fill in for it.

And twitxdandf is ridiculously ubiquitous, with so many thousands of words containing it. In many words it is just doing nothing, just hanging around, showing off. How can it insist on finishing so many words, though no function is brought about? How orally dissimilar would ar and ar★ sound, or hav and hav★: so why that concluding and wholly gratuitous twixtdandf?

Not just that. Why do you and I not insist on confining twixtdandfs to obligatory occasions and words? Grammarians should insist on writing 'futur' and 'captur' and 'raptur' and 'impassabl' and 'surpris' without such arrogant intrusions from that lazy, good-for-nothing show-off suffix, which is always turning up in words, but hardly brings much about with all its arrogance.

Okay, such words without concluding twixtdandfs might look odd, possibly sick, but that's simply out of visual habit: if from now on words always show up without that concluding non-consonant, nobody would think it mad or bad or unusual. In fact, soon it would turn out as our visual norm, and infants acquiring a grasp of calligraphy would know no dissimilar way of writing. It would grow into an all-dominating standard, and this world would know total logic in writing words.

But what is going on in Poland or Italy or Russia or Spanish? Is our chum, twixtdandf, constantly intruding in such lands, lodging in words without pronunciation? Just think about all that scriptural work – involving so many folk with so many ways of talking – which is invariably a by-product of such unsought arrival of twixtdandfs in words: nothing is brought about orally or aurally, but any word containing this irritating non-consonant must still command vast but wholly surplus inscriptional labours.

But not now. For as you will now know, you and I can pass through our days and nights, communicating without any confusion, and without a solitary twixtdandf in sight or sound. Therefore, A Happy New Year, Readers! Oh fuck, sorry, feck.

[3 January 2003]

VII.5. Apostrophe's

It was the proudest moment of Sam Fletchers' young life when he received his diploma from The League of Signwriter's and Grocer's and Butcher's Assistant's. Not merely was he now qualified to write the price of apple's, cucumber's and potatoe's inside shop's all over the country, but he could also finally propose to the love of his heart, Ermintrude Entwhistle.

She came of a good family, whereas his was of modest mean's. He was deeply aware of the difference in their respective class's, as, no doubt was she: and although he could barely bring himself to speak to her, he felt sometime's that there was a glint of affection in her eye whenever she passed him in the street.

Now that he held a precious diploma in one of commerces' most testing skill's, confidence filled his breast. 'I am your's,' he wrote to her. 'Through the day's of my life, through sunset's and sunrise's alike, I am your's to command. Tell me to swim in Arctic water's, sweet Ermintrude, and I will. Order me to drink a dozen glass's of poison, and I will do so. Your's truly, Sam Fletcher.'

Two day's later he received a message to meet her on Rathmine's Road. Nervously he approached the rendez-vou's. Ermintrude was already there.

'I am your's,' he heard himself repeating, unable to prevent the word's pouring forth.

Ermintrude visibly stiffened. 'It is "yours," she said with a note of asperity. 'Not "your's". That is the very reason why I cannot be yours. Or your's as "The League of Signwriter's, Grocer's and Butcher's Assistant's" would say. Do you not understand? I cannot love a man who does not know where to put his apostrophes.'

'My apostrophe's? What is wrong with my apostrophe's? I came first in all three apostrophe class's during my diploma course. I am proud of my apostrophe's. My lecturer's said I would rise to the dizzy height's of the sign-writing profession's, with my command of apostrophe's.'

Ermintrude winced in pain. 'There you are, you see. You are a good man and a decent man, and I would be paltering with the truth if I denied that I feel for you. But I cannot love a man who does not know where to put his apostrophes.'

'Apostrophe's,' replied Sam absently.

'My point precisely. I have nothing more to say to you,' said Ermintrude haughtily. 'Henceforth we shall be strangers.'

Stranger's, thought Sam miserably. How can we be stranger's when I know nature intend's us to be lifelong lover's? Yet he was not a man to submit to lifes' misfortune's. Back home, he looked up apostrophe in the yellow page's: sure enough, there were companie's offering apostrophe-awareness' class's throughout the country. Next day he signed up for one provided by *Irish Time's* Service's.

'No,' said his Irish Times lecturer on his first day, 'it is not *Irish Time's* Service's but Irish Times Services.'

'*Irish Time's* Service's,' echoed Sam.

'Irish Times Services,' said the lecturer patiently. Say after me: 'Irish Times Services.'

'*Irish Time's* Services,' said Sam.

'*Irish Times* Services,' intoned the lecturer again. Watch my lips. *Irish Times* Services.

Sam sobbed. 'Iv'e watched your lip's, and I ca'nt help it. Every time I see the letter "s" at the end of noun's and pronoun's, I want to put apostrophe's in. Its' human nature after all, do'nt you agree? Its' only human, is'nt it?'

The *Irish Times* lecturer repressed a small sob, and said: 'Lets' beg', I mean, let's begin again.'

Two years later, Sam emerged with an M.Ap. There was nothing he did not know about the apostrophe. Joycean scholars deferred to him, Beckettian ones revered him, Nabokovians did dances of Lolitian propitiation. And as he walked along the quays, he reeled at the apostrophic atrocities he beheld: Potatoes' 10p/lb, Flat's to Rent, House's for Sale. He was filled with shame as he thought of his own once heedless violence towards the English language, and to that precious little grammatical tadpole, the apostrophe.

Suddenly, he heard a scream. A man rushed over to him, crying: 'A young womans' fallen into the Liffey at Bachelor's Walk.'

'Tut tut,' reproved Sam. 'Surely you mean woman's and Bachelors Walk. It is Merchant's Quay but Bachelors Walk,' and Sam proceeded on his way, quietly deploring the abominable decay in the linguistic standards of today's youth.

'Help, help,' came a female voice, 'Im' drowning, Im' being sucked down by undercurrent's.'

Even as he was about to deplore the apostrophic deluge engulfing the girl's last words, Sam froze. There was something familiar about the voice and yet the apostrophes were a violation of all that was decent, all that was pure! Surely it could not be Ermintrude? And how could he possibly want to save a creature who so despoliated the English language?

Yet some ancient, pre-apostrophic Sam remained within him. With a bound, he had leapt into the Liffey and was swimming powerfully to the struggling figure in the river. 'The wave's are dragging me out to sea,' trilled the girl, 'and I ca'nt fight them any more.'

With a manly grasp, Sam seized Ermintrude – for it was she – and swam strongly for the shore.

'You are one of my lifes' heroe's,' gasped Ermintrude, once again on terra firma.

'Life's heroes, I think you mean,' replied Sam modestly.

'Whatever,' said Ermintrude, shuddering with desire. 'I missed you so much that I went to The League of Signwriter's, Butcher's and Grocer's Assistant's class's to win you're love. Take me. Help yourself to my ample breast's, my ardent loin's.'

'Oh, all right,' said Sam, sinking his face into her glorious apostrophe's.

[18 October 2000]

VII.6. Schmeernoff Kwollity Vodqa

If there was any good news this week, it was that an illicit vodka-distilling operation was smashed in County Tyrone after the word 'quality' was misspelt on the label. Yes, Sinn Féin-IRA can kill, can torture, can abduct and bury secretly, and can absolutely run rings round the unionists and the British and the Irish governments in negotiations: but the poor dears still can't spell – which is why P. O'Neill and others, have recently been attending English-language classes.

Students were asked to leave their spades at the door and their guns at the ready.

'Let's start with a song,' said their teacher. 'Seamus O Wail-on, give me a line from a favourite love ballad, if you please, and then spell it'.

The TD opened his throat, and crooned, 'Aisle bee seaing yew in awl thee oughld phagmiliar playsays.'

The teacher's jaw fell open as he shushed the eminent Shinner statesman with a wave of his hand. 'My God,' he said, 'you even misspell English when you speak it. I love the "old", by the way. As in "though", yes?'

'Possyblee. Thew itts knot migh phawlt that thuh langwidge ov the oapressor is sew illodgical. Thanx to thegm bleading Britts, I cann nevur rememnbur whitch spelling goze with whitch wurd.' He sobbed, and then cried: 'Uh Nayshun Wunce Agenn!'

'Amazing!' cried the teacher. 'You do it so seamlessly, so … He paused, and allowed a small smile to come to his lips before he finished, ' ... sew dieutleagh.'

The class stared blankly, uncomprehendingly, at him. He searched them with his eyes. Nothing. No one seemed to understand his 'deftly', though he thought it was rather clever. He began to explain. 'The final gh is silent, as in thorough or though. The first syllable is deft, as in lieutenant ...'

He was instantly interrupted by a roar of disapproval. A Sinn Féin-IRA leader festooned with campaign ribbons – crossed spades for secret burials, several little baths to denote interrogations, a dozen kneecaps hanging from little tassels, five hoods, six slices of orange skin representing dead policemen, and a few trombones, for army musicians blown up – rose, snarling.

'Excyoose mee,' he barked. 'Wee dugh do not pronownse lootenant with an "eph". Thatt is a marque ov Brittish ymnperalizm. Up thu rupublick!'

Their teacher – a new recruit to the cause, he had not been fully indoctrinated in the rubric of the movement – blanched. 'It's not just the British who say 'lieutenant' with an 'f'. Our Army does too.'

'Are Armeagh? Are Armeagh? What the phuque dough yough mene, are Armeagh? Weagh argh thee Armeagh ov thee Rupublick and wee seigh lootenant.'

Overwhelmed by all those 'gh' letters, silent but nonetheless sensed at the end of so many words, and aware of his gross military solecism, the teacher's face went from white to grey. Up until recently, he had been a card-carrying member of Fine Gael. His wife was called Jennifer. His children – Simon, Richard, Emily – could all play the piano. Nocturnes and so on. Poor, deprived infants! Why, they had never celebrated a murder in their lives. Oh, would he ever get this patriotic thing right?

'Kweight,' he said. Suddenly there was a ripple of approval through the room at the vowel sound, as in 'sleight'. Clearly, Sinn Féin-IRA members were connoisseurs in such matters, and relished an elegant misspelling whenever they heard one.

Feeling a little easier, he continued: 'However, we must get the spelling right, if our businesses are to make money. Repeat after me, and make sure you spell it right as you say it, 'Smirnoff Quality Vodka.'

'Schmeernoff Kwollity Vodqa,' intoned the class.

'No, no, no,' he said, perhaps a little more testily than was prudent. 'Smirnoff Quality Vodka.'

'Shmearnough Cwalliteagh Voldcagh,' they repeated solemnly, the room replete with unspoken consonants.

'Jesus Mary and Joseph!' he screamed. 'That was even worse. Are you utterly dumb or what?'

'Knot dumm,' said another Shinner festooned with medals for every conceivable kind of atrocity. 'Thysse is uh gunne. And this is uhspayed. Nough. Whott dough wee mayque in Tirrown?'

'Timearnough Ckwolliteagh Voughldkalgh,' he cried, an army of silent consonants and vowels filling the air, with the opening sibilant being stolen from the heart of 'position'.

'Weal mayq uh a troo rupiblicann of yew yette,' declared one hero.

'Erin go brath,' murmured the teacher weakly.

[14 May 2004]

VII.7. Homophones

Well come two An Irishman's Diary's camp pane for Homophone Eek-quality. This a grate chance four stew dense hoo have failed there Leaving bee cause of they're spelling! We have especially in mined awl those who hoped four hire Marx in they're English eggs am. Are intention is to show yore fail you're is sir ten lee dew two home oh foe bee a: a refusal to axe sept the parity of a steam four awl homophonic sounds, wreck guard less of spell ling, provide dead the word has a plaice inn the Dick shun nary. After awl, we awl have are own lexicality: its finally thyme to ex press it.

Bee cause, when wee speak, hoo nose the difference between too dear here and two deer hear? Hoo can actually here it? How can any won bee sir ten that when aye say wun thing eye do knot mean an other? How does the hew man brain no that I mean won and knot the other? Sew equally, when aye an ounce that something is dew in the morning, and u here me, how can yew bee shore that aye do not inn tend to say that it is due in the morning? Yew can knot, eve and though the difference is mass if.

At a thyme of grief, eye mite say that the undertaker is due in the morning rather than dew in the morning. Conversely, if eye actually wish two say that the undertaker arrives lightly during a bereavement, I could say that he is dew in the mourning: and regardless of his wait, I could say he was due in the mourning, which is all sow true. Awl the same sounds, but lodes of different mean pings.

Won second. What's that term, 'mean pings'? Don't yew mean meanings?

I, aye do: but the 'p' is psilent as in psalm or psychiatry. Yew psea, they're is the basic homophonia, and their is complex homophonia which employs the baffle ling rules of English; and since wee R still speak king English, then the psame rules a ply. In deed, we have to a ply them, other wise the rules come plane to the Equality Commission that their know longer bee ying given work.

Sew, it goes like this. Their our cert ten groups of letters which won mite reed, but which won would sell dumb prone ounce. Think about rhythmn. It has too complete lee unused letters, the first 'h' and the 'n'. Won rites them butt won never says them. Why restrict them two that word? Why knot say chown for cow, or phuddern for udder?

Pleas. Their awl sorts of sigh lent letters in English. Yew don't have to in cert them inn Homophonia, shore lee? How can any won understand yew?

Wee our knot trying two bee under stood. We are speaking Homo phone, a chording two the biz our rules of English. Let me revert to English hear, oops, I mean here. What are poor foreigners to make of a language which pronounces the final syllables of borough, tough, though, through, bough, slough, cough and hough differently?

Sew! What rite has any language two does side to limb it the free dumb of home oh phone? Nun! Four what wood yew have then but an ark quay? When I here such stuff, aye'm tempt Ted two spell how hough, and throw through, and then maybe through in a cup pull of silent consonance, so that how becomes phohughn.

If yew want, aisle bee really violin-case peep pull think aye'm turning soft; sew isle unleash the dreaded 'phthisis' prince supple on yew. This is the won which perm it's a word to have a hole lee redundant lexical cup let in nit. Better still is phthisicky, 30 purr sent of hoos letters won does not prone ounce.

Stop! Gnome ore! Aye no what's a foot now! This is a sill lee see son Colm, write? Yew khan take us that frivolously, shore lee? This is a groan up news pape per. Four wee doughn't pain nothing four such rubbish ewe no. No, each cop pea setts a reed da back wun you're roe anther tea pensive yew bye it new: sec and hand its knot sew deer, awl write. But who cells yes two daze pub lick asians thee zzz daze?

Awl write, aisle com Kwai it lee, its a fare cop guv, and jew got me bang two rites. Eve en sew, yew khan tall ways sucks cede in you're criticisms. Aye doughn't want peep pull tooth ink that this Colm is with out intellectual dime mention.

Four what about awl those stew dents – mails, most lee – hoo have awl weighs thought know won would ever right like them in new spay purrs, hoo assumed that own lee they rote homo phone, and that they were all a loan. Brothers! Bee at piece! The daze of the homo phones have a rived! Wee be leave that we *may* say what wee here; that is why we cawl ourselves maize!

A rise, home oaf phones and fell low maize! Hour our has fine Nelly Qum!

[23 August 2002]

VII.8. Miguyse

One thing that the return of rugby internationals confirms is that the word 'guy' has almost completely colonised mid-Atlantic English, rather like rhododendron throughout the glens of Killarney. All rugby players now refer to their team mates as 'guys', eliminating those other amiable and traditional synonyms for man – 'lad', 'bloke', 'chap'. Indeed, the last word now has the whiff of shabby and slightly absurd gentility: for anyone to refer to a young man as a chap is to invite parody, as if the term were just a little Brigade of Guards and the Mall.

But it isn't, because in the Brigade of Guards they all refer to one another as 'guys' too. 'Bloke', 'lad' and 'chap' are rapidly going the way of 'wight', 'swain' and 'cove', and the complex thickets of the termonology of familiarity – a curiously male collection of words – are yielding to the verbal rhodendron of 'guy'. And there is absolutely nothing anyone can do about it. Language goes entirely its own way: influences pass through it as if by a vast and unconscious act of group will.

For no one decides that young girls will start saying, 'I'm like, omigod, no way, I *so* do not believe you.' To be sure, it helps if a scriptwriter puts an expression into a hit television show: hence *Friends* and *Neighbours* are probably the most influential linguistic power stations in the English language over the past decade. *Neighbours* has universalised the rising lilt at the end of ordinary indicative moods, as if they are questions. *Friends* has introduced a little army of linguistic devices to common English, the most common being the use of 'so' as an adverbial intensifier.

Most of these will pass, and join 'groovy', 'far out', 'hep to the jive', 'daddy-oh' and 'sock it to me,' in the museum of fad words that belonged to a particular time, but lacked the essential vitality to survive the change in culture that followed. They lost the Darwinian contest, and linguistic palaeontologists can pore over their fossils and wonder what it was that brought about their demise.

'Bloke' and 'chap' seem not to have travelled across to the US. The former is almost certainly Irish, and is probably a Shelta corruption of *buachaill*, for 'boy'. There is a theory that it was introduced by tinkers recruited into the Royal Navy in the eighteenth century, and it remained a naval word like 'mate' until a critical mass of ex-sailors in population centres like Liverpool, Dublin and London made the term commonplace in English and hiberno-English.

'Chap' is like 'fellow' – it was originally a commercial term. It is the same word as 'cheap', when the latter simply meant a deal, a trade, and before it took its present meaning from 'good cheap', meaning inexpensive. A trader was known as a 'chapman', which truncated gave us 'chap'. Far from being the caricature word it has since become, it was once commonplace in working-class areas of Belfast. Similarly, 'fellow' – which, curiously, appears in robust rude health – comes from the Old Norse for *fee-lay*: someone to do business with.

For some reason, 'chap' became associated in the popular mind with upper-middle-class twits, and rapidly fell out of favour, even in its heartland, the rugby clubs. Those stout garrisons would, one might have predicted, have clung onto the word 'lad,' especially in its plural form, as an invocative term. Moreover, the word had currency in the US, the main cultural engine of contemporary English. President Reagan used 'lad' frequently, and it was a standard term in use for American soldiers in the film *Apocalypse Now*.

That was written in 1979. Now the word seems virtually to have vanished from the US and is vanishing in common anglo- and hiberno-English – though in both, it retains particular specific meanings. In anglo-English, 'laddish' is a largely uncomplimentary description of young male behaviour, and here 'lads' it retains a grisly presence as an affectionate euphemism for the IRA.

Not long ago, an Irish rugby captain would have effortlessly referred to his fellow players as 'chaps' or 'lads' – and would have urged them to fresh heroics with 'Come on lads!'

Not any more. 'Lad' is probably trooping off the linguistic stage, and much as we might deplore it, we can do little about it while 'guy' takes over completely. Guy comes from Guy Fawkes, and originally referred to the effigy that was burnt on the anniversary of the Gunpowder Plot of 1606. I don't know whether the early English settlers celebrated Guy Fawkes night in the US: if they did, it was in time supplanted by the roughly co-synchronous Hallowe'en, introduced by Ulster immigrants. Yet the effigy-concept of the word 'guy' remained in American-English, and in time mutated into meaning 'man'.

It certainly wasn't a common word up until relatively recently. John O'Hara never seems to have used it, and if Dashiell Hammet did, I haven't been able to find where; however, Raymond Chandler and Damon Runyan certainly did use it. In those days, it was an emphatically demotic term, and propriety would have prevented it from being used by the professional classes.

Now the word is everywhere, and something within me dies whenever I hear a man of a certain age walk into a room and, instead of saying, 'Hello everyone, nice to meet you,' he waves a cool hand, and says, 'High guise.' Or something like that.

Thus it is almost precisely four hundred years after his death, Guy Fawkes has finally achieved not the destruction of a Protestant parliament, but the destruction of almost every other synonym for man. Makes you rather sorry he didn't succeed in the first place.

[ND]

VII.9. Hurling

Last weekend provided the autumn climacteric with the first of all the All-Ireland finals. This is the evensong of summer, our September vespers, and the great glories of hurling, with comparable sporting-cultural events occurring at the Oval in

London, prompt certain questions. Because for all the mythology of Cuchulainn and hurling, the truth is that hurling is not played where Irish is spoken: it is associated largely with areas of Anglo-Norman settlement, and with the exception of Antrim, is essentially confined to semi-rural areas south of a line running from Tullamore to Gort.

Even this simplification doesn't convey the full truth. In Leinster, the Wicklow-Kildare-Carlow quadrant is virtually free of hurling. Whether this is any way related to the fact that those counties were so deeply involved in the '98 Rising might be purely coincidental. After all, Wexford was both the home of the Rising and is the quintessential home of hurling. On the other hand, it is possible that the manner of landlordism in the hurling-free quadrant did not encourage the sport, even as it provoked insurgency.

Landlordism was certainly a key to the agrarian success of both cricket and hurling – and in Ireland for a while both sports overlapped. Where landlords encouraged the games, the sports flourished. Yet questions remain. Why should Lincolnshire, alongside Yorkshire, be relatively cricket-free? Why should Westmeath alongside Offaly be almost hurlingless?

The two sports have come to stand for their countries – and though I dislike the concept of 'national character' – what has a Louth man in common with a Kerry man? – each manages to convey something of that elusive abstraction. Hurling requires three-dimensional, multi-facetted, intuitive genius. Cricket requires patience and stolidity. Hurling is certainly the fastest field game in the world: but cricket achieves astonishing speeds also. Just .3 of a second elapsed between the ball leaving the bat and it being caught in the slips during the test match at the Oval last week. Balls from 'slow' bowlers move at over 40 mph; from fast bowlers, at well over 90 mph, which means that half a second elapses between delivery and bat.

The two sports have something else in common. They are based on counties, and their culture is still fundamentally amateur. They celebrate local loyalties, local identities, local traditions, in sporting, team-based ways that are unknown in the rest of Europe. For we in these islands, probably driven by the example of the English, invent team sports: and wherever English is spoken, indigenous team sports flourish. In the US, baseball, football, basketball; in Australia, Australian rules: in Canada, ice hockey; in Ireland, Gaelic and hurling; in England, two rugbies, cricket, hockey, soccer.

The entire Latin world over two continents, the Slavic world covering two-thirds of the Eurasian landmass, the Indians and the Chinese with their heaving billions, have not invented a single such sport. Though, let us not forget the Afghans, and the chukka with the head of the defeated chieftain: however, hardly cricket, old fellow.

Last weekend saw public enactments of different forms of the same rituals of comradely hostility in the two islands. In London, the most mesmerising cricket series that has ever been played for the Ashes drew to an enthralling close. In Dublin, the hurling season came to a nail-biting, helter-skelter conclusion; but perhaps we had already feasted too well at that banquet of extravagance in the Galway-Kilkenny match.

These encounters are celebrations of kindred rivalry: of kith and kin and cousinhood, vindications of the sporting spirit that grew in English schools, and which Ireland then consciously emulated, if only to show the English that anything they could do, we could do better. This is precisely why the Australians feel such passion about the Ashes: it is the post-colonial Oedipal urge, but tamed so that the ocular orbs become merely objects of contention.

Was I the only person in Ireland who last Sunday was fretting over the rival attractions of the All-Ireland Hurling Final and the final test at the Oval? Probably not, though as it happens, needlessly: rain in London made the choice simple. We might pretend as a people to be indifferent to the fortunes of the England cricket team, but ours is the only European country outside the UK to carry major coverage of the Ashes match. When this newspaper carried an interview with the great Ian Botham recently, it felt no need to explain who he was.

For decades, the GAA cringed behind the barriers of exclusion and hostility, convinced, in a very typically post-colonial way, for fear that if it let down its guard for a moment, it would be overwhelmed by the game of the imperial master. The truth was otherwise. This summer has proved to be one of the most glorious in the history of the Association, as it has been for cricket.

And so it goes; sunset moves north each eventide and the sun at noon daily lies a little lower in the sky. We learn a little, and forget more. Yet this much is obvious, as autumn seeps through our trees. The largely synchronous political and sporting cultures of Britain and Ireland are like similar emotions and desires, but which have different ciphers. One is encoded in cricket: the other in hurling. They are two beautiful expressions of similar yearnings, similar civilities, similar loyalties. Indeed, there is perhaps no finer venue in Ireland for cricket than Croke Park: for the willow and the ash both prosper on the same riverbank of common sporting decency.

[13 September 2005]

VII.10. Irishness in Sport

What is this mercurial substance 'identity'? What is it that brings rugby supporters from the four nations, 'the Home Countries', together in the B&I Lions, and to cross the world in their support, or gather by the hundred in pubs across the country? And how can this commonality be seen by some to be a national compromise?

'It's an anachronism,' roared my friend Proinsias, who is from Ulster, where they are well acquainted with anachronisms. 'There's no reason whatever for players from this country to be playing in the same team as those…' I think the word he used here was 'phuqqing', one I'm not acquainted with – 'Brits. It's an anachronism, so it is.'

Perhaps; but that union created enduring resonances. We know that we can slice an Englishman in a certain fashion and produce an Irishman, if only for the purposes of sport. John Aldridge or Tony Cascarino were as Irish as the Tower of London, but it was possible for our imaginations to accept them as Irishmen-of-convenience, in a way which wouldn't really be possible with a Russian or a German. Simply, there are areas of commonality and confluence that bind the Irish and the British peoples, regardless of whatever it is you might want.

'Phuqq commonality!' roared Proinsias, slamming his fist onto the desk and breaking it. 'What about the Black and Tans? The Famine? Why should we be playing rugby with that shower?'

It's not just Proinsias, of course. The GAA community probably viewed the Lions tour of Australia with a diffidence that might have been sublime, if it hadn't been tinged with a certain hostile perplexity. What business have Irish players submersing themselves within a broader British and Irish identity, this B&I?

Good question: another question. Why does the GAA have a London team? Why do hurlers play a composite rules games with shinty? When two English gunmen shot an Irishman on 22 June 1922, how was it they were members of the IRA and he was a British field marshall? Reggie Dunne and Joseph O'Sullivan were born in England; their victim Sir Henry Wilson was born in Edgeworthstown.

Loyalties can be complex structures of opposing forces, like suspension bridges. David Beckham in the shirt of Manchester United, one of the most powerful and all-conquering teams in the world, will have the impassioned support of vast numbers of Irish people, who normally love an underdog, against a team which hasn't got a chance; put him in the white shirt of England, an underdog team which hasn't won a sausage in thirty-five years, and most of those same Irish people would support a Gestapo team in preference.

The IRA sniper who would happily shoot a teenage soldier from Leeds in the morning that afternoon could be cheering on the team the dead man would have been cheering too, if he wasn't in a morgue with a tag on his toe. And many of the stoutest opponents of B&Iism will as casually watch British television, buy British newspapers, consume British footstuffs and be aware of British politics in a way that has simply no equivalent across Europe.

Identity doesn't merely bind, it excludes, often on spurious or ludicrous grounds. When delegates from the different tribes met in Sarajevo to discuss their future ten years, they decided that they couldn't understand one another without interpreters, and insisted on Serbo-Croat, Serbo-Bosnian and Croat-Bosnian translations of everything that was said, though they understood one another perfectly.

This is an acute version of the phenomenon of finding tiny differences and turning them into talismans of identity. Part of this process requires a denial of commonality. Hence the furious rejection in some quarters in Ireland of the term 'Home Countries', even though it is radiantly clear that the relationships between the people of these islands are more Scandinavian in their intimacy and their complexity than the relationship between Ireland and any other foreign country, or Britain and anywhere else.

This isn't to deny differences, only to state that they exist at levels that usually deny simple description. And we can put these differences away for an hour and a half for the duration of a football match, and then resurrect them with all their ferocious integrity at the final whistle, just as we can invent them for the same period and then abandon them.

Part of us knows such differences can be dangerous things, a social plutonium that we confine within the lead-lined containers of things like the EU, the UN, and in more informal alliances, such as in football crowds and social clubs, which are as much about uniting as they are about dividing. In fact, we move in a swirl of conflicting loyalties, some of which are based on a created memory, others on geographical propinquity, and some – the Leeds-supporting IRA sniper – merely prove the strength of our desire to belong to some community, though it might exist entirely within our imaginations.

'Aye, but what about 1798?' rumbles Proinsias menacingly. 'And what about 1916? Give me one good reason why an anachronism like the Lions is tolerated.'

I can't, other than that rather like the giddy whirl of sub-atomic particles, we are bound by anachronism and accident, collision and contingency through time and space, endlessly creating and recreating differing loyalties; and the Johnny Wilkinson whose boot I was cheering last Saturday, this coming October, I will be praying he misses every kick. For we humans like our many packs; and the BandI Lions is just another one.

[20 July 2001]

VII. 11. The Grand Slam Supporters' Club

The survivors of the 1948 Grand Slam Supporters Club gathered as usual after the match last Saturday in their little clubhouse, a mashie niblick chip nor' nor' west of the Royal St George. There was a curious kind of exultant despondency in the air, the masochistic joy of valetudinarians that their worst predictions had once again come true.

'What the dickens,' murmured the Grumpiest Member as he looked around in bewilderment for the coat hooks, as he always did ever since they had been moved in 1973. The club secretary silently took the coat to the cloakroom. 'Always shifting things round, never the same from one year to the next,' the Grumpiest Member continued. 'Why do we bother?'

The Cheeriest Member blew in. 'Another disappointing result,' he chuckled, rubbing his hands and holding them against the fire. 'Never mind. There's always next year.'

'Next year? Next year? Do you know how many years we've been saying next year for?' snarled the Grumpiest Member. 'Where's the damned barman? Never around when you need them.'

'If we make it through without winning the Grand Slam to 2008,' said the Coolest Member, who being an accountant, slowly did his sums on his fingers, 'it'll be, ooh, about sixty years.'

'No,' said the Mathematical Member. 'It will be *precisely* sixty years.'

'As it is,' mused the Historical Member, 'the fifty-seven years since our last Grand Slam is greater than the amount of time between the battle of Waterloo and the Franco-Prussian War.'

'If we manage to fail for just one more year,' added the Gloomiest Member, 'and we unquestionably shall, then we'll match the passage of time that elapsed between the Wright Brothers' first flight and Yuri Gargarin going into space.'

'But we've had some great occasions, nonetheless,' chortled the Cheeriest Member. 'A few Triple Crowns here and there.'

'And some terrible times,' the Gloomiest Member interjected, with deadly effect. The room went silent as they thought of the appalling eighties and nineties.

'The defeat by Tibet was the low point for me,' said the Mathematical Member. 'With the Dalai Lama at scrum half, and a couple of yaks in the centre, I thought we might manage that one. I think what did for us was the Abominable Snowman on the wing.'

'Only to a degree,' said the Historical Member. 'Remember he died of heat stroke and oxygen poisoning before half time.'

'Is this a clubhouse where alcohol is served or a Sistine Monastery?' came the impatient cry of the Grumpiest Member, who being of the Reformed Faith was a little vague on such ecclesiastical matters.

'Cistercian monastery, I think you mean,' corrected the Mathematical Member, an adherent of Opus Dei. 'Was that worse than the defeat by Mother Teresa's orphans? God help us, three of them were lepers.'

The Gloomiest Member cut in: 'No, the direst moment for me was when we were beaten by the Lithuanian Blonde Beach Volleyball Team.'

'They cheated,' declared the Historical Member with some warmth. 'Insisting on sharing the same dressing-room with our boys, and giving one another nude warm-up massages and bikini waxes before the match. Bloody hell, our chaps could barely walk onto the pitch, never mind play rugby.'

'Chaps,' said the Cheeriest Member wistfully. 'Back in '48, we used to say chaps. And blokes. And lads. Now it's all guise.'

'Guys,' corrected the Historical Member.

The Mathematical Member, whose Opus Dei loyalties prevented him from knowing about such matters, suddenly asked in baffled tones: 'I've always wondered. What precisely is a bikini wax?'

The slightly heated silence that followed was interrupted by the Grumpiest Member hitting the bar with a half crown. 'Service! Bloody hell. This place is like the *Marie Celeste*.'

'So Irish Rugby has achieved almost nothing during all those decades,' observed the Historical Member, who was a Dublin Jew.

'Just about nothing,' agreed the Cheeriest Member, who was a working-class Catholic from Limerick.

'Looks like that,' concurred Grumpiest Member, who was a member of the Ahoghill Church of the Seventh Day Adventist Elim Latter Day Saints.

'Wasted years,' mused the Mathematical Member, a Cavan Catholic.

'So little achieved,' added the Coolest Member, a republican from Portadown.

'Roll on next year,' the Cheeriest Member suddenly cried. 'And maybe the next Grand Slam!'

And with that, the barman arrived, and the 1948 Grand Slam Veterans Supporters once again looked forward to yet another campaign to emulate the triumph of all those decades ago.

[15 March 2005]

VII. 12. The Winter Olympics

And welcome to the Winter Olympics, where we have had an enthralling opening couple of days, beginning with the men's blood test, which has already seen a dozen contestants eliminated. One athlete blamed the positive test on a pedicure a year ago. Another blamed the fog. Another said it was his toothpaste. A fourth said it was his time of the month. A fifth said – ah well, you can guess the rest: proof, yet again, of how the true Olympian spirit lives on in the test tubes and the laboratories of the world!

All talk today is on yesterday's polar triathlon, in which contestants wrestled a walrus into submission, plucked its whiskers, then swam a mile beneath an ice sheet, before finally using the whiskers to floss the teeth of a polar bear. However, not merely did the reigning champion in this event, Knut Fittelikkir, fail the blood test, so too did all the walruses. The polar bear ate the first three blood testers who approached it – a welcome development that many athletes have observed with interested approval.

Favourite for the ladies' uphill bobsleigh is Ulrika Reindeerdottir, whom nature has particularly favoured by giving her four legs and some antlers – highly unusual in the female of the species in the animal world, and relatively rare even amongst human athletes. Those antlers, and the aggressive manner with which she wielded them, have been a primary reason why she did not fail her blood test, the handful of surviving testers having decided that since their job was to take blood, not give it, they didn't give her the test.

Norway's prime contender for the 100 kilometre anvil-carrying marathon over broken ice is Harald Sphagnum-Moss. But strong competition is expected from the Swedes Carl Gustav Barrel and Magnus Opum. The Danish outsiders are Nils Desperandum and Viggo Vereyougo. A team of naked pygmies from Botswana has also arrived for this event, but never having seen ice before, and with an average height of four-foot-six, hopes of their triumphing over the Nordic countries are not widely entertained.

Excitement has reached fever pitch over the Polar Triathlon. This involves athletes on ice skates hauling a Volvo containing ten tons of well-meaning Scandinavian platitudes up a glacier. This is followed by the luge, in which each contestant descends down a vertical ice sheet on a coat hanger with a bazooka on his back at 200 mph, stopping every quarter mile to fish for cod with his bazooka. The final leg occurs in the Olympian cemetery, where the athletes' colleagues from less demanding sports – the downhill three-legged race and the ice-rink foxtrot – bury them with full Olympian honours: crossed syringes, a volley of testosterone over the coffin, and with ovaries at half mast.

In tune with attempts to give the winter Olympics broader appeal, beyond the reach of performance-enhancing drugs, yet nonetheless locating the events in the homelands of the winter sports, the Arctic Knitting triathlon has been introduced. Here contestants' hands are immersed in ice-cold water for half an hour, after which they have to knit the Icelandic Constitution. Points are deducted for

for any missed amendments, or failure to purl Iceland's undisputed fishing rights over its entire continental shelf.

After their hands are refrozen in liquid nitrogen, athletes must crochet Sibelius's 'Finlandia', with points being deducted for the wrong key, or for straying into the 'Karelia Suite.' Finally, after immersing hands in liquid carbon dioxide for a further half an hour, they must execute an embroidery of the Regency of Sten Sture the Elder of Sweden (1501–03), with – naturally – points deducted for any confusion with the hopelessly corrupt Regency of Svante Nilsson Sture (1504–12).

Bookies' favourite for the moment is the only Irish hope for the games, Sister Hibernia Irridenta, the 108-year-old lace-making nun from Carrickmacross. Her body temperature has never risen above 2 degrees centigrade since her order – The Impoverished & Wizened Little Sisters of Arachnia, of which she is the youngest member – renounced money, food and warmth of any kind in protest at the shamefully liberalising measures of Vatican II.

But the event that is really seizing the imagination not merely of traditional supporters of the Winter Olympics, but of a far wider audience than ever before, is the Danish flag-burning competition. A slightly less popular variant – the slalom compared to the downhill, if you like – is the Norwegian flag-burning competition. These enthralling contest are giving cultures that have felt themselves unfairly excluded from the Winter Olympics in the past – because they don't have real winters – a real sense of belonging. Kuwait, Saudi Arabia, the United Arab Emirates, Sudan, have all sent enthusiastic teams for this event. So too has the Gaza Strip, which many athletes – not being too interested in politics – hitherto had thought was a dance by a drunken English footballer. However, despite this strong competition from the Middle East, the favourite for the gold in Danish flag burning is actually a Swede: Sven-Abdul Hammerskjold.

There is also a ladies' Danish flag-burning competition, in which the contestants are all dressed entirely in black burkas, with no other markings, inscriptions on female attire apparently being regarded as sacrilegious. Drug testing of blood would of course mean baring a body part; and as for acquiring a urine sample …

No matter! After a break of what seems like all of several weeks, the Olympic Games are back at our throats, once again. Time to stay glued to the television, reading a book.

[13 February 2006]

VIII. People

VIII.1. *The Great Leveller*

In July last year, Alice Wardle, aged 67, and her sister Mildred Bowman, 61, of Gateshead in England, both widows, flew to Benidorm for a two-week holiday. They always did everything together: both their late husbands had even been called Ronnie. On this holiday, they were sharing a double bed. As they flew to Benidorm, Lieutenant Martin Farkas of the army of Slovakia was flying to Kosovo on peacekeeping duties. The sisters and the soldier arrived safely at their destinations, and while Martin began a six-month tour of peacekeeping, Alice and Mildred checked into their room in the Levante Club apartments.

Martin and his men were serving with Echo Company in the Trebisov Battalion, alongside members of our own Defence Forces, and US national guardsmen from Indiana. That American state has a close relationship with Slovakia, from where the ancestors of many of its residents emigrated a century ago. Moreover, Slovakia is not merely a distinguished peacekeeper with the UN, but also a fervent ally of the US in the war on terror. No doubt Martin was pleased to be with the nice Americans in Kosovo: he might otherwise have been with some nice Americans in Iraq.

Alice and Mildred spent their first night in their apartment, and rose the next day. With them on holiday, but in a different apartment, was Alice's daughter Alison and her family. They all met at the poolside. Later, having arranged to all meet up the next day, the two sisters retired for a nap. They didn't even undress, but simply lowered the fold-up double bed from the wall, and then lay on it.

But they had neglected to erect the legs at the end of the bed. It seems that the torque created by the bed being at the wrong angle to the floor, and the fact that the wooden wall frame that enclosed the bed when it was upright hadn't been properly screwed to the wall, caused what happened next: the frame fell onto the bed, trapping, but not injuring the two sisters.

In Kosovo, Martin and his fellow Slovak soldiers found that their duties consisted largely of protecting Serbs from Albanian attack, around the villages of Plementina and Obilic, where they also distributed aid. There were many minor incidents, but no serious ones, and finally last week their six-month tour ended.

The day after the wooden bed frame had fallen from its wall, enclosing the sisters, Alison Gibbons and her children waited for her aunt and her mother to show up for the planned meeting. They didn't arrive. She was puzzled, but not alarmed. Meanwhile, the two sisters were still alive under the bed frame, enclosed as if a wardrobe had fallen on them.

On Thursday, some 28 men from Echo Company – no doubt excited at the imminent prospect of home – boarded an Antonov AN-24 transport aircraft, along with eight crew and seven military co-ordinators, bound for Kosice, in Slovakia. Air traffic controllers tracked the Antonov's flight progress, through a narrow valley of the Hernad River. The AN-24 strayed off course, and before air traffic controllers could warn the pilot, at 19.30, Greenwich Mean Time, the plane vanished off the radar screen. It had flown, at full speed, into the side of a mountain, detonating into a fireball. It was simply impossible for anyone aboard to survive such an impact

But impossible or not, Martin Farcas was alive. He had survived the 300 kmph impact into solid rock, which shattered the bodies of his fellow soldiers into their component parts. He had survived the inferno that had then consumed the fuselage. Surrounded by simply unimaginable scenes of carnage, he was even able to phone his wife on his mobile phone, and tell her what had happened. Then the batteries failed. So he was in the middle of a forest in the steep foothills of the Carpathian Mountains in knee-deep snow, with no communications, with no torch in the pitch dark, without an overcoat, and without a chance of anyone finding him before first light. The temperature was −18 degrees Celsius, and falling. He had survived the crash: he could not survive the night.

He survived the night. Hours later, not knowing where he was or where he was going, he blundered into the path of the very first search party tentatively setting out to look for the site of the disaster. Had he chanced to go in any other direction, he would certainly have died of the cold.

In Benidorm, Mildred and Alice were strangers to cold, lying on their bed, with the wooden case enclosing them, as July became August. No doubt they shouted for help and tried to push the box off them, consoling themselves with the thought that either Alison, Alice's daughter or the daily maid would surely raise the alarm. But the door was locked from inside, and neither did.

On 4 August, however, an increasingly worried Alison persuaded the apartment managers to force the door open. Initially, there was no sign of the two women, because the bed was completely enclosed in the fallen wall frame. But the rescue party finally found their dead bodies. After days of being trapped, the inseparable sisters had inseparably suffocated.

Martin Farkas was in a plane that crashed at full speed into a frozen mountainside, instantly killing all his companions, but leaving him wholly uninjured. Two sisters went briefly to bed, and spent the last days of their lives trapped there. What does this tell us? Merely that death is lord of all, undisputed master in both its manner and its moment.

[25 January 2006]

VIII.2. George Best

Now that George Best is dead, those old television clips of him can't even begin to convey the truth of the man's genius, for his talent was so full, so flowing, so majestic, that no single game could encompass all his mesmerising qualities. Certainly no footage exists of perhaps his most amazing match, which lives on only in the memories of the survivors of the 35,000 people there.

You have to be a certain age to have been present then, when Manchester United visited Leicester City in November 1965, and I have that melancholy distinction. Leicester were – briefly – a modest power in the footballing world: they had reached the FA Cup Final twice in the previous four years, and were above Manchester United in the First Division. Early in the match, George Best, just turned nineteen, was injured. In those days, substitutes were not allowed, and since his injury merely slowed him down rather than incapacitated him, he dropped back to midfield.

There followed the most sublime individual footballing performance I – or anyone in the ground – have ever seen. Unable to dribble or run, he orchestrated affairs from the centre of the pitch with a vision that was quite unearthly. He simply passed the ball, because that was all he could do; but with those strokes of matador's steel, he cut Leicester to the heart.

It was not that Leicester didn't play well; they were good enough to beat most teams that day. But there was nothing they could do about Best. He saw possibilities where others merely saw pitch. Soon a deadly chill settled on the home crowd as they watched their team being routinely, systematically and irresistibly slaughtered by a midfield cripple. An extraordinary buoyancy took hold of the Manchester United forwards. All they had to do was to wait for Georgie to plant the ball in some wholly unexpected position behind a flailing Leicester full back or neatly over the head of a floundering centre half, for them to run onto.

There was nowhere to which he could not lob or slide the ball, and in order to prevent themselves being made utter fools of, the Leicester defence dropped back, making their offside trap quite redundant. The result was that United scored two swift goals, forcing Leicester to counter attack. God help them: lambs to the slaughter. In a bewitching display that combined a profound grasp of trigonometry with the insight of the chess grandmaster, George Best sent ball after ball through the Leicester defence from impossible angles into even more impossible destinations, to an appreciative, if slightly stunned, applause from the Leicester crowd. The match ended, Leicester City 0 Manchester United 5. The following Saturday Leicester won away at Newcastle 5–1.

In having it all, George Best had too much. Had he been a less brilliant dribbler, a slower man on the ball, he could have been forced to play midfield, where his incredible footballing brain could have more fully expressed itself. As it was, he played forward, where he was not given the service that his intuitively insightful mind knew was possible. But of course, that would only have been so if the George Best who put Leicester City to the sword was playing at midfield, while the other, more usual George Best, the striker, waited for the sublime through-passes upon which to feast. He once described the despair he felt at match after match at endlessly seeing unexploited opportunities, whose existence no one else remotely suspected. Intellectual frustration, quite as much as drink, was the rock upon which his career perished.

For all the words that have been uttered about him, few have dwelt upon his integrity. He was often fouled, and though he was a persistent and courageous tackler, he never intentionally hurt anyone in revenge. There was a strangely fitting congruence that as his sublime career at Manchester United ended, that other great Irish player, Roy Keane, was born; and as his life ebbed away, so too ended Roy Keane's often thuggish career at Manchester United. The differences between the players were many, but the most important was that George Best was genetically incapable of performing the infamously dreadful tackle which Keane intentionally inflicted on Alf-Inge Haaland, and which effectively ended the Norwegian international's career.

Each player was a refutation of stereotypes. The ruthless hard man who deliberately hurt people came not from east Belfast but from a pleasant Cork seaside town. The creative genius, whose personal gentleness was testified to by the tears of the medical staff who treated him, came from the brutal shipyard streets which produced some of the most depraved, morally insensate killers of the Troubles.

Best's character was dwarfed by his talent, his beauty, his brain, his incredible sexuality. The person has not been born who could cope with all of his gifts. The only way that as a player he could have been intellectually content was for another couple of George Bests to be playing alongside him. And what young man could resist the insistent advances of the scores of beautiful young women who, scorning all the pretence of courtship, sought only the sexual recreations of his body and his bed? Four Miss Worlds sampled those pleasures; and for another three, he forgot to turn up.

George Best was burdened with more talents, and graced with more temptations, than mortal man can bear. All in all, he bore them well, gave great pleasure to millions of fans and hundreds of women, and has finally gone the way of all flesh. No reason to grieve; none at all.

[29 November 2005]

VIII.3. Joey Dunlop

There are many creeds in Northern Ireland, many sects, and most infused with tribal animus and regional memory: for they all have their heroes and their foes, which they regularly gather to revere or to curse in the strange covens of that place. But there is a seldom-mentioned sect that unfailingly cures those it recruits of all sectarian taint. In place of poison, it blesses them with the magic wand of enthusiasm and of personal loyalty, thereby recruiting them into a brotherhood bound by rules and rites that are barely a century old.

The church of these adherents is the workshop, their communion host the carburettor, their communion wine the cylinder oil in which they spend their days. They might be illiterate in politics and history, and their vocabulary in ordinary English be possibly less impressive than that of an average ten-year-old Swede. But in what they know, they are experts; and their understanding of the dialect, liturgy and rubric of the internal combustion engine is as exhaustive as the College of Cardinals' mastery of the complexities of Thomism. Joey Dunlop was their pope, their moderator, their archbishop, their pastor.

Like all binding religions, its hold on its adherents is quite mystifying to outsiders: but like all great religions, outsiders could see and be impressed by the effect that it had on those who worshipped within its rules. And those who gathered around the dismembered engine parts of Nortons, BMWs, Kawasakis, BSAs, were bound by an eternally combustible loyalty to one another, and to the secret scripture of their creed: the motorbike manual.

The petrol-burning engine has a remarkably ecumenical effect on those drawn to its influence, and its loyalties are curiously regional. Cork – for some reason – is one such area where worship of the motorcar is very powerful. Henry Ford's family were poor Protestants from Cork, and Ireland's most distinguished home-born car magnate, Sir Patrick Hennessey, was of equally poor but Catholic background. You must go to the opposite corner of Ireland to discover an internal combustion engine culture as strong, to Antrim, and the tiny, hill-locked communities where the particular form the worship takes is an obsessive dedication to the species of beast first created by Gottlieb Daimler 115 years ago.

North Antrim has a reputation for sectarianism, not least because it is the heartland of Paisleyism. Yet the complexity of loyalty, the subtle nuances of local tolerance and respect within a broader picture of what to the outsider seems like intolerable bigotry, means that even the most divided communities find a modus vivendi for everyday life. Differences are concealed; strategies of language are invented to avoid points of conflict. People agree to differ by not talking about their differences.

But that is not how the brotherhood of the motorbike conceal their differences. Simply, there are none. All those Herbies and Wilburs and Wesleys, the Seanies and Seamies and Paddies, with their spanners and their wrenches and their oil-saturated overalls and with fingernails which haven't been clean in ten years: they have found their grail of commonality, and not merely are they not participants in the sectarian conflict of the past thirty years, they are so absorbed in the mysteries of the poppet valve and camshaft that they are barely aware of the sectarian gale that has been howling outside their garage doors for so long. Philip Allen and Damien Trainor, murdered in the Railway Bar in County Down two years ago, were fine examples of the carburettor-innocence which has managed to survive amid so much death.

That was what made the local tributes to Joey Dunlop so very striking. Normally when such an eminent person dies, testimonials refer to 'both sides of the community'. Not in Joey Dunlop's case; there was only one community, which worshipped around engine block and crankshaft: small-town working class, highly skilled technically and conservative in its ways. Its members have their dinner in the middle of the day, they drink alcohol sparingly or little at all, and their few non-motorbike conversations will probably be conducted in a singular and largely incomprehensible variant of Lallans.

They know their own community, and their own community knows them, and they are content that it is so. That their heroes are the most technically skilled, physically courageous sportsmen in the world is beyond doubt. Their incomprehensible addiction to speed unites them as it eliminates all subsidiary selections difference. There is neither east nor west, border nor breed nor birth when motorcyclist meet motorcyclist, though they come from the ends of the earth.

Every TT racer knows of the certain annual cull in his profession, sudden death or terrible, life-shattering injury. Were racers drawn from a higher social bracket, as grand-prix drivers are, Joey Dunlop would long ago have been Sir Joseph Dunlop, and he would not have owned a wee bar in a North Antrim village but would have been a tax exile in Monte Carlo, with long-legged blondes simmering gently beside a blue swimming pool.

But he was in fact Joey Dunlop, of Ballymoney, County Antrim, the greatest sportsman Ireland has ever produced, not merely five times world champion in the most terrifying sport of them all, not merely world leader in his sport for thirty years, not merely such a technical genius that he understood the witchcraft of his motorcycles' carburetion better than Honda's experts, but a kindly gentleman of Olympian modesty.

Those who worship in the church that Joey Dunlop led wipe a tear or two away with oil-impregnated hands, say not a great deal, and return to their poppets and their cams. That was Joey Dunlop's way. It is their way too.

[ND]

VIII.4. E.H. Gombrich

It is idiocy to be sentimental about the past, but one largely departed feature of the childhood of earlier generations was the role of books in our lives. All middle class children had at least one children's encyclopedia, or sets of encyclopaedia: every household had Arthur Mee's *Children's Enclopaedia* and H.G. Wells' *The Outline of History*. Whenever the weather was wet, in the days before daytime television, children found refuge in reading.

By the time we had reached adolescence, most of us had grasped a rough narrative of the history of the world, from ancient Greece, to Columbus, to the industrial revolution, the age of empires and the world wars of the twentieth century. We didn't even think of what we knew as knowledge, any more than knowing the way to school was 'knowledge'; it was part of what we were.

I suspect that is no longer the case: that although computers and the net have opened vast new worlds of information for children, they have not created a simple historical narrative for them. No doubt this is one reason why Yale has republished E.H. Gombrich's *A Little History of the World*, which though it has appeared in eighteen languages, had never until now never been translated into English.

In his lifetime, Gombrich personally embodied two distinct intellectual traditions. The first was very much that of the Viennese Jew of Mittel-Europa; this was the man who wrote *A Little History* over just six weeks in 1936 when he was just 26. The Nazis later repressed the book, and it vanished, almost without trace, for over forty years; and then, in a move which should give heart to all authors of forgotten works, it was rediscovered by a German publisher, who reprinted it – with enormous success. By this time, Gombrich was a citizen of the Anglophone world that was to inherit the mantle of cultural tolerance and curiosity which had defined Mittel-Europa, and which the twin abominations of Nazism and communism had destroyed.

Bizarrely, Gombrich's new nationality was one reason why *A Little History* did not appear in English, though it was published in a dozen and half languages. Gombrich insisted that if there was to be an English-language edition, he would have to be responsible for it – yet he found it difficult to reconcile English history with the very Eurocentric themes of *A Little History*. Indeed, like almost everyone of his background, he believed – even to the end – that the Enlightenment was the source of European freedom.

It was not. It was the source of some freedoms – but it was also the source of the lunacies of totalitarianism. Real freedom, in the sense that the world now understands it, was a gradual growth within the English parliamentary system, which took its fullest form in the USA. It is no coincidence that the Eurasian landmass, which in 1942 was – with the exception of the Indian subcontinent – controlled entirely by perverted, totalitarian descendents of the Enlightenment, was within 50 years liberated by the Anglophone world which surrounded it.

No, E.H. Gombrich does not make that point – for he remained an intellectual citizen of Mittel-Europa to the end of his days, even when he had British nationality – and he remained wedded to the standard mainland belief that modern western civilisation grew out of the Enlightenment. And in all truth, my reservations about the true significance of the Enlightenment are neither here nor there, for it is easy to see why Gombrich's book has swept the world. It is a joy to read, not merely because of his effortless mastery of global history, but also because he clearly was an enchanting man. His style was amiable without being patronising – a quality which children can detect like a sniffer dog uncovering a kilo of uncut cocaine in a convent.

One subject that Gombrich had intended to write more about, but died before he did so, was the English civil war. By happy chance, his publisher, Yale, has produced a splendid new history of that melancholy affair, Mark Stoyle's *Soldiers and Strangers*. It is a perfectly terrible tale, providing some of the defining, and thoroughly contradictory episodes in the incremental growth of both Anglophone freedom and murderous English hibernophobia.

For example, 150 Irish soldiers bound for service with their lawful monarch, King Charles, were captured at sea by Parliamentarians. Their English captors later celebrated St George's Day, 23 April 1645, by joyfully killing them all at Pembroke. Such murders of Irish prisoners by Roundheads became regular occurrences, and were endorsed by an ordinance in parliament, which ordered its soldier not to 'give quarter to any Irishman, or papist born in Ireland'. After the battle of Naseby, parliamentary troops hacked to death at least 100 women camp-followers in the apparent belief they were Irish, though they were probably Welsh whose language was mistaken for Irish. This massacre was widely celebrated by Parliamentarians.

The great paradox to modern sensibilities is that while English republicans loathed the Irish with a truly racist venom, the royalist leaders often loved them. Prince Rupert regarded his Irish soldiers with particular affection – so much so that he hanged 13 captured Roundheads in revenge for the murder of 13 captured Irishmen by parliamentary troops. And what truly appalled the Parliamentarians was not so much the revenge murders of their men, but the incredible royalist notion that one Irish life was actually deemed equal to one English life. Yet out of this bloodied, fetid sewer sprang the improbable shoot of freedom that would one day flower as parliamentary democracy.

[9 November 2005]

VIII.5. Sir Edward Heath

The Cathedral Close in Salisbury is beautiful, and provides a perfect view of England. The wisteria rambles in fragrant, muscular sinuousness over cottage and glebe house, the hollyhock and lupin riot with English decorum alongside the cut-stone pathways, and the bells of the great spire chime their sonorous melodies, throughout the hour. Daily there is matins and evensong, the choirboys' voices drifting across the lawns of green linen, in the winter the cathedral lights glowing brilliantly through the stained-glass windows.

In that close, beside that cathedral, surrounded by that immaculately trimmed sward, along those elegant cut-stone paths, Sir Edward Heath spent the last decades of his life, alone, all alone. But that was how he had spent his entire life. Solitude was his natural condition, for he was a man of few social skills, and none whatever when it came to women. Possibly he was just neutral, as some men are, with no serious interest in sex or marriage or abiding companionship. He was probably homosexual, but in his working-class adolescence of three-quarters of a century ago, he had repressed those natural instincts that would have enabled him to have been the happier man he should have been.

Instead, he became this other man, one who was driven by single-minded ambition, who became a singular organist, a brilliant yachtsman, a fine conductor and the man who steered the UK, and thus Ireland, into the unprincipled, self-regarding swamp that was to become the EU. Moreover, simple singularity of goal ensured that he was a wretched Prime Minister: he was inflexible, setting goals for his government without understanding how to achieve them. He had a truly wretched inability to assess how other people thought and felt, a Free Presbyterian in Rio.

He was very much of that wartime generation of British politicians who put unity of effort before clarity of thought. He understood in his heart that Britain's true internal enemy lay in the trade union movement, now representing the ex-soldiers whom he had led in action during the war, and from whose social ranks he had himself risen. But he quailed from taking the necessary draconian action to quell it. For he was a political Unitarian, and had little understanding of the nature of enduring social identity or class conflict, remaining beyond all resolution or negotiation.

Thus his stewardship of Northern Ireland was catastrophic, not least because he listened to the advice of soldiers. These were not the grammar-school officers of the people's army of his generation, but the professional military caste whose melancholy duty had been to supervise the imperial sunset upon palm and pine. This was an often brutish, stupid business, and often with brutish stupidity British soldiers set about the task of halting that imperial decline on almost the final frontier, the back streets of Ardoyne and the Falls Road, and the drumlins of Armagh.

The tragedy that resulted was not of Heath's making alone. Armed with all that we know today, not one of us, from Gerry Adams to Ian Paisley, could travel back in time and give the wise counsel that would have halted the Troubles in their tracks. But he had his own contribution, and allowing the Joint Security Committee of Unionist politicians, Northern Ireland civil servants, some RUC officers and a handful of senior soldiers to decide the policy of Her Britannic Majesty's Army, with virtually no input from Westminster, was a truly majestic one. The subsequent glories of the Falls Road Curfew, Internment, and Bloody Sunday were the result.

He was not so inflexible as not to learn, and learn he did: but he learnt little that was wise, and embraced much that was desperate. The Power-Sharing Executive of 1974 was largely his confection. But with nationalist Ireland still refusing to support the very security forces that made the survival of the Executive possible, as terrorists from all sides assailed the settlement, the Executive was doomed in any case.

Heath's defeat in the general election in 1974 hastened the end of the Northern Ireland Executive, as unionist voters virtually extinguished Executive-supporting politicians. His successor Harold Wilson managed to be simultaneously cowardly, inept, provocative, ill-informed, arrogant and foolish: and thus the power-sharing Executive perished, as indeed did all its successors, and as their successors are doomed to do also.

By this time the two countries were within the EEC, which was to be Edward Heath's greatest triumph. Now politically he was fatally wounded, and he withdrew to the long grass where his political career faded and died in the Westminster Serengeti of failure. He was replaced by Margaret Thatcher, who aided by great good fortune and by her considerable tactical skills, took on the very enemies who had defeated him, and in turn defeated them.

So he retired to his close in Salisbury, to his yacht, his keyboard and his podium. One by one these diversions faded, until only the Cathedral close remained. Ted Heath spent his final years in his Avonside house, alone but for his Special Branch officer. The two of them would spend much of the day in a nearby pub, each growing majestically in girth, jowl and chin, where I saw them once. Heath's face had begun to erupt with sunbursts of broken blood vessels and the grim stains of liver spots. Alas, infirmity did not weaken him, nor the years condemn.

Each dawn he woke to another unwelcome day: by noon, he was back in the pub, without conversation, friend or true companionship. And so it went on, year after bell-rung, matins-sung, utterly deathless year. Until now.

The Cathedral Close of Salisbury is beautiful, and provides a perfect view of hell.

[22 July 2005]

VIII.6. Kipling & Yeats

This year marks the 140th birthdays of two of the greatest poets of the English language: W.B. Yeats and Rudyard Kipling. The former is – properly – still revered everywhere, but regard for Kipling remains deeply unfashionable, and is largely confined to British academics and – of course – High Tories. For the much-vaunted and voguish and allegedly liberal 'multiculturalism' does not extend to embracing the imperial culture of which he was the unofficial laureate.

Certainly, Yeats thought highly enough of him to include some of his verse in the infamous Oxford anthology that he edited: but I have no idea what Kipling thought of him in return. I suspect Yeats' early Celtic mistiness would have caused an intemperate rush of blood to the Kipling head; but the meatier stuff of later years would probably have appealed.

They have more in common with one another than the year of their birth (although Rudyard managed to squeak in by a mere day). Both had Yorkshire blood in their veins, but more importantly, both were outsiders in the societies whose virtues they lauded. Kipling was born of British parents in India, moving finally to England only in adult life. Yeats was born in Dublin, of Protestant and emphatically un-Gaelic stock.

Yet each became versifiers of worlds they could only glimpse into from the outside: not knowing those worlds in a truly personal sense, they were able to find beauty and magic where their natural inhabitants might have found merely humdrum mundanity and mediocrity. No farrier writes hymns to the forge, no sailor pens paeans to the sea.

Kipling was actually more remarkable is his emotional transferences, because his were many-directional. His childhood was spent amongst the European merchant classes of Bombay, but he got captivating insights into the real India through the household servants. Similarly, young William Butler Yeats was introduced to that Other Ireland in Sandymount, where the Yeats' retainers usually spoke Irish.

But Kipling was also a stranger in England, which perhaps enabled him to love its ways with the detached enthusiasm of the outsider. Moreover, his enthusiasms were not confined to the peoples of the Raj and of Britain. He had an extraordinarily powerful affection for Ireland, and one of his most famous characters Kim was half-Irish. To be sure, it was an Ireland of his imagination, largely populated by stoutly loyal soldiery: *My name is O'Kelly, I've heard the Revelly, From Birr to Bareilly, from Leeds to Lahore.* But inevitably, when the people of Ireland let his vision down with their ambitions for Home Rule, he felt betrayed and enraged.

Irish nationalists of course remember him for his intemperate poem about the perils of Irish self-government 'Ulster 1912'. But looked at coldly across the ninety years which separated us from then, how genuinely tolerant was Irish nationalism of Irish unionism? Never mind what we all know about the fate of Irish nationalists under a northern unionist government: were public expressions of unionist sympathy freely permitted in finally independent Ireland ten years or more after that poem was written?

Kipling was a man of great anger, and prey to the anti-Semitism that was extremely powerful across Europe at the time. Though this was deplorable, we should not view this bigotry solely through the lens of the Holocaust, nor was it the inevitable precursor of the Final Solution. Yet even in his worst anti-Semitism, Kipling's pen found greater truths. In his froth-flecked fulminations over the elevation of the attorney general Sir Rufus Isaacs – who had benefited financially from insider-dealing – to Lord Chief Justice, he accurately summed up the conduct of all judges who have an eye on preferment.

> Search and probe Gehazi,
> As thou of all canst try,

> The truthful, well-weighed answer
> That tells the blacker lie –

Do these words not strike to the very heart of the Hamilton report of the Beef Tribunal?

His political unionism, both towards India and Ireland, was complex. It certainly was not racist. The often misquoted lines about east and west never meeting goes on: 'But there is neither East nor West, Border nor Breed nor Birth, When two strong men stand face to face though they come from the ends of the earth'. The poem concludes with an Indian and Englishman becoming brothers-in-blood. On the other hand, he was an admirer of that abominable creature, Cecil Rhodes.

But we should not judge Kipling by his friends or by today's political standards. It is as of the coiner of some of the finest expressions in English that we should remember him. 'If' is one the greatest and most irreducible, perfectly pitched poems in the language: but so too is 'The Gods of the Copybook Headings', which combines great wisdom with unforgettable verse. And there is no angrier denunciation of war, and the vanities of generals, than 'Mesopotamia 1917' –

> But the men who left them thriftily to die in their own dung
> Shall they come with years and honour to the grave?

Both Yeats and Kipling receive four pages in *The Oxford Dictionary of Quotations*, though neither gets the length each deserves. Only one poet who was (roughly) a contemporary of theirs gets more, and that is T.S. Eliot, who particularly admired Kipling. He manages over five. No, he was not like the other two born in 1865: but all three have a certain chronological congruity; he died in 1965. Subtract these three great men – all of whose various anniversaries we should be marking this year – from the poetry in the English language of the past century and a half, and barely a threadbare corpse remains.

[13 January 2005]

VIII. 7. *Frank Patterson*

With the passing of Frank Patterson also passes, finally, the era of the Irish tenor. Singers with tenor voices singing the repertoire of Irish music hall ballads no doubt will still be heard; but they will not be of the species, but imitating it, just as some today imitate the three tenors from Italia 90 without convincing anyone that they are of the Latin singing tradition.

Frank Patterson was of the tradition that he so splendidly recreated in the film *The Dead*. It is of music of the drawing room. It is of music gathered around the family piano. It is a celebration of Irishness in what today seem obsolete and irrelevant forms, not least because that kind of Irishness is all but extinct. Frank Patterson could sing the often-winsome anthems of Irish balladry because he was not merely of that tradition, but because he believed in it. He was an authentic exemplar of a musical form; he was raised within it, and adhered to its loyalties and its cultural priorities. That is what made him so popular. It is a music that, for all its naivety, demands authenticity; the bogus, the insincere, the mere imitator are soon rumbled.

So aside from having a lovely voice, he was entirely of the species he represented. He was its laureate and its bard and its ambassador, and if the Ireland that he represented was an invented Ireland, are not all group-identities based on conceits and deceits and the flattering falsehoods of legend? Of course, there was never the blameless, fault-free, unworldly world that is celebrated in the songs of the Irish ballad; and in their hearts, the adherents of that world knew that. But it was an agreed fiction which united audience with singer; and in as much as there will never be another Frank Patterson, nor will there either be an audience which subscribes so whole-heartedly to the amiable fantasies of which he sang. It is not so much that Frank Patterson is dead, as the audience to which he sang is dead also: indeed, in Ireland, he long outlived it.

I met Frank Patterson a couple of times. He was a ridiculously nice man. His niceness in part explains his popularity. He was unaffected and uneffected by shame. His niceness wasn't of the toe-curling glutinousness of Daniel O'Donnell. It wasn't laboured or precious or created or self-conscious or irritating or tiresome or ingratiating. It was what he was. It was the niceness of simplicity and niceness of honesty and the niceness of unfeigned modesty and the niceness of unselfconscious and uncontrived goodness.

I suspect that part of Frank Patterson actually half-believed in the world of which he and others sang: that world of the Kerry dances, and gardens where the praties grow, with Ballyjamesduff waiting forlornly for Paddy Reilly to come back, in which three lovely lassies live in Bannion, where also resided Mary of the Curling Hair and the Country Leitrim Queen, where both Lagan stream sings lullaby and bright waters meet. That world shimmered in the collective folk memory of the Irish people up until a generation ago, a better and more preferable place, an invented Tír na nÓg of gallantry and beautiful women and plaintive love songs.

Though nobody believed in that world in reality, in the séance of a concert hall or a drawing room beside the upright piano, it became possible to subscribe to its fantasies, an agreed myth which united people around a congenial fiction; and there was since John McCormick no finer medium to conjure up the spirits from an invented past, held in common and created in common, than Frank Patterson.

That was why Frank Patterson was better at singing these songs than he was at lieder or the more technically complex music that dominated the earlier part of his career. He was a believer. The church he sang in was the church of other people's imaginations: amongst his audience he evoked memories of things that had never happened and which belonged purely to the realm of the purely fabulous. But while he sang, he and they shared an agreed vision: and in recent years, it was easier to have that vision of a mythic past of Ireland in the US than it was in Ireland itself, with the depraved realities of Irish life, awful and self-inflicted, too inescapable to be removed by song alone.

Virtually no one in Ireland has subscribed to that musical version of Irishness for a generation or more; certainly nobody under the age of thirty would have the least idea of the topography or the population created by Percy French, Joseph Campbell, Johnny Patterson and others. And though that landscape and those people were not real, the idyll they spoke of for decades released generations of Irish people from the irksome captivity of political and economic failure. They were the essential narcotic which made life bearable.

We have no more Frank Pattersons because we need no more Frank Pattersons. But to have lost the childlike belief in a never-never land is not necessarily a good thing. Credulousness makes all art possible, and Frank Patterson was an artist, his singing was artistry: when he sang of Gortnamona or the Green Hills of Antrim or any other mythic place of song, for that brief shining hour his audience believed him. That is art, pure and simple. Of very few people can you say that they were an unmitigated blessing for their country. Frank Patterson was one such person.

[15 June 2001]

VIII. 8. The Queen Mother

She was born the very year before Lord Roberts was made Earl of Kandahar, Pretoria and Waterford, to commemorate the two battles he had won in Afghanistan and South Africa and to mark the ancestral home of his family; and she died in the middle of the latest of the Afghan Wars, after the utterly unimaginable had occurred in those two other places.

In the history of the world there has never been such a life lived within such a lifespan. No heavier-than-air aircraft had ever left the ground when she was born, and the overthrow of the last Manchu Empress of China that August of

1900 left just one empress reigning in the world, the grandmother of her future husband. In time she was to succeed Victoria, to become last queen empress in the world, and the week she died, China hoisted its first unmanned space vehicle into outer space.

Nor was she born to be queen, never mind queen emperor, or queen mother, or to help guide her country through the most atrocious war the world has ever known, or to preside over the diminishing sea of red on the map, nor become loved across her country like nobody in its history, until at vast old age she finally surrendered her life to the call of the clay. Only a churl would deny her magnificence.

But what has been refreshing indeed has been the response in Ireland to her death. The Taoiseach read the occasion exactly right by ordering flags to be flown at half mast, which has sent a remarkably powerful message of friendship both to unionist and the British people. Moreover, RTÉ showed her funeral live; and such coverage of a royal event from Britain not so long ago would have been unthinkable.

And there has been much pride in the Irish involvement at her funeral – at the Irish Guards pallbearers from Antrim, Limerick and Dublin, and the pipers of the Royal Irish Regiment being so conspicuous as the coffin was borne out of Westminster Abbey.

There could never, ever have been a more haunting rendition of 'Oft in the Stilly Night', played by some 180 army pipers, to the solemn metronome beat of a single bass drum, the opening bars being repeated time and time again with an almost hypnotic resonance. Goosepimple time.

It was the greatest funeral London had seen in nearly 40 years. Perhaps there will be one such funeral again, that of her daughter; but after that, who would merit it? And how long will such organisational skills remain? For it was they which produced a spectacle that was as breathtaking as it was complex, something that had to be seen in its entirety in order to understand the point and the power of pageantry, and how extraordinarily good the British are at it.

And there's no point in anyone else trying to imitate this, any more than people can imitate an Irish pub, or a French cafe, or a Brazilian Mardi Gras, or an American baseball match. There are things that seem to come naturally to some people, and organised pomp is what the British do best. The meticulous timing, the organisation of thousands of people in exotic uniforms, the blend of music and march: these, like curry houses, HP sauce and Gentleman's Relish are the legacy of empire.

Because this sort of thing is not European but Indian; it is the durbar, the very rare but hugely exotic display that will leave in the imaginations of the governed a sense of the enormous power and majesty of those who are capable of such lavish feats of ceremony. Asian rulers, with innumerable millions of subjects spread over vast distances, cannot command loyalty by regular visits by a viceroy or some lesser court dignitary, nor by the maintenance of vast and ruinously expensive armies.

The British ruled instead through their local agents, maharajahs and nabobs, who had their local network of loyalties; and it was these agents who would be assembled for the durbar. They would then return to their far-flung palaces and their distant courts, determined never to disturb the peace and order of those who could arrange such vast ceremonial displays. For pomp is war by other means, pageant a peaceful but decorously elaborate statement of military prowess.

So British ceremonial evolved in the Raj, rather like some mysterious beast on a now lost continent, with a different climate and amongst plants that are now extinct. It will be impossible to replicate that continent, that climate, or to recreate that beast. The one creature survives from that time, that continent, and since it is not possible to breed from it, when it dies, it is gone for ever.

But what a sumptuous, exotic creature it is, a wonder to behold, and every bit as much a triumph of civilisation as grand opera or a glorious cathedral. It emerged from its palatial lair once more this week in order to patrol the very streets of London, which the person it honoured once patrolled, in different and darker hours, 60 years ago and more. To watch it upon those streets was obligatory, for it is as rarely seen as the unicorn. Now it has returned to where it lives, and it is unlikely to re-emerge in all its full and glorious panoply more than once or twice in the next half century, as it has appeared only twice in the past half century. And never has a person deserved the wondrous accolade it bestows as she who was buried on Tuesday.

[9 April 2004]

VIII.9. Auberon Waugh

Last week Auberon Waugh, the greatest English columnist of recent decades, died. His death was warmly welcomed by the self-righteously liberal circles of Hampstead, for he tormented their holy cows with fiendish humour and irresistable puckishness; and the hostile obituary from the the most eloquent English ideologue of intolerant liberalism, Polly Toynbee in the *Guardian*, only exposed the world which he loathed and opposed with every braincell of his being.

Auberon Waugh, she said, was merely the worst of 'a coterie of reactionary fogeys centred on the *Spectator* and the *Telegraph* … effete, drunken, snobbish sneering, racist and sexist, they spit poison at anyone vulgar enough to want to improve anything at all.'

Well actually, there is more free speech in the *Telegraph* and the *Spectator* than there is in the *Guardian* set inhabited by such as Polly Toynbee: both publications employ columnists who are ardent supporters of the British Labour party. It is inconceivable that such comparable ideological latitude would ever be shown by the *Guardian*.

The left-liberal orthodoxy that has triumphed in academia and the legislating classes in recent years is no friend of free speech. In this country, a robust protection of intellectual freedom is more likely to come from a conservative Catholic such as David Quinn, an ex-leftie like Eoghan Harris, both in *The Sunday Times*, or a solo player such as Mary Ellen Synon than from the dominant ideologues of the liberal-left.

To judge from the fate of Mary Ellen Synon, Auberon Waugh would not have lasted long in Irish journalism. The lynch mob frenzy that engulfed her after her – admittedly ill-judged – description of the Paralympics suggest that the culture of tolerance in modern Ireland is not even skin deep. The substance of what she was – correctly – saying is that the only true test of true athleticism is in the real Olympics. The Paralympics merely reward effort in adversity. That adversity might be very severe, and the conquest of it quite heroic, or – as we now know from the Spanish basketball team – feigned. But there is no equivalance between the two sets of games, and it is intellectual fraud and moral blackmail to suggest there is.

She fell into comparable trouble – even being investigated by senior Garda detectives – for her observations about Traveller lifestyle. They were robust, but not racist, for Travellers are not a race. I would not have chosen her words, but I understand her sentiments. Though I make no judgment on Travellers individually – and nor indeed did she – I truly abhor the conditions in which so many of them live.

As do those who argue most vehemently that the state should do more for Travellers. Not the least influential factor in the creation of those conditions is a powerful Traveller subculture of illiteracy, state dependency, social exclusivism, domestic violence, high criminality, alcoholism and academic non-achievement. Engels said almost exactly the same of Irish slumdwellers in England in the nineteenth century; but Engels, of course, being something of an icon to left-liberals, is revered for his essays.

Mary Ellen is not for hers. Her reward from the liberal left was best summarised by Fintan O'Toole in this newspaper when he said that he did not see why the mass dissemination of such 'racial insults' should not result in a legal sanction. Where race comes in to this, I do not know, nor do I know what legal sanction he had in mind. It is, however, an interesting day in journalism when a respected columnist wants the courts to be an arbiter over how journalists should express themselves.

Nobody in mainstream English journalism, not even in the most virulently intolerant bastions of liberalism such as the *Guardian*, would have proposed that Auberon Waugh be answerable to the law for the things he wrote in his columns. These were anarchic, perverse, insulting, outrageous, cruel, and often simply wrong. But the willingness to accept another's error, to tolerate loud opinions one despises without throwing offenders into the clink or fining the newspaper they work for, is the price one pays for having a free press.

Nor are the press the sole guardians of that freedom. Did the state-subsidised health boards who threatened to withdraw advertising from *Independent* newspapers unless Mary Ellen were suitably chastised – How? The pillory? The stocks? Ritual strangulation? – give a moment's consideration to the philosophical import of what they were doing? Did servants of the state really think they had the right, on their own whim, to threaten to direct state money away from those newspapers whose columnists they personally disagreed with? Was there a single reprimand for such abuse of power? Was there even a discussion about it?

There was not, merely a nationwide morality competition, judged according to the volume and the vituperativeness with which the many competitors could condemn Mary Ellen Synon. It was *The Tailor and Ansty* or *The Rose Tattoo* all over again, the fount of outraged authority no longer being the Catholic Church but the bishops of illiberal liberalism, smiting opponents with their croziers of mandatory egalitarianism.

Auberon Waugh set his face, his life and his art against the humbug of socialist egalitarianism, and the world is the poorer for his passing. He provoked, enriched and enraged in equal measure. From last week he was doing the same amongst the archangels, some of whom have sent his more outrageous celestial columns to higher authority, demanding downwardly vertical ejection.

[25 January 2001]

VIII. 10. Michael Wharton

Michael Wharton is dead. He was the greatest British journalist of his generation – perhaps the greatest of the twentieth century. That he survived it at all, his quill still conjuring great fantasies from the vellum parchment on which he wrote his copy, was probably a deeply regrettable mystery to him, for he found the present to be an unspeakable horror. His natural epochal home was the pastoral Elysium of his own devising, in which worthy rustics toiled in the fields, yeomen coppiced the woodlands, red-faced squires in tailcoats cracked nuts before the manorial mantel, and noble whigs whigly nobled.

He maintained that the worst thing that ever happened Britain was the industrial revolution, with its ruination of the great estates and the peasant classes that maintained them. Other unspeakable events included the Great War, communism, socialism in all its forms, mass immigration, and any attempt by Ireland to modernise. That he lived in a world of caricatures did not rob his journalism of an extraordinary ability to find the larger truth, which was often generally concealed by the media's unquestioning acceptance of the new. (He would have deplored the term 'media'.)

His support for the white Rhodesian of UDI was quixotically typical: that the Smith regime was militarily and morally unsustainable was barely relevant. The Rhodesia of his mind was like the historical England of his imagination or his equally fictional Ireland: a land of contented peasants, guided by their betters and their clergy. The modern English world of equality agencies, of trendy bishops, of armies of social workers, of police performance targets, of metropolitan parks infested by male homosexuals at night and of the 'outreach' programmes of London boroughs which offered free flying lessons for black lesbians: all this was a hell from which he escaped by taking refuge in his world of fantasy.

Its name was Simpleham, the imaginary country estate unravaged by any event of note since the Middle Ages. Generations of peasants had toiled unbrokenly in the fields since Comte de Simple had arrived, married the widow of the local thane, who had perished guarding Harold's flank at Hastings, and thenceforth, all lived happily ever afterwards. Here, in this demi-paradise, fletchers trimmed heron feathers into arrow-flights for the bowmen limbering in the butts: buxom wenches drew creamy gallons from the udders of fat and affable kine, and cheery farm workers refreshed themselves from their toil with bread and cheese, washed down with cider; at day's end, the church bells rang for evensong, as an auriferous sun sank to the silicate growl of whetstone on sickle and the leaky wheeze of the smithy's bellows. It was the eternal dream of romantics: the lost paradise.

But beyond the stout stone walls of Simpleham existed a world of dragons. Here were the bossy monsters who made modern life in England so disagreeable: Sir Aylwin Goth-Jones, 'the genial, unpopular' Chief Constable of Stretchford, the arrogant motorist J. Bonnington Jagworth, the mad psychiatrist Dr Heinz Kiosk, the agony Aunt Clare Howitzer, and the 'go-ahead' Bishop of Bevindon, for whom a belief in the existence of God was merely an optional requirement for those who aspired to the Archbishopric of Canterbury.

Peter Simple's world was lurid, grotesque, enchanting, a columnar Gormenghast that matched that other and rather similar world of Myles na Gopaleen, whom Michael Wharton revered. Both were socially limited men whose company could – and apparently did – usually disappoint. Did they ever meet? I don't know. Wharton lived for a while in Dublin after the Second World War. Had they encountered one another in The Pearl or McDaid's, they would probably have sat in companionable silence, Brian O'Nolan with his ball of malt and pint of plain, and Michael Wharton with his unfailing brandy and ginger ale.

Michael Wharton was truly a self-invented man. For his family were not Anglo-Norman nobility, but German Jews who had settled in Yorkshire, his real name being name Nathan. With an aptitude that will be familiar to anyone who has studied military history, the British army's Intelligence Corps recruited this fluent German-speaker during the Second World War and then – naturally – sent him to fight the Japanese in the jungles of Burma.

Michael Wharton was right wing, but never predictable. For he was also a conservative, and he hated the American way, was appalled by NATO attacks on Serbia, opposed the US invasion of Iraq, and deplored Ireland's desire to modernise. Few could agree with all he wrote – but his quill never failed to enchant, as he tackled holy cow after holy cow, with never any fear that he might be seduced by the most enervating vice of journalism, the consensus. Not merely did he dwell far away from that abysmal trading stall, which exchanges courageous independence and questioning vitality for voguish timidity and bien-pensant compliance – he wasn't even in the same marketplace.

Now he is gone. So bid the archers string their bows, and let their mournful volley fill the sky! Bell-ringers, toll the parting knell! A riderless Shire, reversed empty boots in its stirrups, is led by a black-clad equerry, in the van of the sorrowing cortege; a single muffled drum strikes the pace; six swaying pallbearers shoulder the box of ancient English elm; and in the rear, comes the wild, broken paean of grief from the massed ranks of war-pipers, as sturdy Rangers from Connaught, kilted Buffs from Ross-shire, and tiny mountainy men from Nepal unleash, in plangent reiteration, that great anthem of bereavement, 'Oft in the Stilly Night'. King Michael is Dead.

[14 February 2006]

VIII. 11. The Curse of Clonycavan Man

On the last night of his life Clonycavan man watched the evening star hanging like a lantern in the southern sky. At dawn, he knew, he would be punished for his failure to cause the crops to grow and the kine to calve. He had been born into royalty, and with that privilege came the burdens of responsibility. Failure in that could only mean the ultimate sacrifice.

And he had failed, as he had always known he would. He was an unlucky man, a comical little antic whom no one respected. He should have been born a simple

herdsman, destined to spend his days minding the long-horned cattle in peace on
the bogs, away from the stern warrior caste who now held him such contempt.
For he was certainly no natural leader. His councils were usually bedlam, his pro-
nouncements often interrupted by jeering, ruffianly young upstarts.

They laughed at his hair too, though it had cost him many gold coins to buy
the resin from the wily Phoenician trader who berthed in the shallows beside the
river estuary, three days' walk away. He thought the hair ointment would give him
height and status, but it had achieved the opposite effect: as he strode through
his royal entourage he could hear giggles behind him, erupting sometimes into
mutinous guffaws.

Nor had his reign had been accompanied by luck. Winters had been cold,
summers wet, the autumn yields parsimonious. The wheat rotted in the fields,
the cattle had the murrain. Famine came, and the young and old died in their
peat-walled dwellings. Women cursed him. Children spat. He put more resin in
his hair, as the Phoenician had advised him to, promising that it would make him
taller, more kingly, more manly when he coupled with his harem.

But it did no such thing. Even his women mocked him, and found succour in
one another's arms. Finally, he had led the cattle raid on the kingdom on the far side
of the Red Lough, but fatally he had hesitated as he led his men towards the cattle
brattice, so allowing the defenders to close the furze shutters. From the safety of that
enclosure they were able to fire arrows at the now-defenceless attackers.

His *slua* had retreated from the hail of arrows, losing many dead. Even more
had died of their injuries on the long haul back home. Back in his royal enclosure,
he found plague had taken half of his harem. The night after his return, he had
woken to the tickle of a broadsword on his throat. He was then bound with hazel
branches and led to the stone altar of the high priest, certain of his fate.

'I am innocent,' he said. 'I tried my best to bring sun in the summer and soft
southern breezes in the winter. I made due sacrifices to the gods. I read the runes
of the night sky, and studied the entrails of slain oxen. All told me that my king-
ship was good, and if my people were patient, my rule would prosper.'

The priest was derisive and impatient. No traders came their way any more,
he said, because it was known this was an impoverished kingdom led by a weak
and powerless king. They must placate the gods by slaughtering him, and burying
his body in the bog-which-preserves, so that though he had been killed, he
would never know death, and would forever be denied the glories of paradise. By
that sacrifice might his people win the favour of the god of wheat and the god of
kine and the sun god in the skies.

He knew what fate awaited him. He had witnessed his uncle being put to
death in his neighbouring kingdom for a comparable failure. Unlike him, his
uncle had been a giant of a man, and his end had been long and agonising. They

had made holes in his arms and pulled branches through them. They had gouged out his eyes. They had cut off his nipples. When he pleaded for death, they kept him alive, until finally there was hardly any life left in that whimpering, wheezing body. Ritual demanded that he not die, but be killed; and so he was, before being despatched to the shameful limbo of a bog grave.

Clonycavan man wept in terror as he contemplated the last ordeal of his life, to be followed by an eternity of his tortured soul being marooned in his incorruptible body.

Briefly, he slept, and his dead uncle came to him in a dream, whispering, 'May no good come to this island which murders and buries the innocent. May its curse be that those who murder and bury their victims in bogs are rewarded beyond all measure, and thus war, murder and secret burial become a regular season here, just as in other, happier lands, golden harvests regularly ripen in the fields, and trees grow heavy with luscious fruit.'

So Clonycavan man woke from his dream, and before going to his terrible end, he laid the curse on the island, just as his uncle had instructed.

In 2003, two thousand, three hundred years later, the ground yielded up the dead. His body, and his uncle's, were separately uncovered in their midland bogs, while the remains of Jean McConville were also finally found in the limbo grave made for her by the IRA. Meanwhile the barbarian responsible for her abduction, torture, murder and secret burial had, like all such heathens on this accursed island, been rewarded with mighty honour and high renown, in strict accordance with Clonycavan's ancient curse.

[12 January 2006]

THE UNDEAD

VIII. 12. Bad, Bad Bertie

The Minister for Education Mary Hanafin walked into Bertie Ahern's office. 'Good morning, Taoiseach,' she offered civilly.

'Good mornin,' he replied in a similarly equable manner. The broad grin of welcome that followed suggested that he had not noticed a slight stiffening about her shoulders at his words.

'Forgive me, Taoiseach, but I failed to detect an apostrophe there. I cannot fault you for employing the vernacular when you speak – after all, you do pride yourself on being a man of the people, and Drumcondra people at that – but the least I can expect is some sort of silent grammatical sign that you have elided the final 'g' of the velar.'

The Taoiseach suddenly had a slightly hunted look, his eyes shifting this way and that before he replied. 'Wha?'

The Minister looked over her spectacles in the fashion of a governess who could have put down the storming of the Bastille with a single focussed stare. 'You did it again. No apostrophe to indicate the missing voiceless alveolar plosive consonant at the conclusion of the interrogative pronoun. Tut tut, Taoiseach, tut tut.'

The Taoiseach ran his fingers through his hair, his face as fretful as that of a plump Christian looking into the tonsils of a peckish lion. 'I'm sorry, I-ah didn't catch most of tha,' he said plaintively.

'Well, I must say, that's a considerable improvement. Well done on that very distinctive apostrophe between first person singular pronoun and the abbreviated first person verb, but I'm afraid, you didn't supply one to indicate the missing voiceless alveolar plosive consonant at the end of the final pronoun.'

The Taoiseach looked as miserable as a little boy who's just had a little accident in his trousers. He cast his eyes around him. 'I should of stayed at home today, instead of tryin to run da goverment.'

Mary Hanafin stamped her foot. 'Taoiseach! How many times! Go and stand in the corner, THIS INSTANT!'

'Yes miss,' he whimpered, casting wistful eyes at his headmistress, like a little Christian koala bear who's making his broadcasting debut on Al Qaeda television. He rose from his desk and shuffled over to the corner.

There was a brief knock on the door, and Senator Martin Mansergh came gliding in. 'Begorrah, and the top of the mornin' to you, Taoiseach,' he purred.

'There!' cried Mary approvingly. 'You see what I mean, Taoiseach? Martin's first tongue is Oxbridge English, to which he has added some idioms that he imagines to be Hiberno-English, and overlaid them with an accent which could certainly be mistaken for Irish, if listened to during a rendition of the Hallelulia Chorus by the Mormon Tabernacle Choir, aided by the massed pipes and drums of the Army Number One Band. But did you note the apostrophe in mornin', so perfectly pitched, to denote the elided final 'g' of the velar? Well done, Martin! Have a sweet!'

'Thank you, teacher. Taoiseach, if I could have your attention for while?'

'I'm afraid Bertie's not allowed to talk to anyone today, not until he's learned to get his spelling and grammar right. Isn't that right, Bertie?'

A small stifled sob came from the corner. 'Yes miss. Ah I-ah was only doin me best. I-ah don't even know what a bleedin postroffy is.'

There was a sharp crack as Mary Hanafin's hand hitting the back of Bertie Ahern's knee, just below his grey flannel shorts. 'Yarooo!' he cried.

'Now, not another word from you young Ahern, or you'll be staying behind tonight, doing lines.'

'But miss …'

There was another crack, like a circus-master's whip, followed by a hideous taoiseachly shriek.

'O I say, steady on, old girl,' interjected Martin Mansergh, reverting to earlier speech patterns. 'The poor little blighter's doing his best, don't you know, what.'

'His best isn't good enough. He's leader of the goverment. He'll get no sympaty from me.'

She paused, whitening at the gills, rather like Pope Benedict upon finding the consistory of African cardinals heaving in a vast homosexual orgy in the Sistine Chapel. 'Martin, write down what I just said in its correct form, would you?'

'Certainly, miss.' He put his tongue between his teeth and wrote: 'His best isn't good enough. He's leader of the goverment. He'll get no sympaty from me.'

Martin Mansergh went the colour of a garrotted slug, and sat down with a bump.

'You see, it's not my fault,' sniffed Bertie, rubbing the scarlet backs of both his knees. 'I-ah just can't help it.'

Mary Hanafin was so distracted she didn't even detect the missing apostrophe. 'Why didn't I spell goverment and sympaty properly? Shit! I did it again!'

'Its contagious,' said Bertie. 'I-ah even went to elocution lessons from Sir John Gielgud but I-ah stopped when he started sounding like ah-Ronnie Drew.'

The phone rang and the senator answered it. He handed the receiver to the Taoiseach. 'Buckingham palace, sir.'

'Good mornin, your majesty,' he began.

'Howrya,' Queen Elizabeth replied.

VIII. 13. Kim & Sin

All you need to know about the fair Kimberley Fortier is that she left hospital with her son William in her arms. William had not been staying with her there, but she nonetheless was carrying him when she came through the hospital doors. Why? Was it because she knew that there would be photographers there, and this was the perfect opportunity to be seen as a good mother?

How right she was. Children can occasionally be remarkably useful little creatures, even if sometimes one has to go to the tiresome business of spiriting one into hospital in order to be seen publicly leaving it with one's arm protectively enfolded around the little dear. Perhaps hospitals might consider renting out small children for photo opportunities for society females who want to be seen as good mothers on the hospital steps. Yet another use for otherwise unwanted asylum seekers.

The speculation in London now is that numerous ex-lovers of the blessed damozel will now step forward from the ranks of British society. One hopes so. It would add enormously to the gaiety of nations if Wayne Rooney, Cliff Richard, Camilla Parker-Bowles, the Dalai Lama and Michael Barrymore were to claim acquaintance with her loins, which, to judge from the lush voluptuousness of her eyebrows, are as bushy as they are busy. Her first husband says that she had numerous lovers during their marriage. Clearly, she is as devoted a wife as she is a mother.

London is full of such women, who are drawn to powerful males like horse-flies to steaming dung. They are clever, witty, attractive, beautiful, ambitious, unscrupulous, and sexually mesmerising. And men – poor dears – are apparently helpless before these creatures. When carnal desire is enchanted not just by overt sexuality, but also by beauty and intelligence, we chaps are like a rabbit being wooed by a cobra's eyes. People with male parts – PWMP – can be as pathetically weak as PWC can be ruthlessly predatory.

Now, here in Ireland, we must not be too, well, pharisaic about this affair. The idea of a minister resigning because he hastened the processing of a visa application is as incredible as the notion of an Iraqi minister for tourism. Fixing things like visa applications and planning permissions is what politicians actually do in this country. For years Fianna Fáil governments treated passports for this Republic – the very concept which their political forefathers had bravely gone to the firing squad – as Monopoly money to be showered on foreigners who had a murky past, smiled obligingly and had made meaningless promises to invest in vital constituencies.

Yet even in all the squalor of our political life, I cannot imagine two children being turned into the pawns that Kimberley and Stephen Quinn's children have by both their mother and their natural father, the arrogant and insufferable David Blunkett. The entire process by which he sought to prove the paternity of the children, and his ruthless desire to assert his 'rights' to have access to them reveal him to be a selfish monster. For the primary rights to be considered here, over-riding whatever feelings, ambitions and hopes of the two unspeakable adults now at war with one another, are the rights of the two children – one of whom proved to be such a splendid post-hospital accessory.

The story of Samson and Delilah hovers over the entire affair, but in a strangely garbled version. In *Judges* Samson found a beehive in a lion's corpse, and stole the honey, thus conjuring sweetness out of strength. A comparable paradox is represented by David Blunkett, the Sheffield loony lefty who became the most right-wing Home Secretary in living memory.

For all his personal strength, Samson's, his wife nonetheless cuckolded him with his infinitely weaker friend, just as the able-bodied millionaire Stephen Quinn was unable to prevent his wife from having a passionate affair with a blind and relatively poor man. Having been abandoned by his wife, Samson took up with Delilah, who was as intoxicated with money as Kimberley Fortier was with power – probably the main reason for the affair with David Blunkett.

The Philistines had been unable to curb Samson's strength – just as the Tory opposition had been unable to damage Blunkett – so the Philistines promised her eleven hundred pieces of silver to bring about Samson's downfall. Yet he never suspected what she was up to, as she repeatedly asked him the source of his strength. Equally, neither did Blunkett doubt Fortier's good faith, even though she worked for a Tory publication, and had asked him to do politically compromising favours to fast-track a visa for her nanny. (And by God if a woman needed a nanny, Fortier did.)

Finally, Samson revealed his fatal weakness to Delilah; if his long locks were cut, this would rob him of his strength. Blunkett had an inverse weakness: his absurd and vainglorious paternal pride. Once his hair was cut, Samson was powerless, and the Philistines blinded him; already blind, Blunkett was made powerless by his own hubris.

Samson's captors unwittingly allowed his hair to grow, and thereby his strength to return. Mocked by the Philistines, he heaved on the supporting pillars of their house, killing both himself and thousands of his enemies. No political death, we are told, awaits David Blunkett. We shall see. I care neither way, either for him or his scheming, abominable floozy. But I wonder about the two children, one of them unborn, who are at the centre of this dismal affair, and for whose true welfare only their home-father seems really to care.

[22 December 2004]

VIII. 14. Michael Jackson

Once again, and almost sublimely ignorant of the fact, the media were on trial during the recent court case against Michael Jackson, as indeed, were the media-consuming public. A man was found not guilty, but his life was nonetheless laid waste, and the American media who would have triumphed at a guilty verdict nonetheless exulted at an innocent one. This was not democracy, nor law, nor decency, nor honour, nor justice: this was the hang 'em high school of due process.

Michael Jackson is a tragic figure, an autistic child who knows nothing of the real world. Where the rest of us might have seen grey and doubt and confusion, he merely saw things with infantile clarity. And only a celebrity-demented culture such as ours has now become could have turned this poor creature into a publicly jeered-at grotesque, whose torment took new turns upon acquittal, as he continued to be hounded by sneering, bullying American comedians like Jay Leno.

No clear evidence has been adduced that he sexually assaulted any of his foundlings. His relationship towards those children he slept with is clearly bizarre – but with equal clarity, many of those children have insisted that his behaviour was playful and platonic. One exception – aided by a few disgruntled domestics – provided the spuriously evidential case against Michael Jackson.

Injustice is a common thing in human affairs, and injustice to a multimillionaire is hardly a repetition of Auschwitz. But the net effect of intent is not the issue: the intent is the key. And quite clearly, large numbers of people were delighted at the thought of Michael Jackson being personally, morally, and economically ruined – even to the point that jurors in his trial were later seduced into saying he might possibly have been guilty of charges they had heard nothing about. Thus those who acquitted him then stabbed him in the back, for it was not sufficient to do legal justice; only lynch mob law matched the need of the hour.

For Michael Jackson was the perfect target, the little black African-American boy who yearns for a face of Caucasian Carrera marble. In all his ambitions, in all he was, he found himself not in his fantasy home of Neverland, but a world of his own devising: Borderland, where the ordinary parameters of boy and man, male and female, black and white, celebrity and nonentity, met like the waters of the maelstrom, and became indistinguishable.

In the righteously vicious attack on his life, logic was abolished and decency murdered. An NBC commentator observed: 'Not guilty, but American parents have no proof of his innocence.' That is right. And they have no proof that Bill Clinton is not a Martian, or that the Pope is not Martin Bormann, or that Queen Victoria is not alive and well and living in Alabama. One cannot 'prove' such things: all that the rule of common law can do is conclude that the prosecution failed to make a case that could be accepted beyond all reasonable doubt.

But there can seldom have been such a prosecution in which the state went to so much trouble, with so little evidence. After all, the investigation was triggered by Jackson's own pathetic admission in the course of a television interview that he likes to go bed with boys, not for sex, but for whatever bizarre companionship he found there. Even this did not trigger a complaint – but it did cause a Los Angeles therapist to violate the rules of his trade and report allegations by the boy Gavin that there had been sexual episodes between himself and Jackson.

Welfare officials tracked Gavin down, and both he and his mother denied Jackson sexually molested him. The case was passed to the District Attorney of Santa Barbara, Tom Sneddon, who clearly is no better than he ought to be. He spent *eight weeks* talking to Gavin and more especially, to Gavin's mother, who, equally, is no better than she ought to be. At the end of which, mother and son changed their story, enabling Sneddon to lead a raid by seventy officers on Jackson's house, which was then torn asunder: mattresses shredded, wardrobes ransacked.

The ensuing case must rank at the very nadir of jurisprudential hokum, with some details deserving a grim little smile indeed. Prosecution evidence included the allegation that he once licked a clothed boy on the head. A couple of staff members, who apparently had the run of the Jackson bedroom, regardless of the presence of his guests, reported signs of an erection beneath the bedclothes. Yes, indeed, gentlemen of the world, erections are apparently entirely voluntary things, which is probably news to Viagra, and constitute proof of criminal guilt: in which case, they'd better start building prisons everywhere, and building them big – very big indeed. So, girls, your big day has finally come: this is where you take over.

Michael Jackson mutilated himself in pursuit of some weird personal goal, and made himself the perfect target for the lynch mob of celebrity culture. He has been harried through the courts and the through the media, and been damaged beyond all recovery. So look at him now, a broken, wizened torso of a man-boy, with his bleached skin, his straightened hair and his sad little fragment of a nose. He is the albino rook that is driven from the rookery and flees to the beach, only to be mobbed by gulls. Thus his life, a stranger to all peace, now and for the rest of his days: God help him indeed.

[21 June 2005]

VIII. 15. Julian Lloyd–Webber

Julian Lloyd-Webber is the lesser known and the poorer of the two Lloyd-Webber brothers – which isn't saying a great deal, because Andrew is richer than Luxembourg. He also collects works by that winsome bunch of simpering sentimentalists known as the Pre-Raphaelites, whose works are just about suitable for inclusion in a thirteen-year-old girl's first diary selections selection, but nowhere else.

Pre-Raphaelites usually painted their subjects with tear-filled Bambi eyes gazing mistily into the horizon, and words cannot convey the winsome ghastliness of this school. Fortunately – for the purposes solely of illustrating what a blot they were in the history of European culture – one of their number, Dante Gabriel Rossetti, turned his grisly appetite for the sentimental to literary expression also. Here follows one of the most egregious pieces of verse in the entire

canon of English literature, and if you cannot find in your heart to forgive me
for inflicting this horror on you, then frankly I do not blame you. Deep breath.
Here goes.

> The blessed damozel leaned out
> From the gold bar of Heaven;
> Her eyes were deeper than the depth
> Of waters stilled at even;
> She had three lilies in her hand,
> And the stars in her hand were seven.

'And the stars in her hand were seven'. Have you ever read such frightful,
bathetic bilge in your entire life? How could he try to rhyme 'even' with 'seven'
without vomiting all over the page? But at least this gives you an impression of
what the Pre-Raphaelites painted, and so you can roughly work out the taste of a
man who has spent scores of millions collecting their works, not for the purposes
of stoking the boiler, but to assault his guests with from their vantage point on
the Lloyd-Webber walls.

You might think that for one brother to have such appalling taste must have
exhausted that family's ration: that there would not be enough bad-taste DNA
within the Lloyd-Webber gene pool to allow any other member of the family to
indulge in more than a questionable tie. Perhaps this was why I attended a Julian
Lloyd-Webber bossa nova concert in Chelsea in London last week. So let me
now tell that if J. L.-W. ever comes to a town near you with his bossa nova concert, lick your tongue along a red hot iron, take an electric fire into the bath with
you, become a Christian evangelic missionary in Falluja, have sex with a Siberian
tiger – anything, rather than going to the concert. Please. Please?

Firstly, his appearance. Julian Lloyd-Webber is, I suppose, in his forties. He
has thinning suspiciously monochrome black hair, which he has brushed forward
in a pageboy pudding-bowl style, hanging across his forehead and over his ears.
Believe it or not – and I know you don't, but stick with me here, because it's vital
that you do – it gets worse. For even worse than the hair was his black headband,
which ran under the 'black' bangs hanging down to his eyebrows.

Is there more? Yes, there's more. He was wearing a billowy white smock, and
tight black trousers, and dancing pumps, and frankly, the moment he walked onto
the stage, I simply wanted to cosh him, put him in a bag, take him home, and free
him in Darndale shopping centre at midnight, and see what happened to him next.
That alas, was not to be. Instead what followed was musical torment as J. L.-W.
led us through – for the most part – the music of Carlos Gilberto.

Now this has already been done definitively and finally by Stan Getz and
Charlie Byrd, collaborating with the Gilberto brothers and Astrud Gilberto in

the 1960s. The fusion of jazz and bossa nova (which is Portuguese for 'new wave') created an entirely new and entrancing musical form. But that was a long, long time ago, when bossa nova was nova: if J L-W wanted to be really trendy, he would have tried to a fusion of rap with his cello.

Ah, his cello. I have not yet mentioned his cello yet, have I? An oversight, although you are probably aware that he plays the cello: it is a Stradivarius, and in order to match the volume of sound coming from his amplified backing band, he played it into a microphone. This is the equivalent of smothering a Clarinbridge oyster with HP sauce.

And so he proceeded to lead us through the exotic semi-samba beat of the bossa nova with his Stradivarius. It was like listening to a bad pub band. Worse than this – yes, I know I keep saying 'worse than ...' but it's my way of dealing with post-traumatic stress disorder, okay? – were the looks of anguished ecstasy that regularly crossed his face. Rock musicians do this a lot, when they hit a riff, or manage to pull off a elusive cord. But in J L-W's case, it merely looked as if he was struggling with a particularly troublesome bowel movement.

Tragically, he paused to give us some unamplified Bach: it was quite beautiful, and showed us what he is capable of; and then even more tragically, he reverted to bossa nova, plus some rock and roll, in the course of which – well, to judge from the expression on his face – he unsuccessfully attempted to purge his colon of a grand piano. He pursed, he frowned, he grizzled, he gurned: but the old Steinway stayed where it was, sideways on, just north of his rectum. It's probably there to this day, and as far as I'm concerned, it can jolly well stay there.

[5 July 2005]

VIII. 16. Nelson Mandela

> For God's sake, let us sit upon the ground And tell sad stories of the death of kings: How some have been deposed: Some poisoned by their wives, some sleeping killed; All murdered: for within the hollow crown That rounds the mortal temples of a king Keeps death his court, and there the antick sirs, Scoffing his state and grinning at his pomp ...

The tale of kings, as Richard II mournfully testified, is a tale of murder, of power usurped and held by violence. Yet sometimes, if rarely, kings must have been chosen from the crowd not because of their violence but for their ability to enchant: magic lay at the command of such creatures. Bewitched, men and women were drawn to obey them, to grant them fealty, to accept them as lords of their lives.

No one who had the enormous pleasure and privilege of being present for Nelson Mandela's address at TCD in the Independent Newspapers Annual Lecture the other night could have been in any doubt about the man's regal presence. He is a king; and we who had the great good fortune to be there were hard put to it preventing ourselves falling on one knee and calling him our liege lord.

He is a Xhosa; yet he does not look like the Xhosa. His skin is not black but yellow-brown, his flat features are not so much Bantu as those of the aboriginal peoples of the Kalarahi, the Koi-San. Like the Koi-San – once wrongly called Bushmen – he has epicanthic eyelids, with a fold of skin on the inner corner of the eye. And though like all incomers, the Bantu Xhosa looked down on the strange people they found in the new lands they conquered; yet they were mystified by them also. For these Koi-San seemed to possess magical qualities which the Xhosa themselves lacked. So too did the Fir Bolg of Ireland once enchant their new Gaelic masters; so also did the Picts of the Scottish Highlands similarly beguile their new lords, giving us, if only in folk-etymology, the word 'pixie'.

'Above all,' observed the anthropologist Colin Turnbull of the Koi-San peoples, 'having mastered the art of exploiting their desert environment so that it always provides with enough for their minimal needs and demands, and having mastered the art of living together without formal government, without law, without mutual recrimination or self-seeking, the Bushmen add something else to life, making of it something far beyond the business of survival. They add an incredibly rich belief, a religious belief in a kind of dream world that beautifies every insect, every leaf, every grain ... Perhaps the very severity of their daily life leads the Bushmen to a greater awareness of the world around them. They see beauty where others would only see ugliness; kindness where others would only see cruelty, for they understand it all. The Bushman sees himself as part of one single universe ... He is not concerned with living this life in an ideal manner so as to win for himself a better life in another world; he is concerned with living this life as effectively as possible.'

Is this not all familiar? Does it not sound almost like a definition of what Nelson Mandela stands for, of tolerance, respect, mutual dignity, rich in so much and poor only in that single quality of recrimination? Yet these words were written about not a single individual but an *ethnos* a quarter of a century ago, when he was languishing in solitary confinement in Robben Island and nobody knew he possessed these qualities. And all that aside, even if he were of Koi-San ancestry, how could he have acquired these characteristics to the point of being their very embodiment if he were raised as a Xhosa?

I haven't a clue. Maybe within his Tembu sub-group, the culture of the Kalahari lived on in covert but powerful ways. Whatever about that, I do know that there are things in this world we do not understand. How is it possible for

Nelson Mandela to magnetise a room by his mere presence? How can his modesty and his self-effacement be so utterly compelling? How can his gentleness be as impenetrable as tempered steel?

Apartheid could not quell him; extraordinarily, invisibly, he radiated freedom from his prison cell. Logic, science, anthropology, psychiatry: all the sciences of humanity could not explain the power of this man, for he was as irresistible in confinement as he had been and would be again when at liberty. Finally, as he walked free from his prison cell, it was as if a new light shone over Africa and the lands beyond, reminding us of Colin Turnbull's words about the Koi-San; '(his) belief brings his dreams down to the world he lives in, giving it colour and shape and meaning, giving this life some special purpose and beauty, making it at the same time more livable and infinitely more worth living.'

What strange instinct of self-survival prevented the Afrikaaners from murdering this man in custody? It would have been so easy: and it would have been their very undoing. That South Africa managed the transition from the tyranny of apartheid to being a multicultural democracy is due to Nelson Mandela alone. By chance, wordlessly was I able to shake his hand the other night; by chance, wordlessly was I at hand to move his chair as he rose to leave the dinnertable. And I am content.

[15 April 2000]

IX. Miscellaneous & Other

IX.1. Teenagers

It is a while since I was mistaken for a young man, and I suspect it is unlikely I ever will be again. The scale of the age gap between myself and those born less distantly was brought home to me last year when in a don't you rock me daddy-oh mood, I bought an Eminem long playing record: a seedy, as I believe it is called nowadays. Well, I couldn't make head nor tail of it. As I listened, I tried the rock and roll, the twist, the jive, the Madison, the locomotion, even the bossa nova and the samba. To no avail. As dance music goes, it went.

Teenagehood has been a mystery land for non-teenagers since the arrival of US youth culture fifty years ago. In the summer of 1955, the best-selling single in the British charts was Slim Whitman's 'Rose Marie I Love You,' a ballad which could have appealed to, and been understood by, any generation over the previous hundred years. Bill Haley's 'Rock Around the Clock' followed it to number one, bringing with it a revolution to this side of the Atlantic. When the song featured in the film, 'Blackboard Jungle', teenagers danced in cinema aisles in Dublin, and the newest craze for girls, figure-hugging denims, so terrified the authorities at UCD that they banned female students from wearing jeans (a rule which remained in force until 1969). Meanwhile, the death of James Dean, and the resulting youth cult based on the notion that death was preferable to age, deepened the split between the generations. It has grown wider down the decades.

A defining feature of this cultural division is the role of urban myth in its maintenance, then and now. Stories have recently been sweeping through our horrified middle classes about what happens at dances at Dublin's comprehensive schools; of how 14-year-old girls arrive wearing miniskirts and thongs, but in the course of the evening, remove the thongs and wrap them on their wrists, as a sign of their availability. What they then offer – according the standard version of the tale, which is, needless to say, all hearsay, but is nonetheless petrifying Irish society – is a non-penetrative sexual deed that – how shall I put this? – depends on friction for its outcome: as it happens, a peculiarly appropriate term.

There is nothing new in this world. That form of sexual activity was known as *Uhulabonga* to Zulus, and was authorised between maidens and warriors as a means of satisfying sexual desire without too much fear of impregnation. Zulu society survived *Uhulabonga*, and no doubt Irish society will survive the thong-on-wrist fad, if, that is, it even exists. No doubt it has occurred, but I doubt it is as widespread as rumour alleges. And that is the point of the myth. The real issue is not the conduct of the teenagers, but the desire of their parents' generation to believe almost anything about them, without having any proof whatever, and then not merely to express shock and indignation at what they have heard, but to pass it on, with all possible haste.

So the really divisive factor in society is not so much what teenagers do – in my case, I haven't a clue what they actually do – but the prurient allegations that their elders and betters eagerly if disapprovingly pass on about their activities. Yet these stories are not about a strange and mysterious people in some distant land shrouded in mystery, the way that China-watchers in Kong Kong and Macao would once upon a time report tales of travellers from Peking. They are instead about human beings who live in the same homes as us, who go to the same shops, who eat the same food (sort of), who speak the same language (again, sort of), and whose appetites are pretty much the same as ours. So why do we revel in such rumours about them? Why do we want to believe that their lives are so much exotic, dangerous, debauched, unprincipled and immoral than were our own adolescences?

No doubt that some things happen in teenage dances that shouldn't. No doubt some girls make fools of themselves to please boys, and the male of the species is seldom at his best when the tropical storm of hormonal attack besets his frame. However, you don't need to come here to hear the tsk tsk tsk, it wasn't like that in my day: you can hear those sounds anywhere.

The real point is that we apparently want to believe these stories. It is a form of compensation for the injustice that young people will outlive us. At least, we can tell ourselves, we have lead cleaner, more responsible lives than they will. This belief in the inferiority of the rising generation actually predates the invention of youth culture. Old men in inns have always grumbled over their ale about the vices of the young: immorality is rampant, learning is non-existent, standards are slipping, and as a society, we are doomed.

The girls in their blue jeans who so terrified the authorities at UCD in 1955 are today seventy, sucking on boiled sweets and sporting what appear to be beige tea cosies on their heads as they wave their travel passes at the bus driver. Society survives. The rite of adolescent passage is more tumultuous than it once was, with more casualties; but in 50 years' time, today's teenagers will hear tales about the antics of their grandchildren's generation, and shake their heads in dismay at what the world is coming to.

[24 August 2005]

IX.2. Thongs

This is delicate. So delicate that I hardly know where to begin. But begin I must, for at the particular request of a female reader, I today am going to touch upon the sensitive matter of the thong.

Yes, yes, yes, I am aware of the side-splitting punning possibilities – the Castlebar Thong Contest, et cetera – but we're trying to be serious here. What is the thong about? Thong shops are opening up everywhere. For €50, you can get a couple of feet of beribboned dental floss attached to a cloth postage stamp, and your lingerie drawer is complete – which confirms, yet again, that men are from Mars and women are from Bonkersville.

And because a Martian is writing this, I have to be careful. Can't stray into that category of expression that feminists created at the very moment they were saying men and women were equal in all regards. This category is a precise refutation of the feminist equality claim, and it is known as 'Offensive to Women'. There is of course no such category as OTM.

Girls, you might be from Bonkersville, but you're still human. Well, some of the time, anyway. I'm trying my damnedest not to be OTW, but let's be frank: the thong is designed to cling to the primary outlets of the human body. I mean really cling, with adhesive attention to detail, in areas where one would have thought loads of fresh air was preferable.

But in addition to the needs of the human body: what about the needs of the thong? How does it feel about a life trapped down there, with no room to move, no sunlight, no air, and maybe just the occasional gust of wind?

We'll take a break here, I think, to talk about Mrs Pateman and her underwear. Mrs Pateman lived across the road from us when I was a youngster, and I had ample opportunity to get to know her underwear from her washing line. Ah, you see, I too have lived. And I freely admit to gazing in horrified awe at her huge pink bloomers. They must have reached from her waist to her knees, and were elasticated at each end. They weren't so much an item of lingerie as a fabric garage. You could have rented them out for weddings. They were quite unspeakable.

But they weren't as unspeakable as the thong. In fact, they were infinitely superior to the thong, because – as I recognise now – they were, for all their aesthetic shortcomings, essentially hygienic items. The thong is the opposite. The thong is hygiene's equivalent of the Red Cow Roundabout. Everything converges there, but nothing manages to escape. The result is your very own personalised germ factory on a string.

So what do you do with a thong at the end of the day? Put it out of its misery with a humane killer? Do you just burn it? Or does one attempt to wash it? And is that even possible, in any meaningful sense? Let us take another break here, because I think we all probably need one.

My German dictionary, second-hand, dated 1958, tells me that the German for thong is *die Peitschen-schnur*, a satisfyingly Germanic name. Since in 1958 our modern thong was about as imaginable as talking cats, the good old *Peitschen-schnur* couldn't have had a clue what future lay ahead of it, the poor bastard.

Peitsche means whip. Schnur means string or cord, but – interestingly – can also mean daughter-in-law. In German, this could imply that your daughter-in-law is wearing a German daughter-in-law as underwear – which is just about as bad as it gets.

What is the thong's name? Heidi? And how does Heidi feel about her current life? Would she like a posting elsewhere, or is she content being a Red Cow Roundabout in the moistest nooks and crannies of a stranger's groin? And as Heidi might say: *warum*? Why do women want to wear Heidi in such numbers that Heidi shops have opened up all over the place? For this is definitely a thing for people from Bonkersville. Yes, I know, we men aren't in touch with our feelings, we don't know the difference between taupe and beige, we don't ring one another on our mobile phones when we're sitting next to landlines. And so on.

But these are not the primary difference between the sexes. Heidi is. David Beckham aside, you could never get a man to wear a thong. Not a thong thong, with the back strap passing up between the buttocks, with all that is delightful residing there, to connect with the waist strap. We chaps simply wouldn't do it. Yet quite clearly many of you girls have no qualms about slipping into a Heidi, and setting off on your day.

Yet why would anyone want to house a bacteria farm close to your nearest and dearest from dawn to dusk? Surely going commando is better than having your own e-coli Montessori down there, with budding young microbes learning how to resist antibiotics, yeasts hitherto unknown to science devising hideously personal ailments and various funguses swapping jokes at the office water warmer.

Women wear thongs, it seems, because they don't want a visible pantyline. But if you girls don't want a VPL, and still insist on underwear of some kind, why don't you all follow Mrs Pateman's splendid example, and opt for vast pink bloomers? Go on. Put Heidi out of her misery. You'll feel better for it. And she certainly will.

[20 February 2004]

IX.3. Viagra Spam

Today's column is for men only. Newsagents, if you please, do not deliver any copies of this newspaper to local convents or girls' schools. Ushers in Dail Eireann are instructed to burn this column, lest my many female TD-admirers be devastated by what follows. Vigilante squads of Christian Brothers are to tour public transport forcibly confiscating any copy of this newspaper found in the possession of a person who does not also possess a penis.

Are we in an all-male zone? We are? Good. Then this column formally begins. This e-mail arrived for me the other day.

Hello, do you remember me?
    I'm Todd from NY, I have taken new email address.
    Remember we spoke about a problem of short penis?
    I have found at last a good product which is capable to correct this problem!!!
    This the best that i ever tried!!!
    My power and pleasure has trippled, [stet] my wife can hardly keep up, my penis has gone from 3.5 inches to just over 6 and is still growing!
    This is More-Size, which I found at http://mutably.net/more/
    Try it necessarily!!!
    The best regards,
    Todd Sands

Well, stap me vittles, but I don't remember ever meeting this Todd Sands fellow, and I certainly don't recall talking to anyone on the sturdy subject which he raises. Nor do I recall giving him my e-mail address – yet there it is, irrefutably, a letter wanting to continue some earlier conversation about penis sizes. Odd how Todd spells the word 'tripple': maybe with the extra size, you also get the extra pee. However, he sounds a personable enough chap, if rather inclined to be, well, a little personal.

But he's not alone. Hardly a day goes by without my being pestered by some worried citizen of the USA expressing concern over my personal dimensions. Morning after morning, fresh e-mails offer me a penile extension. To be sure, it's touching that there are so many Americans are fretting about me, and it's confirmation of what I've always thought about them: they are a concerned and caring species.

But on the other hand, I am also concerned, and I care. For have they got a little camera about my house that prompts them to make these entirely selfless and charitable suggestions? Or are they people I have met on planes and boats and trains whom I have assailed with conversations about the male part, which I have then proceeded to forget?

That is something of a worry. To judge from the many e-mails about penis size, I apparently have discussed the matter with several hundred people in the past year alone; and I remember not one of them. I must be one hell of a dinner-party companion. (Hello. A pleasure to meet you. Tell me: how big is your husband's penis? Really? That large? Alas, mine is one tenth the size. Here. Let me show you …) Or perhaps I have been getting up in the Carnegie Hall and denouncing myself for my penile inadequacies, urging people to send me remedies, and that done, I then popped round to the local hypnotist to make me forget these little confessions.

Thus it is that each morning of my life I open up my e-mail inbox, and there waiting for me like a dog at the doorstep, are yet more anxious enquiries about my penis size, and extravagant offers of help.

Now, if I were receiving comparable e-mails about female needs, this would confirm the hope that these are randomly addressed computer-generated messages bombarding every single inhabitant of cyberspace. Which is why every day I open my e-mails, desperate for an advertisement for a vibrator or a breast enlarger or piece of girlish nip-and-tuck surgery down below which will tell me all is well, all this penis-enhancing stuff is not meant personally: but in vain.

Correct me if I'm wrong, but I don't recall this happening in the days of fountain-pen and ink. I was recently reading the diary selectionses of Field Marshall Haig, and he doesn't ever mention penis size, not once, through either the Somme or Third Ypres. The same for Alanbrooke's diary selectionses, 1939–45. Roy Foster's biographies of Yeats don't raise the topic either. Tim Pat Coogan's studies of Michael Collins and de Valera, first members of the Dail, seem to get by without a single reference to the male member of either male member. T. Ryle Dwyer's comparative biography of the two men is promisingly named *Big Fellow, Long Fellow*, but actually turns out to be quite disappointing in that regard, though in no other. I reached hungrily (so to speak) for Ruth Dudley Edwards' *Triumph of Failure*, sure that the explanation for the Easter Rising (another promising avenue opening up there) must lie in Patrick Pearse's penis size. Nope. Not a word. Indeed, as you might say, not a sausage.

Gentle reader: am I alone here? Am I the only male in the world who tremblingly opens his e-mails each morning to find himself being confronted by utter strangers over some alleged penile inadequacies? Have they nothing better

to do in the shopping malls of Des Moines and Peoria than to gather in babbling assemblies, without regard to age, creed, sex or race, and agree I need some
assistance in most regards, not least of all, lengthening? Or is it possible that you
too receive communications from my friend Todd Sands, et alia? In which case,
I may relax.

[23 September 2005]

IX.4. Ageism

The Irish Gerontological Society has found that, compared to racism, there is
under-reporting of ageism in society. Its researchers went to the trouble of scanning both this newspaper and *The Guardian*, and I'm glad they had nothing better
to do with their time. They found that *The Irish Times* had just 61 articles on
ageism, but 2085 on racism. *The Guardian* had 6252 articles on racism, and only
301 on ageism.

Other researchers did an analysis of 15 British and Irish national newspapers
for references to older drivers. Fifteen references were considered negative, seven
were considered as balanced and four were considered positive, and stay awake at
the back of the class, because even I'm falling asleep here.

Desmond O'Neill, professor of medical gerontology at Trinity College
Dublin, says he intends to send results of his research to schools of journalism and
media studies for a 'module' to be formed around it. If God is good, they will be
thrown into the bin, but more probably, those temples to the politically correct
will grant him his wish. No, I don't know what a module is either. A kind of cyst,
isn't it? No, that's a nodule. Sorry, can't help you.

A suggestion to the gerontologists. Go back to the electronic archives and
tap three words into them 'young male drivers' and what you'll get back is three
zillion articles condemning them unconditionally. Here you have sexism and
ageism at its most flagrant, and moreover, most justified.

When gerontologists start giving us lectures on ageism, I find myself asking
– What kind of patients do they treat? Young motorcyclists injured in collisions?
People with VD? Children with scarlet fever? Rugby players with torn ligaments?
None of the above? Oh. So who do they treat?

They treat old people. Take your child with whooping cough or a steel
JCB he's managed to shove up his nose to a gerontologist, and they will point
you down the corridor to that other inveterate ageist, the pediatrician. Similarly
take your little boy with a urinary infection to the gynaecologist, and they'll
direct to the medical male equivalent, which is, oops, non-existent. Because the

medical profession does not merely define itself on ageist grounds but also on sexist grounds – which apparently qualifies it to wag its collective finger at us in the media on such things.

As a matter of interest, would anti-ageist members of the Irish Geronto-logical Society prefer to be behind an 85-year-old woman driver, or behind a 19-year-old male driver? And on the other hand, which would you prefer to have behind you with a blind bend coming up and a double white line? Answers on one side of paper only please, and no conferring.

Now maybe we in the media should take the gerontologists seriously, and increase the number of stories about ageism. Clear the front page! Eighty-year-old who sought a place in a kindergarten gets short shrift! Undergraduates who presented themselves at the post office for their pension treated to a similarly abbreviated dismissal! Newborn babies rejected for Aer Lingus pilot training!

Yes, our sales amongst gerontologists would rocket, and each morning they would quiver in rage that yet again the Army Ranger Wing has refused to employ a single centenarian. Such worthiness is the brown rice of journalism: nobody buys it, and we journalists who are put out of work can chance our arm enlisting in our primary school or claiming the pension.

Of course, the gerries are right when they say that there are more reports of racism than ageism, because the media, being largely recruited from white, guilty, middle-class left-liberals, probably over-report racism. Racism has become a self-fulfilling accusation. Moreover, Irish newspapers and RTÉ have routinely accepted as 'fact' the false claims of illegal immigrants that they are asylum seekers. In reality, there probably isn't nearly as much racism in Ireland as we self-flagellate ourselves about. There is of course some, as the Labour Court recently revealed with the extraordinary story of the Nigerian Aderonke Rasaq who was sacked for 'stealing' three bananas, which had never even left Campbell Catering premises.

Would an Irishwoman have been sacked in such circumstances? No, and I was delighted she got €15,000 compensation, not least because of the vile Styro-foam cup containing a teabag that I got from a place masquerading as Bewley's at Dublin airport recently. That in itself was worth a €15,000 fine.

But I suspect that Aderonke's was a highly unrepresentative case. However, if in our media we endlessly and inaccurately portray ourselves as bigoted rac-ists, then that is precisely how immigrants will come to think of us. Worse, every group that feels its is being discriminated against will seek parity of coverage with our alleged victims of racism.

For example, a new and vociferous group has emerged in recent times, con-sisting of dedicated vowellists. They ask, pertinently – why has racism no 'e' in it whereas ageism has one? On what grounds can that discrimination against the letter 'e' be justified by the race-relations industry? The concrete noun 'race' depends totally on 'e', for without that heroic vowel, the word would sound like a framed horizontal surface, conjoined ribs of lamb, or an instrument of torture. But when it becomes to forming an abstract noun, with all sorts of exotic theory attached to it and with PhDs galore and all-expenses paid conferences in the Seychelles, the hard-working 'e' is dropped. This is outright discrimination.

The new victimhood discipline of e-ology is studying this scandalous state of affairs. We will e-mail you the results.

[17 September 2004]

IX.5. Mulled Wine

So, now with December, that very Hannibal Lecter of a month, sinking its care-fully filed teeth into our throats, we can decently ask this question. What is it about Christmas that causes people to inflict on their friends and loved ones the liquid atrocity known as 'mulled wine'? Is it a repressed hatred of the human race which, goaded by the egregious jollity of the season, erupts with a vitriolic and homicidal savagery, causing normally honourable people to attempt to poison all they know?

Whatever its cause, the alchemists responsible are usually grotesquely proud of their confections, and after forcing one glass on you, gaze with a dementedly cretinous grin written across their imbecilic faces, like a mother who married late in life and is now watching her tubby son, Cuthbert, win the under-fives' egg-and-spoon race. Worse, this authorial delight has a compellingly ruthless edge to it, such as the mother might exhibit towards the egg-and-spoon race stewards if they suggested that before little Cuthbert got his gold medal, he should take a drugs test. Thus, the wine-muller's eye glints dangerously as you hold the glass without actually drinking it. It is a test of wills. And the muller always wins.

So you put the concoction merely to your lips, but that you drink none makes no difference. Mulled wine can penetrate armour, and mere human flesh to it is as wet tissue paper. So this ochre broth cuts through your chin directly onto your teeth, to which it becomes instantly electroplated in a malignant fur, before swiftly adhering to all the sensitive surfaces of your inner jaws. It doesn't matter how little mulled wine actually enters your mouth, nor how briefly you allow the glass to rest against your chin: the effect is always the same. And you know from previous Christmases that not even an oral fire hose power-jetting hydrochloric acid around your tongue and molars will dislodge the layer of mull now fixed there.

Mull is actually quite a good word for such encrusted nightsoil. The OED lists various meanings for 'mull'. One is that it is finely ground rubbish in suspension. Another, that it is a cold bleak headland. Another, a heifer. Another, that is muslin used in bookbinding. Another, a muddle. Another, mud. Another, 'to stupefy'. Another, 'to fumble'. The last, to treat leather with chemicals.

And that about sums it up: there isn't a single good thing to say about the word 'mull'. Moreover, in addition to the ground rubbish in suspension, with fox-droppings from the Mull of Kintyre, with some heifer manure, and bookbinder's, glue, topped off with acidified leather, mulled wine also tastes of creosote, paraffin, turpentine, a burning oil well, with the strong possibility of what might well be alligator's rectum, if you could be sure what alligator's rectum tasted like. Just like mulled wine, actually.

Now you know that your taste buds have been ruined for the next six months, if not for ever. You know that industrial cleaners are booked out to late spring by people vainly trying to remove the coating of mulled wine from their mouths. You know that Christmas dinner is certainly going to taste like the Tet offensive, a compost heap and the final foot or so of an alligator's alimentary canal. So you have every justification for beheading your assailant with a broadsword, and slaying his wife and loved ones.

Yet what do you? Why, you expose your red-stained teeth in what is supposed to be a smile, though it resembles the bloodied grimace of a vampire cow, and, through the ruined wasteland of mucous tissue that is your mouth, you moo how utterly delicious the concoction is. Around you are your fellow guests, their teeth glued together as a consequence of their host's liquid hospitality, cross-eyed in agony, and semaphoring 'let's get the fuq out of here' signs to their spouses – to the ones that are not dead of course.

'Excellent!' chortles your host, and fills your glass back to the brim, then fixing you with a look of murderously benign expectancy, like Saddam Hussein asking a courtier whether he approves of the Iraqi leader's golf stroke. Every molecule of your being, every follicle on your scalp, every tooth in your mouth, every cell in your brain screams: Brain him before it is too late!

No good. You raise the glass back to your mouth, and once again the warm flavours of Berlin-in-1945, mustard gas and crocodilian back passage, all marinaded in tannin-rich Bolivian red wine, infuse your mouth. Tears trickle down your cheeks. In the green mist that seems to fill the room, figures flounder, choking, guttering and dying, like those unhappy fellows from one of Wilfred Owen's less cheery poems.

You try to still your host's hospitality with the declaration, 'No more thanks. I'm driving,' but instead you hear this mechanical voice from the region of your mouth clearly enunciating the utterly poisonous fiction: 'What delicious mulled wine. Any chance of the recipe?'

There is a rattling noise from the floor: the dying gasps of your wife. Now you really are driving. Your host prattles off the ingredients with a thoroughly depraved self-satisfaction: wine, cloves, cinnamon, lemon, sugar, and not a mention of the vinegar, the third battle of Ypres or carnivore's colon currently coating your mouth.

Worst of all is the knowledge the same fate awaits you the next day, and the next, and the next, until Christmas is finally over. Which is of course why the season is called Yule, abbreviated from, 'You'll be drinking that filth called mulled wine for an entire bloody fortnight.'

[1 December 2005]

IX.6. Nightgrinders

Men, women: black, white; tall, short; fat, thin. These are are some of the binaries of human nature. There is another, far more fundamental one. Nightgrinder and non-nightgrinder. Nightgrinders are physically and mentally superior to the their binary opposites. They are usually people of astonishing beauty, with refined manners and remarkable intellect. Michelangelo was a nightgrinder, as was Leonardo. So was Shakespeare. W. B. Yeats also. Oscar Wilde too. All the Bachs were nightgrinders, save their cousin Peadar, who was a bookie in Mullingar. Handel nightground for Germany before nightgrinding for the Hanovarians in London.

No one is quite sure why nightgrinding is the mark of genius, but it is. The original words of the Angelus ran: 'The Angel of the Lord appeared unto Mary, and declared, thou shalt be a nightgrinder.' And a nightgrinder she became; a Virgin Nightgrinder, to be sure, but a nightgrinder nonetheless. This was why they couldn't get a room in the inn, because the innkeeper, being a backward, non-nightgrinding primitive, had a bee in his bonnet about nightgrinders.

So the Holy family trudged off to the manger, where the three wise men were able to find them by following the din of the Virgin Mary nightgrinding. Admittedly, not all nightgrinders have such a distinguished son as she did, but nightgrinders invariably produce stock of noble quality and lofty mien.

Naturally, most artists are nightgrinders, for nightgrinding is evidence of the mind at work from dusk till dawn, while the body sleeps. Beethoven was able to write the Ninth Symphony when he was stone deaf because his teeth ground it out to him in his sleep, and the entire work passed through skull into his brain, where it stayed until morning came and he reached for his quill.

In the first folio of *Hamlet*, the famous soliloquy was not the essay in existential wistfulness which most people think; originally, it was 'To grind or not

to grind: that is the question.' Cromwell, being a non-nightgrinder, a bore and a
dullard, suppressed the original version, and commissioned Milton to write new
words. Milton wasn't at that point a nightgrinder, but he soon became one: and
he celebrated the productivity of his unconscious mind with the poem 'Comas',
where his restless brain famously asked: 'What hath night to do with sleep?'

Where is all this leading us to? To a confession, that is where. To the admission that I am a nightgrinder. Have been all my adult life. I was nightgrinding
when Seamus Heaney got stuck with his first volume of verse, and I nightground
his way of out of a poetical pickle for him. Bobby Ballagh was sitting for two full
years paralysed before a blank canvas, until I came to his rescue, with a few artistic
thoughts dreamt up between my molars. My bicuspids helped out Neil Jordan
after he'd hit writer's block halfway through his first selection of short stories,
Nights in Termonfeckin.

'No, no, no,' tapped out my teeth – dot dash dash dash dot, rudely, in coarse
mode – to my slumbering brain. *Nights in Tunisia*, it insisted. The rest is history.

The problem for us nightgrinders is there is only so much mortar-and-pes-
tling you can do with your teeth before they begin to wear away. You have never
seen photographs of Leonardo or Shakespeare in middle age because picture snappers were so shy about the steady erosion of his incisor snappers. So it has been with
me; my teeth have been vanishing as I gnashed inventively through the night: grind
grind grind, ghosting *Chinatown*, *Groundhog Day*, *The Usual Suspects*, *Wallace and
Gromit* and of course the *Harry Potter* series, the credit for which I nobly allowed to
be claimed by other, lesser creatures, albeit ones with proper-sized teeth.

Thus came the day when my dentist looked into my mouth, and saw what
appeared to be small knitting-needle heads vanishing into my gums. Worse, all
the creative grinding had wrecked one root-canal, and was threatening to do the
same with the rest of my mouth. Two alternatives lay before me; the first was to
continue to grind my teeth into oblivion, leaving me with a mouth like a frog's:
the other was to get my teeth crowned.

Crowning is a terribly simple business. Step one, enter the Central Bank
with a Kalashnikov assault rifle. Step two, leave with the entire contents of the
main vault. Step three. Go to your dentist. Step four, give him or her all the
money. Step five. Promise to pay the rest later. Step six. He amputates most of
each tooth. Step seven. He puts temporary crowns on the stumps he has artfully
left protruding from your gum. Step eight … well, actually, step seven is as far as
I've got. (Step eight is when the final crowns arrive).

But I can tell you this for nothing, the aftermath of step seven reminds me of
a friend who, after bathing in a bitterly cold sea, looked downwards when he was
changing and realised in wild dismay that he'd got someone else's willy.

That's the way I feel about my mouth. It's not mine anymore. It feels as I've had a mouth swap with President McAleese. If we don't see any of her in the next few days, that'll be the explanation. She's gazing at the mirror, horrified, wondering where these gums with tiny protruding white maggots came from.

From me, Your Gracious Majesty.

But *my* mouth now looks as it did when I was a young man. All I need now is a doctor who crowns bodies and a hairdresser who crowns scalps.

[17 November 2005]

IX.7. Having the Builders In

Friends have announced that they are having builders in. One beseeches them to change their mind, but in vain. For wisdom cannot be retained, only forgotten. Each morning Aristotle would ask the young Plato: 'What was I going on about yesterday?' And the young P would reply: 'Dunno boss, haven't a clue.' This is the human condition, which explains the continued existence of builders.

Nobody who has had builders in would ever freely allow the experience to reoccur. I recollect friends in Belfast whose builders arrived in October, demolished the entire rear wall of the house, erected a large plastic sheet, and then left, saying they'd be back the next day. They actually returned in April. In the intervening months, the house came to resemble Stalingrad, but without the charity one associates with that little affair. My friends spent the long winter wrapped in old newspapers and gnawing on the bones of migrating moose they had trapped in the Alaska of their kitchen.

Experience of builders should prevent anyone from ever putting on another wing, installing double-glazing, or erecting a conservatory. The recollections of builders' veterans usually cause them to lie palely awake through the night, gazing at the ceiling with tormented halibut-eyes until just before daybreak, when sleep finally arrives. At which point, the god of builders arrives and cascades his evil honeydew upon his victim: a tincture of optimism there, a small dose of stupidity there, and the stardust of amnesia everywhere. Dracula wasn't a vampire, but a builder's deity.

So dawn, and the exhausted home-owners wake, now bewitched by the notion of calling in the builders, again. Appointments are made for contractors to come and give an estimate for some wholly unnecessary job, and on the appointed day, the home-owners wait. And wait. And wait. Thus their apprenticeship into how their relationship with builders will henceforth be.

Now, it's not widely known that there is a corner of the Toyota assembly-line that is reserved solely for making pick-up trucks for Irish builders, all with identical specifications. Even new, they must be decrepit, with one wheel wobbly on a half-flat tyre, giving them the directional stability of a duck amputee on ice. Such trucks must be white and have no windscreen wipers, indicators or brakes. The driver is standard issue too: lopsided spectacles, mouth agape, and an ancient tweed cap, which he scratches in perpetual bemusement.

Our builders' driver sets off in his brand-new, battered old truck, managing a rather hesitant speed of 40 kph as he slowly wonders if he should turn left, or right, or do a u-turn, or, I don't know, maybe just stop. So he does a little bit of everything. In the back of his truck, he has an uncovered heap of gravel and sand, several of his former clients' buckets and spades, and on top, a long, unflagged ladder protruding several feet front and rear. If he comes to a Garda roadblock, he is certain to be waved right through, scattering sand and gravel as he goes, possibly with a kicking cyclist or two impaled on his ladder.

Do these trucks have particular destinations? Or do they just stop whenever they see a building site and offer whatever it is they have in the back? And does the builder just take what is on offer regardless of whether or not his client has asked for it, or whether it even fits? Probably. Because builders' clients – now possessing the individual willpower of the living dead – will usually take anything that the builder installs; moreover, anything can be made to fit with a hammer, if only the once.

You can always spot the clients. They look like Silesian refugees in 1945, dressed in rags, with bits of cloth wrapped around their frost-bitten hands. They're usually huddled before their tent in the front garden, beside the rubble where the prize-winning roses used to be, making tea for the builders on a primus stove. They originally only wanted a small kitchen fan installed, but one thing led to another, as it does once you allow builders over your threshold, but now the house is being moved six inches backwards, for no reason that anyone can now remember.

'Oh look,' says the foreman cheerfully. 'The roof's on fire. Well that's that. No point in calling the fire brigade. We'll just have to put on a new roof. Never mind. It'll only add twenty thousand to the bill. Ah well. Time to be off. See you tomorrow.'

'See you tomorrow': the builders' equivalent of airport security announcing that you are going to be given a thorough cavity search – 'For your own good.' It is no more for your own good than you will see them tomorrow. You'll be lucky to see them again this year. Now bend over.

With the builders gone, our famished, wizened little Silesians wander forlornly around their former home. The Victorian mahogany chairs made splendid firewood for the lads working indoors, and the matching table proved to be a steady platform for the ceiling plasterer in his hobnailed boots. There are hundreds of teabags everywhere and scores of ancient milk cartons churning out streptomycin from their multicoloured contents. The precious Persian carpet is

IX.7. HAVING THE BUILDERS IN | 267 |

now cushioning a load of bricks, and – look! – the lucky homeowners can see the stars from the basement, which wasn't always the case.

Will they learn from this? Well, in about five years' time, Dracula will kiss them one dawn, and they'll wake up with brilliant notion of installing a new shower unit. They're doomed. Silesia, 1945, beckons yet again.

[29 July 2005]

IX.8. Thinkers & Feelers

A question, which you must answer instantly. Which is more important: mercy or justice?

One of the world's largest management consultancies asks its recruits that question to decide whether they are thinkers or feelers, separating them accordingly. It then asks the two groups firstly to describe themselves, and then to describe the other group. It finds that thinkers invariably describe feelers in pretty much the same language as the feelers use when describing themselves: they are compassionate, caring people who allow their hearts to govern their conduct

In other words, thinkers – though disagreeing with feelers – are inclined to think well of them. Feelers, however, when asked to describe thinkers, generally used extremely hostile, even vicious language; right-wing, uncaring, *laissez-faire*, devil-take-the-hindmost. In other words, the people who think of themselves as being most compassionate are actually extremely uncompassionate towards the very people who to tend to regard them with compassion.

This is because feelers usually consider themselves to be morally superior to those they disagree with. In an orderly, democratic and law-abiding society, such arrogance is just one of those dynamics which can be controlled through schools, the media, courts and parliaments. It is when those protective institutions are removed that some feelers become dangerous people, with no check upon their emotional urges and their boundless self-righteousness.

The great tyrants of the twentieth century were feelers. Nazi Germany was a great festival of feelery, with the Fuehrer leading by example. The Nuremberg rallies, the heathen cult of the SS, the anti-Semitism that increasingly infused German life: these had nothing whatever to do with 'thinking' and everything to do with 'feeling'. Yet having emotions-driven policy did not exclude genius. After all, the governance of the Third Reich from 1933 to 1941 was amongst the most brilliant in world history – if you go in for that kind of thing, that is.

Moreover, revolutionaries are feelers: hence, Robespierre, Lenin, Mao, Guevara. This is why the division between 'left' and 'right' is essentially bogus. It is said that the concepts of left and right resulted from the position that members of the assembly took their place after the French Revolution. However, I suspect that the notion of 'right' predates that. The right of the line in battle was reserved for the most loyal knights of the king: that was where the heaviest blow inevitably fell, because the advancing enemy, being right-handed swordsmen, were inclined to wheel to their left, falling on the enemy's right.

Is the right of the line held by thinkers or feelers? Loyalty is surely an emotion, and therefore a feeler's quality. On the other hand, a thinking man will realise that his personal interests are best served by conspicuous devotion to the ruler: so the right of the line can be held by either thinkers or feelers. In other words, categorisation as feeler or thinker doesn't always lead to opposite destinies.

Politicians tend to be compulsive feelers – Bill Clinton spectacularly so. Fianna Fáil is considerably more a feelers' party than Fine Gael – indeed, the appearance of empathy is a defining characteristic of Fianna Fáil, and is what makes Bertie Ahern such a formidable political force. The Labour Party is ideologically constructed on 'feeling', though Pat Rabbitte is far too thinker-argumentative to appeal to the insatiable Irish appetite for a feeler-leader.

About 60 per cent of journalists are feelers, and I suspect that 90 per cent of columnists are. Most priests are feelers. Interestingly, nuns – and 85 per cent of management consultants – are thinkers. General practitioners are feelers, psychiatrists are thinkers. However, the thinker/feeler division is not a simple binary system but a spectral one: the issue is really one of degree. Which extreme tends to predominate in the analysis of and resolution of problems?

Thinkers don't form lynch mobs. They don't write impassioned or denunciatory letters to the *Irish Times*. They don't get nasty or personal in debate. They don't feel hatred; in their most extreme position, they are without any moral or emotional dimension at all. Werner von Braun, the most brilliant scientists of the twentieth century and the inventor of the V2 rocket, was a classic thinker. So too was Boris Fischer, the greatest chess Grand Master of all time. He was so without feeling as to be apparently autistic – indeed, some think that autism is merely an extreme form of mechanistic, 'thinker' cerebration.

On the other hand, great scientific theorists cannot be thinkers alone. Isaac Newton had a very powerful feeler side, which he expressed in venomous enmities. No unfeeling thinker could have devised the theory of relativity – and Albert Einstein was at times passionately pacifist, passionately Zionist, passionately socialist.

Women are much more feelers rather than thinkers, which perhaps explains why so many women get angry during arguments, as if there were a moral component to a difference of opinion. Such intellectual sexual dimorphism might also explain why autism is so rare amongst women: one woman suffers from the condition for every eight men. Perhaps this is because women's genetic inheritance from the Neolithic was based on bonding and consensus-formation within the family group, while the male hunting party were off thinking just how to catch up with and kill that bloody great mammoth.

So: what did you answer to the opening mercy-justice question? When I was asked, I instantly said justice, which apparently means I am a thinker (for without justice, there is no mercy). Feelers *always* say mercy, even if they don't mean it, as anyone at the receiving end of a feeler's froth-flecked frenzy can testify.

[11 October 2005]

IX.9. Hell-o-oo? Is There Anybody Out There?

Even by the wretched standards of tedium to which this column normally aspires, and usually succeeds triumphantly, what follows is pure anaesthesia, which may more properly be employed upon patients in the Blackrock Clinic awaiting amputation of their feet at the umbilicus. For I have a secret vice, which I will now share with the dozen or so readers who have stayed with me thus far.

It is this. I adore old aeroplanes. I have been to therapy about this, have attended counselling, have been psychoanalysed till my shoulder blades are glued to the couch, and I know the shrink's ceiling as astronomers know the night sky, but all to no avail. Some strange chemical within me stirs whenever I hear the sound of an aircraft piston engine; an almost adolescent ardour fills my soul when I glimpse an airframe of sixty years ago or more; even the Air Corps Marchetti, which on occasion – and rather obligingly – performs aerobatics in the sky above my house can reduce me to a gibbering heap of ecstasy.

Last weekend I was invited to attend a dinner in Cambridge, where I discovered to my joy that the next day, the nearby Imperial War Museum, Duxford, was hosting an air show to commemorate the sixtieth anniversary of the end of the last world war. Perhaps some of my readers – all ten of them – will understand what the prospect of such an airshow – full of Spitfires and Hurricanes, Flying Fortresses and Lancasters, Mustangs and Catalinas, can do to a human soul. Girls, imagine you've found a brand new Nigella Lawson cookbook: boys, you have found the most corpora cavernosa-engorging erotica ever – well, the prospect of Duxford and its ancient aircraft does the equivalent of all that to my brain.

Nine readers is not bad. Nine, as you know, is divisible only by three, and its threefold multiples remain immune to division by any other number. Nine is faithful. Nine is fine. We'll settle for nine. There's a special Irish reason to visit Duxford, which is that the latest exhibit there is a faithfully restored Air Corps Supermarine Spitfire, complete in proper livery, including the exact shade of a strangely attractive pea-green of Baldonnel 50 years ago or so. Alas, it was not flying last Saturday: if it had been, I fear would have passed away from sheer happiness. As it was, my contentment was almost terminal.

Ah. Have you to leave so soon? What? You have to see a man about a dog? I see. Very well. Eight readers is a more than adequate. And however peculiar the eight of you might consider my appetites for such things, I was like Eamon de Valera himself compared to other people present, for anniversary airshow day at Duxford combines Anorak Central with Nerdsville.

Half the males there were apparently on day-release from the Home for the Bewildered, where they are being treated for terminal lack of irony. Many of them were strutting around in air force uniforms of various nationalities from the last world war, and not all allied by any means: the struttingest of all was apparently a Luftwaffe fighter ace, with a Knight's Cross, with Oak Leaves and Swords. One group of men were dressed as a complete RAF bomber crew, complete with leather helmets and fur-lined boots, though the temperature Celsius was more than four times the numbers of readers I have kept with me so far.

Which is fine. Seven is a lucky. Seven is prime. My Magnificent Seven will understand the echoing surge in my heart as the Lancaster surged into the air, followed by the Flying Fortress. You ask: what kind of Flying Fortress? Well, it was without the chin-turret, which made it a B-17E or -F, rather than the B-17G, which of course – as you all know – has the chin-turret.

But though a Lanc and a Flying Fort will be expected to reduce strong men to tears and bring even the most resolutely chaste member of an enclosed order of nuns to an earth-shattering climax, they are as nothing to the effect achieved by a formation of six Spitfires, one for every one of my readers. Have you the least idea how seldom this will ever happen again? Six Spitfires, curving and swooping and diving, their beautiful scimitar-wings scything majestically through the air – can you imagine the unadulterated wonder that that represents?

Five North American Mustangs also took to the air: these were perhaps the most important aircraft of the Second World War, and just enough to give readers one each.

Then there came the Grumman family of fighters – four of them, the Wildcat, the Hellcat, the Tigercat and the Bearcat, which served in the US Navy in the Pacific War; and ah, how fortunate, yet again, one per reader.

Alas, as you both know, almost no German aircraft from the Second World War have survived, and the picture is barely better for Soviet aircraft. Still, Duxford managed to show a Yak fighter – a composite confection made from several different marks – and a Polikarpov biplane, originally designed to compete in the 1940 Olympics. Yes, in the 1930s the IOC was contemplating making aerobatics an Olympic sport.

Strictly between the two of us, the day was concluded with a fly-past of some 50 Second World War aircraft, while down on the ground, I was sounding like Madonna, just back home from a trip to Ann Summers. And you know, I have exactly the same sense of solitude now. Hello? Hell-o-oo? Is there anyone out there?

[13 July 2005]